FAITHLESS EXECUTION

ANDREW C. McCARTHY

FAITHLESS EXECUTION

BUILDING THE POLITICAL CASE FOR OBAMA'S IMPEACHMENT

ENCOUNTER BOOKS  NEW YORK • LONDON

First American edition published in 2014 by Encounter Books,
an activity of Encounter for Culture and Education, Inc.,
a nonprofit, tax exempt corporation.
Encounter Books website address: www.encounterbooks.com

Manufactured in the United States and printed on
acid-free paper. The paper used in this publication meets
the minimum requirements of ANSI/NISO Z39.48 1992
(R 1997) (*Permanence of Paper*).

FIRST AMERICAN EDITION

LIBRARY OF CONGRESS CATALOGING-IN-PUBLICATION DATA
is available for this title.

ISBN 978-1-59403-776-4 (hardcover: alk. paper)
ISBN 978-159403-777-1 (ebook)

CONTENTS

Lawlessness in the use of raw power, or "direct action," is central to the training and practices of community organizers

The dictatorial potential inherent in the power to enforce or not enforce the law makes impeachment a crucial check on presidential power

Unmoored from the president's constitutional duty to execute the laws faithfully, law is a weapon in an ideological crusade; the president becomes a ruler, not a public servant

PART I

President Obama's policies are deeply unpopular and his imperialism is alarming

A summary of the president's extensive violations of law and derelictions of duty

There is a worthy case for impeaching the president due not to political or philosophical disagreements but to his violations of law, which threaten our constitutional framework

As a practical matter, impeachment is the only plausible congressional remedy to stop systematic presidential lawlessness

The courts are impotent to stop systematic presidential lawlessness

Impeachment is a political remedy, not a legal one; it is a question of the public's will to remove the president, not a matter of whether impeachable offenses can be proved

The Framers sought to ensure that the presidency's enormous powers would be checked and that presidents would be held accountable for abusing them

The Framers saw impeachment as an indispensable protection against executive lawlessness

The constitutional standard of "high crimes and misdemeanors"—in addition to treason and bribery—was adapted from British law to address profound executive maladministration

High crimes and misdemeanors are not necessarily statutory crimes; they are offenses political in nature that involve "the misconduct of public men" and subversion of the Constitution

The president is fully responsible for the misdeeds of his subordinates (or "co-adjutors")

Impeachment is one of three ways the Constitution reins in executive lawlessness; the others—elections and the power of the purse—no longer perform this function as originally envisioned

The modern left's drive to centralize power confirms the Framers' fear that factions would endanger the Constitution's framework of divided, competing powers

The aggressive passivity of Republicans also frustrates the Framers' constitutional design

The failed Clinton impeachment did not involve willful, systematic subversion of our constitutional framework and is thus not a precedent against impeaching President Obama

True lesson of Clinton impeachment: A principled political case for impeachment should be made, but the House of Representatives should not file articles of impeachment unless there is a reasonable chance of conviction in the Senate

Impeachment is innately political, not a legal process; it has more to do with the public's investment in preserving our system of government than with proving impeachable offenses

The House's power to impeach does not create a duty to file articles of impeachment if there is no realistic prospect that the Senate will vote to remove the president

Drawing an analogy to the work of a police officer or a grand jury does not support the argument for an immediate impeachment by the House, in part because police do not make an arrest and grand juries do not indict every time a crime is committed

The requirement of a two-thirds Senate supermajority ensures that a president will not be removed in the absence of broad, bipartisan public support for the action

The Senate acquittal of a president who has been impeached before there is public support for his removal would encourage more presidential lawlessness, just as the contempt citation of Attorney General Holder, showing a lack of resolve to remove him, encouraged more executive malfeasance

Impeachment is a political procedure for stripping political power; portraying it as a legal process is insidious because legal gamesmanship vitiates political will and accountability

There are salient differences between criminal justice proceedings, which are essentially legal, and impeachment, which is essentially political

The legal grounds—provable high crimes and misdemeanors—are vital to building a political case for impeachment, but the fundamental question is whether the president's conduct is so egregious that the public will support his removal

The movement left, though a minority, is united in vigorous support for President Obama's anticonstitutionalism in pursuit of its objectives; whether the remaining vast majority of the public is committed to preserving our constitutional framework is open to question

Under the camouflage of "prosecutorial discretion," President Obama has claimed the power to dictate law

A president may decline to execute laws he believes are unconstitutional, but Obama refuses to execute incontestably constitutional laws on policy grounds, and he extorts states to observe his policies rather than federal law

Prosecutorial discretion is a commonsense resource-allocation doctrine related to criminal law enforcement, not a generalized license to ignore congressional statutes

Under the guise of "prosecutorial discretion," President Obama delegitimizes and effectively reverses laws he opposes on philosophical grounds

Rebuking the Obama administration's obstruction of the Yucca Mountain nuclear waste project, a federal appeals court explains why prosecutorial discretion is not a rationale for violating the president's duty to execute the laws faithfully

President Obama's illegal waivers and edicts do not relieve citizens of the duty to comply with congressional statutes; they place citizens in the intolerable dilemma of incurring executive wrath or behaving illegally

PART II

To build the political case for impeachment, it is essential to illustrate that high crimes and misdemeanors—the legal predicate for impeachment—can be proved

The legal case that President Obama is guilty of high crimes and misdemeanors is overwhelming; it illuminates the systematic threat to our constitutional framework; and it solidly supports the political case for removal

THE ARTICLES OF IMPEACHMENT

The president's unilateral amendments of Obamacare legislation (the Patient Protection and Affordable Care Act)

The president's unilateral amendment, on the eve of the 2012 election, of federal law mandating notification of impending layoffs

The president's unilateral amendment of the federal law requiring welfare recipients to work

The president's unilateral amendments of federal immigration law, including decrees of amnesty for various categories of illegal immigrants

The president's unilateral amendment and maladministration of the Clean Air Act in destructively regulating carbon dioxide

The president's defiance of congressional law and court orders in obstructing the Yucca Mountain nuclear waste project

The president's defiance of federal law requiring the president to address the impending insolvency of Medicare

The president's usurpation of Congress's constitutional war powers in instigating an undeclared, unauthorized, unprovoked, and ultimately disastrous war in Libya

The president's making of "recess appointments" when the Senate was not in recess

The president's undermining of, and contempt for, Congress's constitutional duty to conduct oversight of executive agencies created and funded by the American people's representatives in Congress

CONTENTS

The president's imposition of unconscionable combat rules of engagement that recklessly endanger and cost the lives of American troops

The Benghazi massacre: The president's reckless stationing of American government personnel and provision of grossly inadequate security for them in Benghazi, Libya, resulted in a foreseeable terrorist attack in which the U.S. ambassador to Libya and three other Americans were murdered, and numerous other Americans were wounded

The president waged the Libya war under false pretenses and denied that bombardment of a foreign nation's government forces, resulting in thousands of deaths and the killing of that nation's head of state, constituted "hostilities" under federal law

The Benghazi fraud: The president's fraudulent claim that the Benghazi massacre was caused by an anti-Islamic film, including the willful misleading of the American people, the provision of false information to Congress, and the scapegoat prosecution of the film producer

The Obamacare fraud: The president's willful misrepresentations that Americans would be able to keep their health insurance and their doctors, and that they would save rather than lose thousands of dollars, in order to secure political support for Obamacare's enactment and conceal damaging information that would have threatened his reelection bid

The president's enabling of Iran's nuclear program while publicly vowing to prevent Iran's acquisition of nuclear weapons

The president's fraudulent claims about enforcement efforts against illegal immigration

The Solyndra fraud: The president's provision of subsidies to a failing solar energy company backed by a prominent donor, his deceptive claims about its financial condition when it was preparing to sell stock to the public, and his imposition on taxpayers of millions of dollars in company losses in violation of federal law

The president's unlawful grant of amnesty to categories of illegal immigrants by executive edict

The president's unlawful conferral of amnesty on categories of illegal immigrants by executive order, administrative regulations, and the invocation of prosecutorial discretion

The president's extortionate pressure—by expensive litigation and the withholding of federal resources—on states attempting to enforce laws against illegal immigration

The president's rewards—refraining from litigation and continuing the flow of federal resources— to states that decline to enforce laws against illegal immigration

The reckless Fast and Furious operation intentionally armed criminals, foreseeably resulted in violent crimes that include the murder of at least one U.S. Border Patrol agent, and has been covered up by the attorney general's contemptuous obstruction of a congressional investigation and the president's specious invocation of executive privilege

The willful denial to Americans of equal protection under the law by the Justice Department's racially discriminatory enforcement of federal civil rights law

The systematic politicization of hiring at the Department of Justice

The politicization of investigation and prosecution by the Department of Justice in order to coerce compliance with administration policy, to punish critics, and to appease political supporters

The sweeping investigation of journalists in contravention of Justice Department guidelines, and the attorney general's misleading testimony to Congress regarding the investigation of a journalist as to whom the Justice Department had obtained a search warrant

Coercing state compliance with Obama administration policy by politicizing enforcement actions and encouraging state attorneys general to abdicate their duty to defend valid state law

The systematic stonewalling of Congress

CONTENTS

ARTICLE VII
Willfully Undermining the Constitutional Rights of the American
People That He Is Sworn to Preserve, Protect and Defend

The president's selective targeting of political opponents for harassment and abuse by the Internal Revenue Service, and obstruction and corruption of the resulting investigations

The president's abridgement of First Amendment free-speech rights in order to appease Islamic supremacists by adopting repressive sharia blasphemy standards

The president's suppression of information about Islamic terrorism, including its occurrence in the Fort Hood massacre

The president's abridgement of First Amendment free-speech rights by selectively and vindictively prosecuting a high-profile critic

The president's denial of First Amendment religious liberty under Obamacare by gratuitously imposing an abortifacient and birth-control mandate on conscientious objectors

The president's infringement of Second Amendment firearms rights through an international treaty he joined despite widespread congressional opposition

INTRODUCTION

THE RULER OF LAW

"Be careful how you make those statements, gentlemen." Barack Hussein Obama had been president of the United States for all of two months. He was lecturing the titans of American finance who were struggling to explain to him, a man with no meaningful business experience, how high salaries are necessary if American companies are to compete for talent in a global market.

"The public isn't buying that," scoffed the president. He wasn't talking about *the* public, though. "My administration," he warned, "is the only thing between you and the pitchforks." The pitchforks: that's *his* public.

Obama's formative background is the left-wing fever swamp of Chicago "community organizing," a gussied-up term for systematic rabble-rousing that has now become acceptable enough to put on a résumé. The pursuit of raw power is the gospel according to the seminal organizer, Saul Alinsky—if we may use "gospel" in connection with an atheist whose most famous book, *Rules for Radicals*, opens with an ode to Lucifer for winning his own kingdom by rebelling against the establishment.

In Obama terminology, "hope" is the possibility that power may be wrested from society's "haves" by infiltrating their political system. Just as Willie Sutton robbed banks because that's where the money is, organizers must target and enter the very system they reject in order to acquire power. They must make themselves attractive to the great mass of society despite having "contemptuously rejected the values and the way of life of the middle class," as Alinsky put it. This is the formula for transformational "change": the acquisition and exploitation of power so as to redistribute wealth and elevate the left's professionally aggrieved vanguard.

Though the quest for "social justice" must wend its way through regular politics, the goal cannot be reached by regular politics. That's where the pitchforks come in. "Direct action"—as Mr. Obama's long-time confederates at ACORN (the Association of Community Organizers for Reform Now) euphemistically put it—is the organizer's signal tactic. *Action*, Alinsky taught, is the very point of organizing. "Direct action" is barely disguised code for the occasional use, and the omnipresent threat, of mob mischief against the law-abiding bourgeoisie. The organizer prospers by defining down our ethical boundaries—or, looked at the other way, by legitimizing extortion.

"Grass-roots community organizing builds on indigenous leadership and direct action," Obama wrote in his contribution to *After Alinsky: Community Organizing in Illinois*, a retrospective published fifteen years after Alinsky's death in 1972. In another revealing passage, the up-and-coming organizer elaborated:

The debate as to how black and other dispossessed people can forward their lot in America is not new. From W.E.B. DuBois to Booker T. Washington to Marcus Garvey to Malcolm X to Martin Luther King, this internal debate has raged between integration and nationalism, between accommodation and militancy, between sit-down strikes and boardroom negotiations. The lines between these strategies have never been simply drawn, and the most successful black leadership has recognized the need to bridge these seemingly divergent approaches.

Breathtaking! No wonder that Obama's media allies resisted reporting on these cogitations, even as they scoured the earth in search of Sarah Palin's third-grade report card. Lawfulness and lawlessness, thuggery and regular politics—we're not to divine any moral or ethical differences. They are just different "approaches" to empowerment. They only "seem" to be "divergent." It may be important to maintain the veneer of respect for legal processes, but it is just as legitimate to stretch or break the rules whenever necessary to achieve social justice—a higher form of legitimacy than society's rule of law. Separatism, menacing action, civil disobedience: none of these is beyond the pale. They are simply choices on the hard-power menu that Obama "bridges" with soft power (i.e., the system's mundane legal and political processes).

As recounted in Stanley Kurtz's *Radical-in-Chief*, the definitive political biography of Obama, the young organizer's formative experiences included the use of Alinsky's "direct action" tactics—alliances with aggressors like ACORN and the SEIU (Service Employees International Union). Indeed, Obama personally orchestrated a demonstration in which scores of protestors broke into a private meeting between bank executives and local community leaders, menacing them as they tried to negotiate a controversial landfill deal. As Obama earned greater prominence through his organizing activities, especially in the field of registering thousands of ne'er-do-wells to vote, he was invited to sit on the boards of left-leaning foundations, enabling him to steer funding to notorious direct-action practitioners. One of his close allies in that endeavor was the avowed "small-c communist" William Ayers. The former Weather Underground terrorist knew a thing or two about direct action.

In the short run, the goal of direct action is sheer extortion: to coerce capitulation in the controversy of the moment, be it over a private business's right to compensate employees or build production plants as it sees fit, a state's sovereign power to defend itself by enforcing immigration laws, or Leviathan's grab (under the cloak of regulation rather than outright seizure) of one-sixth of the U.S. economy in the name of "health-care reform." Over the long haul, the goal is to demoralize civil society, to convince opponents that regular processes—particularly, reliance on the law—will be unavailing. This is the distinctive slice of Chicago that Obama has brought to the White House. Administration officials monotonously invoke the "rule of law" even as they use law as a cudgel, run circles around it, and ride roughshod over it.

The power to enforce the law, which carries with it the equally salient power not to enforce the law, is a president's most imposing domestic weapon, rivaled in importance only by the awesome authority inherent in a president's status as commander in chief of the U.S. Armed Forces. After a Supreme Court ruling that angered him, President Andrew Jackson is said to have scoffed, "John Marshall has made his decision. Now let him enforce it." Though the story may be apocryphal, the lesson it conveys is only too real. Congress writes laws and courts assess the laws' validity, but neither has the power to breathe life into the law. Absent executive action, the exertions of the other branches arc dead letters.

In various justice systems, particularly in Europe, prosecutors share powers with judges, and, at least theoretically, are duty-bound to charge crimes whenever there is sufficient evidence. Not so in the United States, where prosecutorial discretion is the rule of the road. Through public hearings and withering opinions, Congress and the courts can try to pressure the executive into enforcing particular laws, investigating potential violations, or staying his hand. But they cannot compel a president to act or refrain from acting. They cannot force a president to abide by his constitutional obligation to execute the laws faithfully. They have no means of taking enforcement action on their own. The judiciary's capacity to halt capricious executive action is entirely dependent on the administration's willingness to honor judicial directives. Congressional oversight requires an administration's cooperation. A president of dictatorial persuasion who coopts the media in his disregard for the system's checks and balances is nigh impossible to contain.

Nor is there reciprocity any longer in our separation of powers. While the executive now legislates and rules, the other branches cannot enforce their own statutes and decisions. The imperial presidency has become the administrative state, the legacy of progressive fondness for a metastasizing government whose purportedly expert, apolitical bureaucracies supplant popular sovereignty. The Wilsonian vision was installed through the ceaseless exigencies of Roosevelt's twelve-year reign; and long before Rahm Emanuel came along, FDR knew that a crisis was a terrible thing to waste.

Today, well beyond the New Deal and the Great Society, the administrative state is socializing health care, micromanaging industry, dictating education standards, taking over automotive and insurance giants, underwriting mortgages and student loans, borrowing trillions of dollars from itself (i.e., printing trillions of dollars for itself), and even mandating coverage for contraceptives and abortifacients. The president oversees a vast expanse of executive agencies, and exercises enormous influence over ostensibly independent commissions, to which Congress delegates seemingly limitless legislative authority in the form of regulation-writing power. Much of the resulting tens of thousands of pages is insulated from judicial review. Presidents issue executive orders to shape Leviathan's priorities and procedures. The lines blur, and it becomes increasingly difficult to stop a president hell-bent on imposing his political aims as if they were legal duties.

Congress is endowed by the Constitution with the power to impeach a president for serious violations of law ("high crimes and misdemeanors"). Impeachment is a grave remedy on the order of a nuclear strike. It has been sparingly invoked against presidents—only three times in our nation's history. Andrew Johnson and Bill Clinton were impeached by the House but acquitted in Senate trials; Richard Nixon resigned to avoid sure impeachment and removal. As we shall see, impeachment is a *political* remedy: even if palpably guilty of profound transgressions, a president will not be ousted without a groundswell of public ire. It has thus been thought impractical as a response to all but the most egregious abuses of executive power, involving attacks on the constitutional foundation of our liberty.

It is the burden of this book to persuade readers that President Obama and his administration are engaged in just such a campaign. That said, impeachment is not a plausible response unless the American people become convinced not only that the campaign is real but also that a governing system they wish to preserve is mortally threatened by it. Are we still a self-determining people resistant to the freedom-devouring proclivities of an imperial presidency? That is much harder to answer than the question whether "high crimes and misdemeanors" have been committed.

If a president is the type of man who couples his hope with audacity, if he is willing to play Alinsky-style hardball despite his oath to uphold the Constitution and faithfully execute the law, there is little that can stand in his way—not if Congress is unwilling to use its competing constitutional powers. Law becomes a dispositive weapon in the service of the president's ideological crusade, never a brake against the crusade's advance. In the Obama administration, "rule of law" talking points are just rhetorical camouflage. *True* law is the moral and ethical consensus of a civil society, reflecting the conscience of a free and virtuous people; but to Alinsky, "conscience is the virtue of observers and not of agents of action." For his disciples, the agent of action must be the Ruler of Law—its master, not its servant.

American constitutional republicanism has been strong enough to survive over two centuries of self-governance, civil war, world war, terrorism, social upheaval, and periodic economic calamity. But can it survive a Ruler of Law and his trusty pitchforks? The Constitution says we need not be put to that test. The Framers gave Congress checks to combat executive lawlessness. The ultimate one is impeachment. There is a rich legal case for using it. But impeachment is not about what the law allows. Impeachment is a matter of political will.[1]

PART I

CHAPTER ONE

———

WE DON'T
HAVE THE VOTES

"It's a good question."

Ted Cruz was answering a query from a woman in the audience for a dinner speech. His topic was lawlessness in the Obama administration. This being Montgomery County, Texas, rather than the Beltway or the Upper West Side, the subject was deemed fit for respectable discussion. The woman's question specifically concerned the president of the United States, and it was succinct:

"Why don't we impeach him?"

Senator Cruz was right: It *is* a good question.

Impeachment, after all, is not a high mountain to climb. The Constitution vests in the House of Representatives "the sole power of impeachment."[1] Currently, the House is controlled by President Obama's opposition: Republicans hold a comfortable 33-vote majority, with reasons for optimism that their ranks will swell after November's midterm elections. Formal "articles of impeachment" require just a simple majority for approval. The historical rarity of impeachment owes to its gravity, not its difficulty.

Besides, despite the GOP's seething intramural divisions, there is nigh unanimous revulsion when it comes to Obama's agenda. In fact, even Democrats—especially those facing tough reelection races in the fall—have taken to avoiding joint appearances with the president. His poll numbers have tanked. Hope-and-Change delirium has given way to the hard reality that we really can't keep our health insurance policies and our doctors if we like them. The public grows angrier with each insurance cancellation notice—or is it, each *million* cancellation notices?

Even Obama sympathizers at the *Washington Post*, putting their best spin on the matter, concede that 21 million people are out of work, not the 10 million grudgingly acknowledged by the administration.[2] In fact, the real unemployment rate of about 13 percent is double the rate routinely reported by the media.[3] By December 2013, the population of Americans over the age of sixteen without a full-time job had climbed to a staggering 92 million—far exceeding the total population of Germany, the world's fourth largest economy.[4] In a nation that has grown by nearly 10 million people since Obama took office, 11 million fewer people are working today than in 2009—marking a nadir in American workforce participation not seen since the Jimmy Carter malaise.[5]

Remarkably, prominent liberal law professors—a core Obama constituency—have even begun speaking up about the administration's abuses of power. George Washington University's Jonathan Turley describes Obama's imperialism as the "uber-presidency," conceding in congressional testimony that the president has enveloped the nation in "the most serious constitutional crisis . . . of my lifetime." (Yes, Professor Turley did live through Nixon.) In more recent testimony he added, "The president has in fact exceeded his authority in a way that is creating a destabilizing influence in a three-branch system."[6] Harvard's Alan Dershowitz has slammed the Justice Department for its "outrageous" and "selective prosecution" of a conservative Obama critic—a case that reportedly put Professor Dershowitz in mind of Lavrenti Beria, Stalin's infamous secret police chief, who said, "Show me the man and I'll find you the crime."[7]

The alarm is way overdue, but it is not surprising. So rampant are President Obama's violations of law and derelictions of duty that it has become a chore to summarize them. But let's give it a shot.

The president has assiduously ignored the chief executive's fundamental constitutional obligation to "take care that the Laws be faithfully executed."[8] He has repeatedly violated the oath that the Constitution requires only of presidents:

> I do solemnly swear (or affirm) that I will faithfully execute the Office of President of the United States, and will to the best of my Ability, preserve, protect and defend the Constitution of the United States.[9]

The president has serially usurped the power of Congress to write and amend the laws. When Congress has declined to enact his unpopular policy initiatives, such as the legalization of illegal immigrants and a cap-and-trade law that could fatally cripple the coal industry, he has presumed to legislate unilaterally and unconstitutionally, under the guise of executive orders and agency regulations.

The president has willfully defrauded the American people in the enactment and implementation of Obamacare. In addition, he has unilaterally and unlawfully amended and "waived" the statute's terms—guided by his knowledge that timely, lawful application of the deeply unpopular law would be devastating to his party's electoral prospects and would have made him a one-term president.

His administration has sicced the Internal Revenue Service and other government agencies on his political opponents—frustrating the capacity of conservative groups to have the powerful impact on the 2012 presidential election that they had on the 2010 midterms. Simultaneously, the administration has manipulated the law and the public fisc for the benefit of Obama's political cronies. Contrary to the impression Obama conveys when his subordinates are caught using bureaucratic muscle to reward friends and harass foes—a frequent occurrence—the president is principally responsible for the misfeasance and malfeasance of his administration. He is not just an innocent bystander.

On Obama's watch, the Justice Department has enforced the laws in a politicized and racially discriminatory manner. It has, furthermore, filed and threatened vexatious lawsuits against sovereign states to obstruct their lawful execution of public policy— particularly, the enforcement of laws against illegal immigration and election fraud. The president's attorney general, Eric Holder, has exhorted state attorneys general to become more like him—to adopt the practice of ignoring the laws they are sworn to enforce when those laws depart from Obama's progressive pieties.

Holder's department orchestrated the astounding "Fast and Furious" operation, in which large quantities of firearms were knowingly sent to vicious drug gangs in Mexico. Top administration figures are, of course, rabidly anti-gun. Yet the Bureau of Alcohol, Tobacco, Firearms and Explosives (ATF), in collusion with Justice Department lawyers, encouraged arms dealers to make illegal gun sales to "straw purchasers"—faux buyers whose true intention is to transfer the weapons in bulk to persons (usually illegal aliens and other criminals) who are not legally eligible to obtain them.

At best, the ATF agents foolishly believed the straw purchasers would lead them to violent gangs against whom they could make a splashy case. More plausibly, the ideologues expected that the guns would end up tied to various atrocities, thus bolstering their political argument that America's gun culture fuels international violence. Thousands of guns were allowed to walk, no meaningful prosecutions were developed, and, predictably, things went horribly wrong: some of the ATF guns have been tied to the murder of Brian Terry, a U.S. Border Patrol agent.

Congress has tried to investigate Fast and Furious, just as it tries to investigate a web of administration scandals that would make Richard Nixon and John Mitchell blush. The president frivolously invoked executive privilege to stall the probe, after Holder was held in contempt of Congress for his misleading testimony and refusal to turn over Justice Department memoranda.

That, by the way, was before Mr. Holder provided misleading testimony to Congress about his role in the investigation of a Fox News journalist—right around the time the Justice Department secretly issued sweeping subpoenas for the phone records of Associated Press reporters, flouting the department's traditional deference to free-press rights explicitly protected by the First Amendment.

More recently, the department has embarked on an invidious felony prosecution against Dinesh D'Souza for allegedly illegal contributions to a Senate campaign. D'Souza, an influential conservative, is the author of *The Roots of Obama's Rage* and co-producer of the related movie, *2016: Obama's America*, both of which were popular with the public and despised at the White House. The D'Souza case is the one panned by Alan Dershowitz as "selective" and "outrageous." The piddling sum allegedly involved, $15,000, is well beneath the Justice Department's norm for criminal enforcement; it falls into the category that is routinely settled with a fine paid to the Federal Election Commission. Certainly it is not in the same stratosphere as the Obama campaign's own *multimillion-dollar* campaign finance violations, which are felonies that the same Justice Department opted not to prosecute.

The president instigated a war, unauthorized by Congress and in the absence of any threat to the United States, against the Libyan regime of Muammar Qaddafi. At the time, the Obama administration was supporting Qaddafi's government with public funds and portraying it as a key American counterterrorism ally. As is the president's wont, the war against Qaddafi was fraudulently conducted: the public was told that the military assault was an impartial humanitarian enterprise to halt fighting between the Libyan government and insurgent forces; in fact, the American-led coalition one-sidedly bludgeoned the Qaddafi regime, while the administration secretly green-lighted arms shipments and funding for the jihadist-ridden insurgents.

As was easily foreseeable, the unprovoked military adventure empowered anti-American terrorists. In addition to facilitating the arming of jihadists during the war, in violation of American criminal laws against material support to terrorism, the president's policy enabled jihadists affiliated with al-Qaeda to seize parts of the regime's arsenal in the chaotic aftermath of Qaddafi's assassination. Thus fortified, terrorists conducted violent operations against American and other Western targets in the region.

Despite the threat to the United States exacerbated by his policy of empowering Islamists, Obama repeatedly claimed to the public, in the run-up to the 2012 election, that his leadership had "decimated" al-Qaeda and left the terror network "on the path to defeat."[10] His administration, meanwhile, facilitated the virulently anti-American Muslim Brotherhood's rise to power in Egypt and, again in violation of American laws against supporting terrorists, issued a visa to a member of an Egyptian terrorist organization—formally designated as such under U.S. law—so he could consult with top administration officials at the White House.

At home, the administration consulted with "experts" it has refused to identify in purging information about Islamic supremacism—the ideology that drives our enemies—from materials used to train law enforcement, intelligence, and military personnel responsible for our security. The obsession with bleaching the Islam out of Islamic terrorism reached mind-boggling lengths with the administration's refusal to brand the Fort Hood massacre—in which thirteen Americans, mostly military personnel, were killed and dozens more wounded—as an act of terrorism.

For a year leading up to the attack at Ford Hood in November 2009, the gunman, Nidal Hasan, a psychiatrist and commissioned officer in the U.S. Army, had been exchanging international emails with Anwar al-Awlaki, a top al-Qaeda terrorist who had ministered to the 9/11 suicide-hijackers. Breathtakingly, government investigators who knew about these emails, and were also aware of lectures in which the psychiatrist spewed anti-American jihadist rhetoric, dismissed all this as "academic research" that indicated no terrorist threat. After the massacre, the worst domestic terrorist attack since 9/11, General George Casey, army chief of staff, bleated that a "greater tragedy" than the mass murder and maiming would be "if our diversity becomes a casualty." The administration fraudulently labeled the killings of U.S. troops who were about to deploy to a war zone as "workplace violence," not international terrorism—a finding that denied Purple Hearts to the soldiers killed and wounded in the attack.

Meanwhile, Obama was imposing unconscionable rules of engagement on American combat forces in Afghanistan. Our troops are now expected to fight a war against terrorists who hide among (often sympathetic) civilians while not engaging the enemy if there is a possibility that civilians could be harmed. U.S. ground forces are also routinely denied air cover, again for fear of harming Afghan civilians. Since Obama took the helm and incoherently announced a troop escalation coupled with a troop withdrawal, American combat deaths have more than doubled, while the Taliban has surged and stands poised to retake Afghanistan after the imminent U.S. pullout.

President Obama turned a blind eye in 2009 when the Iranian people were brutally crushed in an uprising against their totalitarian regime—jihadist terror's leading state sponsor, whose anthem for over thirty years has been "Death to America." Then, in 2013, he reached out to President Hassan Rouhani, the mullahs' new front man. After years of lip-service assurance that Iran would not be permitted to become a nuclear-weapons power, Obama has cut an "interim" deal with the regime that enables Iran to continue enriching uranium and eviscerates years of UN Security Council resolutions barring Iran's uranium enrichment activities. Rouhani triumphantly boasted in a tweet that the United States had "surrendered to Iranian nation's will," while the regime's chief negotiator bragged that Iran "did not agree to dismantle anything": not its centrifuges, not its ballistics program, not its nuclear program.[11]

The interim agreement is to be implemented under the terms of a memorandum of understanding between the two sides. Tehran insists that if people want to know what this memorandum says, they should read it—but the Obama administration refuses to release the text to the American people. You'll just have to trust them. We do know for certain that Obama demanded no concessions on Iran's promotion of jihadist terror, the main reason why allowing it to become a nuclear-weapons power is unacceptable. At least, it used to be.

Back in Libya, Obama recklessly neglected the duty of a president and commander in chief to protect Americans serving overseas, a negligence that included the shocking failure to take responsive action while Americans were under a terrorist siege in Benghazi on September 11, 2012. The president, whose White House has refused to account for his whereabouts and activities during the hours of the Benghazi attack, was evidently busy preparing for the Las Vegas political fundraiser he flew off to the next day. Subordinates were left to sort out the jihadist murders of a U.S. ambassador and three other Americans, and the severe wounding of many others.

With the November election looming and the president's campaign rhetoric about decimating al-Qaeda becoming laughable, the White House endeavored to defraud the American people into believing that the Benghazi massacre was not a terrorist operation foreseeably carried out by al-Qaeda affiliates on the eleventh anniversary of the 9/11 atrocities, but a spontaneous riot provoked by an anti-Muslim video. Susan Rice, Obama's confidante and ambassador to the United Nations, went on the Sunday shows to weave the video yarn. Meanwhile, Michael Morell, a top CIA official with close ties to Secretary of State Hillary Clinton, obligingly purged references to al-Qaeda in agency talking points used for briefings on the massacre. Morell later deceived Congress about his edits and the fact that they were done in coordination with the White House. The deceptive scheme included a trumped-up prosecution of the video producer on charges related to parole (or "supervised release")—though obviously his real "crime" in the administration's eyes was exercising his First Amendment rights.

The Obama administration has also conspired with foreign elements to reduce the constitutional liberties of the American people. Since the start of his presidency, Obama has colluded with the Organization of Islamic Cooperation (a 57-member bloc of countries with large Muslim populations plus the Palestinian territories) on an international resolution prohibiting speech that casts Islam in a negative light. Following the Benghazi massacre, Obama shamefully compounded this campaign with not only the heinous prosecution of the aforementioned filmmaker but also (a) a television commercial (directed at Middle Eastern, not American, audiences) in which both he and Secretary of State Clinton slammed the film, and (b) an indignant proclamation in his annual United Nations speech that "the future must not belong to those who slander the prophet of Islam." Quite apart from their transparent suggestion that the film, not Obama's policies, triggered the murders of American officials, these gambits continued the administration's campaign to erode the First Amendment's protection of free expression.

The Second Amendment is threatened by the administration's signing of a United Nations treaty on arms regulations in 2013, despite warnings by substantial bipartisan congressional majorities that there is no prospect of approval by two-thirds of the Senate, as constitutionally required for the pact to be ratified. The treaty would impose weapons-transfer regulations concocted by international bureaucrats—many of whom are anti-American and rabidly opposed to American firearms rights.

Finally, the administration has exploited Obamacare to impose regulations that run roughshod over the First Amendment's freedom-of-conscience guarantee. Religious believers, including religious organizations that self-insure, have been required to provide coverage for abortifacients (as well as other forms of birth control) despite their religious objections and the inexpensive, ubiquitous availability of these substances to those who desire them.

There is more to say, in due course, about the administration's performance. But this synopsis is enough, again, to press the question posed at that Montgomery County dinner gathering: "Why don't we impeach him?"

Senator Cruz's response that evening was just as Lone Star blunt: "I'll tell you the simplest answer. To successfully impeach a president you need the votes in the U.S. Senate. With Harry Reid and the Democrats controlling the Senate, it can't succeed."[12]

Truer words were never spoken.

Time to put the cards on the table: There is no doubt in my mind that President Obama ought to be impeached and removed from office. I believe the Constitution's framework—in particular, the Framers' ingenious separation and balancing of competing powers within the central government, and between that government and the sovereign states—is indispensable to liberty, which is so central to the American character. The Constitution, moreover, is the social compact. It established the solemn terms that induced the states to ratify our fundamental law and form a more perfect union. It answers the aspiration of our Declaration of Independence: to institute a government the powers of which derive solely from the consent of the governed and the limited purpose of which is to secure our unalienable rights to life, liberty and the pursuit of happiness—not to rule us. It is history's greatest proven generator of prosperity, security and human flourishing.

The rise of the administrative state over the last century has profoundly challenged the Constitution's framework, but President Obama has quite intentionally undertaken to dismantle that framework. That is what the president's commitment to "fundamentally transforming the United States of America" is all about. President Obama seeks to agglomerate power in the federal executive branch, enabling him, without meaningful opposition, to remake our nation. No longer would it be based on liberty, with the citizen guaranteed protection from oppressive government. The Obama dream is the nightmare about which Alexis de Tocqueville warned: a comparatively soft tyranny, in which the individual serves an "immense and tutelary" state and its centrally planned, punctiliously regulated society, enjoying only as much liberty as the government deigns to grant him.[13]

While I vigorously oppose it, I do not begrudge the president his vision of the just society: government redistributing wealth, hyperregulating property so it is no longer *private* in any real sense, enforcing a perverse notion of equality in which unequal treatment is applied to achieve a humanly unachievable equality of outcomes, and dramatically downsizing America's role on the world stage. What I object to is the president's pursuing these ends by violating his oath to preserve the Constitution, shredding the separation of powers, using the vast bureaucracy to repress his political opponents, and misleading the public about both his objectives and his failures. I believe the president should be impeached because I am not confident the nation can withstand nearly three more years of his governance. Oh, we would still be here, of course, but it would be a very different country, with the president having set precedents for worse to come.

Many Obama critics look hopefully to the 2014 midterm elections, calculating that a Republican landslide will put the GOP in control of both houses of Congress, which would purportedly derail Obama's onslaught and end the constitutional crisis. This is wishful thinking. Even if we assume for argument's sake that Republicans will have a big electoral victory in the fall, there would be little prospect of stopping the president.

Right now, Republicans control the House of Representatives, in which the Constitution vests primacy on taxing and spending. With forty-five seats in the Senate, where minorities enjoy parliamentary advantages they do not have in the House, Republicans also have the votes, right now, to stop new Obama initiatives and to support the House were the latter to stop financing the president's excesses. And yet, cowed by the Obama-friendly media, they have offered nothing but token resistance. Republicans are paralyzed at the very thought of using the power of the purse. The one time that House conservatives did so—in attempting to defund or delay the implementation of Obamacare in 2013—they were savaged by the Beltway GOP leadership.

I do not see any of this changing after the midterm elections. Even if Republicans win, the same Republican leaders will still be running the show. Moreover, Republicans are not going to come close to winning the lopsided majorities necessary to override Obama vetoes. As a practical matter, that means the president will not need to veto many bills. Democrats, unlike Republicans, would stick together in the Senate and coordinate closely with House progressives to kill any GOP-sponsored legislation aimed at rolling back Obama's agenda. If past is prologue, Republicans will rarely even attempt such legislation. They will shrug and tell us that resistance is futile.

Perhaps more significantly, American presidents have enormous power over the conduct of foreign affairs and over the direction of the sprawling executive bureaucracy. If Congress becomes more of a dead end for Obama than it is now, he will simply redouble his determination to rule by international agreements and executive orders—to be imposed on Americans by the administrative agencies that run the country day to day, and by the federal courts whose benches the president has been filling with hundreds of like-minded progressives since 2009.

The Constitution provides two congressional avenues for reining in presidential lawlessness: the power of the purse and the authority to impeach the president. They are extraordinarily powerful remedies—and they are the only remedies available. Some lawmakers appear to think there is a third: Unwilling or unable to persuade their colleagues to use the constitutional powers available to the legislature, they hope to have the courts do the work for them, and to look as if they are mounting real resistance by filing their bal-lyhooed lawsuits against the administration. It is a feeble strategy.[14]

It is not the purpose of the federal courts to resolve national controversies. They were created to remedy individual injuries but given no power to enforce their judgments. That, indeed, is why Alexander Hamilton anticipated that the judiciary would be the "least dangerous" branch: Controlling neither sword nor purse, it would be "least in a capacity to annoy or injure" the "political rights of the Constitution."[15] In fact, the law of "standing," which addresses what grievances litigants may bring before courts, teaches that the more a controversy affects the body politic rather than the individual citizen, the less appropriate it is for judicial resolution. It is for just such controversies that we have political rights.

American jurisprudence counsels the judiciary to stay out of "political questions," disputes between the two political branches over the extent of their competing authorities. Most judges will not give such suits the time of day. Even if some unexpectedly do, litigation takes years to resolve. When it finally ends, we are reminded that courts are powerless to give effect to their own orders. Indeed, the Obama administration is already scoffing at judicial rulings that, for example, stripped the federal government's power (under the 1965 Voting Rights Act) to "preclear" state election laws, such as new voter ID provisions; and that invalidated the president's "recess" appointments—*when Congress was not in recess*—to the National Labor Relations Board.[16] When a federal judge in New Orleans ruled that the administration's announced moratorium on deepwater drilling following the BP oil spill in the Gulf of Mexico was illegal, the administration simply stopped issuing drilling permits—in effect, imposing an *unannounced* moratorium that continued the lawlessness.[17]

In the unlikely event that judges presume to rule against the president, they must depend on his executive branch subordinates to enforce their directives. Good luck with that.

If Congress is unwilling to use its command over the treasury to coerce the president into heeding the limits of his power, impeachment is the only other alternative to the current Congress's obviously preferred course of abdication. If you won't defund malfeasance, you have to remove it—or accept it. There is no other course. Plus, as we shall see, the Framers saw impeachment as the appropriate response to presidential corruption, lawlessness, and infidelity to the Constitution. It is the designed tonic for faithless execution.

In the final analysis, though, my belief that President Obama should be impeached counts for nothing (beyond the duty of full disclosure to the reader). In fact, it counts for very little that members of Congress may believe that they can prove numerous impeachable offenses, and thus that the president should be impeached. Impeachment is not a *legal* matter of proving "high crimes and misdemeanors." It is a *political* matter of will.

Senator Cruz was right. Although it is true that a simple House majority can vote out articles of impeachment, *successfully* impeaching a president means *removing him from office*—actually purging the lawlessness. Removal requires, in addition, the president's conviction on articles of impeachment by a two-thirds vote of the Senate.[18] That vote will never happen in the absence of extraordinary political pressure on these elected officials. That is, there would have to be such a robust national consensus that the president must be ousted that at least 67 of the 100 senators would vote to do it, notwithstanding the partisan and ideological ties many have with the president, the security of the six-year term that tends to make a senator (especially in the early years) less responsive than a House member to his constituents' wishes, and the guarantee of media demagoguery over the very thought of impeaching a liberal Democrat.

At this point, while there is increasing angst over Obama's policies and growing disapproval of his presidency, there is no public consensus that he should be removed from office. The legal case for impeachment is very strong. The political case lags far behind—and it is the only case that matters. Political cases have to be built.

CHAPTER TWO

THE MISCONDUCT
OF PUBLIC MEN

"Shall any man be above justice? Above all, shall that man be above it who can commit the most extensive injustice?"

These epigrammatic questions were posed by George Mason at the Philadelphia convention in 1787. They elucidate the Framers' rationale for including in the Constitution a procedure for the impeachment and removal of a president.[1]

Few matters at the convention addled the delegates as much as the dangerous potential that the president of the United States—the powerful new position they were creating, the single official in whom they decided to vest the entirety of federal executive power—could become a king. The purpose of the Constitution was to safeguard liberty, not sow seeds for the very tyranny from which the American colonies had liberated themselves. Much of the convention, therefore, was dedicated to foreclosing that possibility.

First, the president would have to face election every four years. He would have immense authorities as the chief executive, but they would be checked in every important particular. For example, the president would be commander in chief, but Congress would retain the power to declare war and hold both the purse and significant powers over the armed forces. The president could make treaties and broadly conduct foreign affairs, but international agreements could not amend the Constitution (there being a separate process for that), treaties could not take effect unless approved by a Senate supermajority, and Congress was empowered to regulate foreign commerce. The president would appoint major government officials, but they could not take office without Senate approval.

While the Framers took care to set limits on executive powers, they also sought to ensure accountability by vesting those awesome powers in a *unitary* executive rather than a committee or a minister advised by a privy council.[2] Ultimately responsible for all executive conduct and unable to deflect blame for wrongdoing, a single president would be amenable "to censure and to punishment," Alexander Hamilton argued.[3] The future Supreme Court justice James Iredell likewise observed that a president would be "personally responsible for any abuse of the great trust reposed in him."[4]

For the unitary executive to be truly accountable, the Framers provided a mechanism to hold him to account. It would be "indispensible," as James Madison put it, for Congress to have the power to impeach and remove the president in order to protect the nation against "the incapacity, negligence or perfidy of the chief Magistrate." At the Commonwealth of Pennsylvania's later debate over ratification of the proposed Constitution, James Wilson explained that the imperative of a removal power stemmed from both the concentration of executive authority in one public official and the principle that no man was above the law:

The executive power is better to be trusted when it has no screen. Sir, we have a responsibility in the person of our President; he cannot act improperly, and hide either his negligence or inattention; he cannot roll upon any other person the weight of his criminality; no appointment can take place without his nomination; and he is responsible for every nomination he makes. . . . Add to all this, that officer is placed high, and is possessed of power far from being contemptible, yet not a single privilege, is annexed to his character; far from being above the laws, he is amenable to them in his private character as a citizen, and in his public character by impeachment.[5]

Support for the impeachment remedy was overwhelming, though not unanimous. Gouverneur Morris and Charles Pinckney, for example, worried that impeachment proceedings might interfere with the president's effective performance of his duties. Moreover, because chief executives would always have subordinates in the commission of any crime, they thought it sufficient that these "coadjutors" could be punished during the presidential term. Morris also offered what may be the ultimate argument for the political rather than legal essence of the matter: If a president were reelected, he opined, that would be sufficient proof that he should not be impeached.

Quite rightly, the other delegates were not moved by these qualms. After all, a president who was corrupt in the execution of his duties would spare no corrupt efforts to get himself reelected, especially if winning would immunize him from impeachment. His perfidy might not be discovered until after reelection was secured. These all too real possibilities, Mason pointed out, "furnished a peculiar reason in favor of impeachments whilst [the president was] in office." Plus, the law regarded principals as responsible and thus punishable for the wrongs of their coadjutors; manifestly, this should no less be so when it came to the president—the principal capable of doing the greatest harm to the republic. It was, unsurprisingly, Benjamin Franklin who offered the convention's most bracing point in favor of impeachment: Historically, when no impeachment remedy was available to a society, "recourse was had to assassination" in cases where "the chief magistrate had rendered himself obnoxious"—an intolerable outcome that not only "deprived [him] of his life but of the opportunity of vindicating his character."

Ever concerned about the balance of powers among the branches that is the Constitution's genius, the Framers did worry that granting impeachment authority to Congress could give the legislature too much power over the executive. Any governmental power can be abused, and impeachment is no exception. But though this danger could not be discounted, it would be mitigated by the unlikelihood that a large bicameral legislature drawn from different states with divergent interests—as opposed to a single chief executive—could be broadly corrupted. Moreover, the high hurdle of a two-thirds supermajority needed for conviction in the Senate would guard against wrongful removal.[6]

History attests to the Framers' wisdom in this regard. In over two and a quarter centuries of constitutional governance, articles of impeachment have been formally voted by the full House of Representatives against only two American presidents, Andrew Johnson and Bill Clinton. In each case, there were insufficient votes in the Senate to convict and remove the incumbent from office. A third president, Richard Nixon, would surely have been impeached and removed had he, like Johnson and Clinton, chosen to fight to the bitter end.[7]

The convention delegates concurred in the principles that the United States is a nation of laws not men and that the potential for abuse of the presidency's awesome powers required making provision for removal of an unfit incumbent. This consensus, however, did not immediately translate into agreement on an impeachment standard. It was assumed from the first that a president would be removable for "malpractice or neglect of duty." Yet, consistent with the concern that the executive not become too beholden to Congress, some delegates suggested a narrower and more objective standard that stressed the gravity of impeachment: The president would be removable only for treason or bribery. But this was clearly insufficient, failing to account for an array of corrupt and incompetent actions not necessarily related to either cupidity or treachery.

Such condemnable conduct was not merely foreseeable in the abstract. The Framers had a concrete, contemporaneous example: the sensational impeachment trial in Parliament of Warren Hastings, Britain's governor-general in India. The primary proponent of Hastings's impeachment was Edmund Burke, the renowned Whig parliamentarian, political philosopher, and supporter of the American Revolution. Burke extensively charged Hastings with "high crimes and misdemeanors," the ancient British standard for removing malfeasant public officials. While some of Hastings's offenses involved bribery, most related to extortion, heavy-handed corruption, trumped-up prosecutions (resulting in death and other severe punishments), the allegedly reckless conduct of warfare, and what we would today call "human rights" abuses against the indigenous people of England's Indian domains. Far from treasonous, Hastings's actions were intended to preserve and strengthen the British Empire's position (even if, to Burke's mind, their wanton immorality and disregard for Indian sensibilities arguably weakened it).[8]

The impeachment inquiry on Hastings's governance formally began in 1786, and articles against him in the House of Commons were voted the next year, only a few weeks before the Philadelphia convention. Mason noted the spectacle in positing that the executive would be inadequately restrained if impeachment were limited to treason and bribery: "Treason as defined in the Constitution will not reach many great and dangerous offenses. Hastings is not guilty of Treason. Attempts to subvert the Constitution may not be Treason[.]"After the delegates finally agreed to add "high crimes and misdemeanors" to treason and bribery as grounds for impeachment, Hamilton explained that Great Britain provided "the model from which [impeachment] has been borrowed."[9]

"High crimes and misdemeanors" was not Mason's first choice. He argued for "maladministration," the term used in the impeachment provisions of several state constitutions. Blackstone's *Commentaries on the Laws of England*, a magisterial legal treatise that profoundly influenced the Framers, described "maladministration of such high officers, as are in public trust and employment" as the "first and principal" of the "high misdemeanors"—offenses "against the king and government" that were punished by "parliamentary impeachment."[10] "Maladministration" was indeed close to the concept the delegates had in mind, but Madison had reservations about its vagueness. A promiscuous construction of the term could devolve into legislative *dominance* over the executive, going well beyond the objective of empowering Congress to deal decisively with a president who had demonstrated himself truly unfit. Mason responded to Madison's concerns by amending his proposal to "high crimes and misdemeanors," which had the benefit of being a venerable term of art.[11] This standard was adopted by the convention and enshrined in the Constitution.[12]

All public officials are certain to err at times, and chief executives, who make the most consequential decisions, can err egregiously. Nor will it be uncommon for presidents to abuse their powers to a limited extent, whether because of venal character or because it is often the president's burden to navigate between Scylla and Charybdis. Comparatively few presidents, though, will prove dangerously unfit for high office. Thus, impeachment was designed to be neither over- nor under-inclusive. "High crimes and misdemeanors," complementing treason and bribery, was an apt resolution. It captures severe derelictions of duty that could fatally compromise our constitutional order, but eschews impeachments based on trifling irregularities.

As Burke made clear, "high crimes and misdemeanors" had been used by the British Parliament for centuries. The Constitutional Rights Foundation elaborates:

> Officials accused of "high crimes and misdemeanors" were accused of offenses as varied as misappropriating government funds, appointing unfit subordinates, not prosecuting cases, not spending money allocated by Parliament, promoting themselves ahead of more deserving candidates, threatening a grand jury, disobeying an order from Parliament, arresting a man to keep him from running for Parliament, losing a ship by neglecting to moor it, helping "suppress petitions to the King to call a Parliament," granting warrants without cause, and bribery. Some of these charges were crimes. Others were not. The one common denominator in all these accusations was that the official had somehow abused the power of his office and was unfit to serve.[13]

"High crimes and misdemeanors" is a concept rooted not in statutory offenses fit for criminal court proceedings, but in damage done to the societal order by persons in whom great public trust has been reposed. Hamilton described impeachable offenses as those which proceed from the misconduct of public men, or in other words from the abuse or violation of some public trust. They are of a nature which may with peculiar propriety be denominated POLITICAL, as they relate chiefly to injuries done immediately to the society itself.[14] [Emphasis in original.]

Mason fixed on betrayal of the president's fiduciary duty and oath of allegiance to our system of government, saying that "attempts to subvert the Constitution" would be chief among the "many great and dangerous offences" beyond treason and bribery for which removal of the president would be warranted. It is noteworthy for our purposes that the Framers regarded the mere attempt to subvert the Constitution, whether successful or not, as a sufficiently heinous breach of trust to warrant removal by impeachment.

What distinguishes impeachment from judicial proceedings and technical legal processes is its *political* aspect. As the Constitution Society's Jon Roland points out, it was immaterial whether the offenses cited in articles of impeachment "were prohibited by statutes"; what mattered were "the obligations of the offender. . . . The obligations of a person holding a high position meant that some actions, or inactions, could be punishable if he did them, even though they would not be if done by an ordinary person."[15]

This explanation echoes Joseph Story's elaboration on the "political character" of impeachment in his seminal 1833 treatise, *Commentaries on the Constitution*. Justice Story noted that while "crimes of a strictly legal character" would be included, the removal power

has a more enlarged operation, and reaches, what are aptly termed political offenses, growing out of personal misconduct or gross neglect, or usurpation, or habitual disregard of the public interests, various in their character, and so indefinable in their actual involutions, that it is almost impossible to provide systematically for them by positive law They must be examined upon very broad and comprehensive principles of public policy and duty. They must be judged of by the habits and rules and principles of diplomacy, or departmental operations and arrangements, of parliamentary practice, of executive customs and negotiations of foreign as well as domestic political movements; and in short, by a great variety of circumstances, as well those which aggravate as those which extenuate or justify the offensive acts which do not properly belong to the judicial character in the ordinary administration of justice, and are far removed from the reach of municipal jurisprudence.[16]

An essential attribute of criminal laws is definitiveness. Our jurisprudence mandates that the laws put a person of ordinary intelligence on notice about what is prohibited. Otherwise, law enforcement becomes capricious and tyrannical. "High crimes and misdemeanors," by contrast, is a concept neither conceived for nor applicable to quotidian law enforcement. It is redolent of oath, honor, and fiduciary obligation. These notions, conveying positive duties, are more demanding of the public officials than the clear prohibitions of the criminal law. They are also more abstract: It is not as easy to divine what duty calls for in the various situations a public official confronts as it is to say whether a given private citizen's course of conduct satisfies the essential elements of a penal statute.

This distinction makes impeachment rare—a process reserved for grave public wrongs. It does not make impeachment arbitrary, as implied by the deservedly maligned claim that "an impeachable offense is whatever a majority of the House of Representatives considers it to be at a given moment in history." It is one of history's curiosities that this assertion was made in 1970 by Congressman Gerald R. Ford during his failed effort to impeach William O. Douglas, the irascible liberal Supreme Court justice. Ford would replace Spiro Agnew as vice president before the end of 1973, and Richard Nixon as president eight months later—Agnew and Nixon both having resigned to avoid impeachment and removal.[17]

It is odd that politicians, law professors, and plaintiff's lawyers have been known to complain that "high crimes and misdemeanors" is too amorphous a notion to apply to political wrongs. They rarely think twice about dressing down, condemning, or filing suit against a corporate CEO for breaches of fiduciary obligations. Do they really think a president should be less accountable than a CEO? In truth, the president, the commander in chief, is akin to a soldier in that his duties make him punishable for actions that would not be offenses if committed by a civilian: such things as abuse of authority, dereliction of duty, moral turpitude, conduct unbecoming, and the violation of an oath.[18]

The delegates to the Constitutional Convention were adamant that impeachment not reach to errors of judgment, or what Edmund Randolph described as "a willful mistake of the heart, or an involuntary fault of the head." On the other hand, betrayals of the constitutional order, dishonesty in the executive's dealing with Congress, and concealment of dealings with foreign powers that could be injurious to the rights of the people were among the most grievous high crimes and misdemeanors in the Framers' estimation. The concept also embraced the principle that "the most powerful magistrates should be amenable to the law," as James Wilson put it in his "Lectures on Law," delivered shortly after the Constitution was adopted.

For example, in response to a hypothetical in which a president, to ram a treaty through to ratification, brought together friendly senators from only a few of the states so as to rig the Constitution's two-thirds approval process, Madison remarked: "Were the president to commit any thing so atrocious . . . he would be impeached and convicted, as a majority of the states would be affected by his misdemeanor." Iredell made clear that the president "must certainly be punishable for giving false information to the Senate. He is to regulate all intercourse with foreign powers, and it is his duty to impart to the Senate every material intelligence he receives." It would be untenable to abide a president's fraudulently inducing senators "to enter into measures injurious to their country, and which they would not have consented to had the true state of things been disclosed to them."

Finally, the Framers stressed that the impeachment remedy was a vital congressional check on the executive branch as a whole, not just on the president's personal compliance with constitutional norms. The chief executive, Madison asserted, would be wholly "responsible for [the] conduct" of executive branch officials. Therefore, it would "subject [the president] to impeachment himself, if he suffers them to perpetrate with impunity high crimes or misdemeanors against the United States, or neglects to superintend their conduct, so as to check their excesses."

What would the Framers have made of a U.S. attorney general who practices racial discrimination in executing the civil rights laws, politicizes law enforcement, and urges state attorneys general to ignore the laws they are sworn to defend? Of a Homeland Security secretary who obstructs sovereign states trying to defend themselves from illegal immigration? Of a secretary of state who collaborates with foreign governments to diminish American constitutional rights and recklessly neglects to provide adequate security for American officials, who consequently get killed serving in the perilous foreign posts to which she has irresponsibly dispatched them? What would the Framers have made of a Health and Human

Services secretary (perhaps I should end the question right there) who energetically violates and rewrites congressional statutes in the simultaneously fraudulent and incompetent implementation of a government plan to seize control of the private economy's health-care sector? What would they make of the habit the president's "coadjutors" have made of misleading and stonewalling Congress?

They would have made a case for impeaching and removing the president.

CHAPTER THREE

THE I-WORD

"I don't think you should be hesitant to say the word in this room."
The room in which Georgetown law school's Nicholas Rosenkranz
was sitting was on Capitol Hill, specifically, the room where the
Judiciary Committee of the U.S. House of Representatives conducts
its hearings. The word he was referring to is *impeachment*.

Professor Rosenkranz was mildly chastising Rep. Steve King,
an exceptional Republican congressman from Iowa. Unlike most
of his colleagues, Congressman King has exerted himself mightily
in search of practical ways to combat the Obama administration's
lawlessness. Yet he was tongue-tied at the prospect of uttering, let
alone seriously discussing, the Framers' carefully tailored solution
for incorrigible presidents.

Professor Rosenkranz must have thought he had already broken
the spell. Earlier in the session, a hearing on the president's constitutional duty to execute the laws faithfully, he had been unrestrained:

"The ultimate check on presidential lawlessness is elections and, in extreme cases, impeachment," he testified. But his clarity just seemed to spook senior Republican staffers, who winced at each invocation of the i-word.[1]

The GOP had better get past its angst—either that or be prepared to accept a government that is more a centralized dictatorship than a federalist republic under the rule of law. Congress has only two means of checking presidential lawlessness: the power of the purse and the power to impeach and remove. If the opposition party in Congress finds it inconceivable that these powers should be used, it is effectively abetting and institutionalizing the imperial presidency.[2]

Elections are also a check on presidential excess, but more so as originally conceived than as they occur today. In the first elections under the Constitution, each state would choose prominent, knowledgeable citizens to sit in the Electoral College (in direct numerical proportion to each state's congressional delegation), and these electors would vote for the president and vice president. The rise of political parties caused this system to be frayed after only four election cycles, and the historical trend toward popular elections has rendered the Electoral College largely a formality.

The original Electoral College had been modeled on the Centurial Assembly system of the Roman Republic precisely because the Framers were suspicious of the mischief that political parties could make.[3] The idea was to conduct elections without parties or national campaigns: have statesmen elect a president invested in preserving the constitutional framework, rather than indulge the spectacle of candidates promising the moon as they barnstorm the country vying for power. The rapid ascent of partisan politics—in which James Madison and several other Philadelphia convention delegates were key figures—illustrates that the Framers' lofty goal was unrealistic. It does not discredit their suspicions.

The Framers were particularly attuned to the timeless challenge of managing factional strife.[4] They feared that ideological factions, through the machinations of political parties, would be intent on acquiring power and imposing their pieties. They would not prioritize preservation of the Constitution's delicate balance of power. It is this separation of powers—among the branches of the national government, and between that government and the sovereign states—that guards against any single governmental component's accumulation of tyrannical power. The competition between authorities, their monitoring and checking of one another, ensures freedom by protecting the citizen from oppression.

The modern left proves how prescient the Framers were. The left's class warfare strategies mean that election campaigns are actually conducted against the Constitution's safeguards of freedom. Supporters of the Constitution's federalist framework of limited central government and its protection of liberty and property rights are demagogued as enemies of social justice. Statist candidates construe electoral victories as a mandate to undo constitutional constraints that impede their authority to do "the right thing," as Obama puts it. Winning office becomes a license for lawlessness.

The power of the purse, too, has been eviscerated as a practical check against an outlaw president. The Constitution presumes that the different branches of government will protect their institutional turf. The Framers reasoned that Congress, faced with a president who usurps legislative prerogatives, would fight back by cutting off money the president would need to carry out the usurpation.[5] Even after partisan politics took over, it was assumed that politicians took their constitutional responsibilities seriously, either out of noble statesmanship or in the practical calculation that voters expected the Constitution's protections of liberty to be honored. A congressman of the president's party would see himself, first and foremost, as a congressman. Valuing the duties of his office over party loyalty, he would join with other legislators to rein in executive excess.

Today's Democrats, however, are members not just of a party but, perhaps even more, of the movement left. Their objective, like Obama's, is fundamental transformation of a society rooted in individual liberty and private property into one modeled on top-down, redistributionist statism. Since statism advances by concentrating governmental power, Democrats—regardless of what governmental branch they happen to inhabit—rally to whatever branch holds the greatest transformative potential. Right now, that is the presidency.

Congressional Democrats want the current president to use the enormous raw power vested in his office by Article II to achieve statist transformation. If he does so, they will support him. They do not insist that he comply with congressional statutes—which must be consistent with the Constitution in order to be valid, and thus may reflect the very constitutional values the left is trying to supplant. Democrats will get back to obsessing over the "rule of law" if and when Republicans win another presidential election.

While Democrats quite intentionally defy the Framers' design, Republicans frustrate it by aggressive passivity. They incessantly tell supporters that they are impotent to rein in Obama's excesses because the GOP controls "only one half of one third of the government."[6]

This argument ignores the fact that the Constitution divides power by subject matter, not percentage of governmental control. The party that controls the House has full primacy in taxing and spending, every bit as much as the party that controls the executive branch has plenary control over prosecution decisions. Constitutional authorities are not contingent on how much (if any) control the party in question has over the rest of government.[7] In theory, then, nothing in government can happen unless the House, with ultimate power over the purse, agrees to fund it. If a corrupt administration uses the IRS as a partisan weapon to audit and harass its detractors, the House can refuse to fund the IRS—or other parts of the executive branch—in order to curb executive overreach.[8]

Historically, congressional Democrats have used the power of the purse to stop Republican presidents from, say, prosecuting the Vietnam War or aiding the Nicaraguan Contras. Yet when today's conservatives in the House or the Senate urge fellow Republicans to use their command over the purse to stop Obama's excesses, the GOP leadership turns on them with a ferocity rarely evident in their dealings with the president.

The late political scientist Aaron B. Wildavsky noted that "the power of the purse is the heart of legislative authority and thus an essential check on the executive branch." Indeed, he observed, "An executive establishment freed from dependence for funds upon the legislature (and hence the public) would be a law unto itself and ultimately a despotism."[9] Alas, with Democrats energized by Obama's law breaking and Republicans paralyzed by fear of being blamed for government shutdowns if they use their constitutional muscle, there is no realistic prospect that Congress will starve Obama of funding.

That leaves impeachment as the sole remaining constitutional safeguard against executive imperialism. There is nothing else.

Republicans have talked themselves—*petrified* themselves— into the canard that the failed Clinton impeachment effort cautions against *any* conceivable impeachment scenario (just as they construe the mid-nineties budget showdown with Clinton as a caution against any conceivable government shutdown scenario). At the aforementioned hearing on presidential lawlessness, Congressman King steered awkwardly around the elephant in the room.

After lumbering through other theoretical checks on the executive that had, as a practical matter, proved impotent against President Obama's enterprising lawlessness, King finally muttered, "Then the next recourse is, as Mr. Rosenkranz said, the word that we don't like to say in this committee and that I'm not about to utter here in this particular hearing."

Well, the word needs uttering. Absent a frank discussion of what impeachment is, what it's for, when it should apply, and why it is necessary (that is, why other remedies are inadequate), we will never know whether political support for impeachment can materialize. Analyzing constitutional remedies for executive lawlessness without discussing impeachment makes as much sense as analyzing Islamic terrorism without discussing Islam—and the fact that the latter is Obama administration policy ought not elevate incoherence into binding precedent. We must not fear the word, Rosenkranz aptly insisted. "A check on executive lawlessness is impeachment," he said. "And if you find the president is willfully and repeatedly violating the Constitution. . . . I think that would be a clear case for impeachment."[10]

A clear *legal* case, to be sure. Willful and repeated violation of the Constitution is *the* textbook example of high crimes and misdemeanors. But the legal case is not the half of it when it comes to removing a president.

Unlike the simple majority vote required for the House to approve articles of impeachment, a conviction by a two-thirds supermajority of the Senate is necessary to impose the Constitution's impeachment penalty: "removal from office, and disqualification to hold and enjoy any office of honor, trust or profit under the United States."[11] Unless the point of the exercise is mere partisan foot stamping, it is not enough to have sufficient legal grounds for impeachment, even lots and lots of grounds. *Real* impeachment, removing the president from power, requires political support.

On that score, Republicans have vastly overinterpreted the Clinton impeachment episode. They construe it to mean that the societal turmoil inevitably caused by attempting to impeach a president—a cynic might say, the bad press ensured by any effort to impeach a left-wing Democratic president—is so much worse for the country than any offenses the president might be committing that it is simply not worth the effort—cynic again: simply not worth turning the Republican Party into the media's punching bag. Such thinking results in paralysis, and thus in abdication of Congress's duty to protect the constitutional framework—a duty just as solemn as the president's.

This does not mean that Congressman King is wrong when he asserts, "You'll never get an honest [impeachment] verdict out of the United States Senate if Harry Reid is going to be the majority leader."[12] But someone like Reid will always be the majority leader if the minority party is too craven to make a dynamic stand against unprecedented executive lawlessness. Changing the dynamic requires moving public opinion, which in turn hinges on forcing the president's myrmidons to defend his high crimes and misdemeanors under an intense spotlight.

The decision whether to remove a president is political. As Senator Cruz said, you need to have the votes. Not just enough votes to win in a squeaker; you need 67 out of 100. As we've seen, the Framers did not want impeachment to be a power play. The assent of an overwhelming majority of senators is mandatory because impeachment must be tantamount to a proclamation of overwhelming public sentiment. It must reflect the desire of the American people that the president be removed.

At the moment, there are effectively 55 Democrats in the Senate: 53 party members plus two ostensible "independents" who caucus with them. Besides being extraordinarily partisan, they are a very disciplined voting bloc. Even if all 45 Republicans were persuaded to convict the president of high crimes and misdemeanors, 22 Democrats would have to break ranks and join with them for the president to be removed. And if the current crop of GOP senators were to engage in their familiar parliamentary gamesmanship, you might not even get 45 Republicans voting to convict—unless they were sure the president would prevail and that their futile votes could be good campaign fodder in their particular election races.[13]

Right now, conviction in the Senate is a pipedream, and therefore one cannot reasonably expect the House to file articles of impeachment. The process of impeachment will always be an ordeal, regardless of how necessary it is. Americans may be convincible regarding the need to oust a lawless president, but they will never be happy about it. Nor should they be. Even the president's most zealous detractors should prefer that he mend his outlaw ways and finish his term than that the country be put through an impeachment process that would be painful in the best of times. And these are not the best of times: today, the pain would be exacerbated by the vulgar propensity of the left and the media to demagogue concern for the nation's well-being as racism. Consequently, impeachment entails substantial political risk for the protagonists, even if they are clearly right to seek it. House members have no incentive to push for impeachment charges unless conviction in the Senate is within the realm of possibility.

Of course it matters that the president has patently and routinely violated his solemn oath to preserve, protect and defend the Constitution. And of course it matters that the president has willfully betrayed his constitutional duty to take care that the laws

46

be faithfully executed. Still, the real significance of these facts lies not in their legal qualification as impeachable offenses but in their solidity as the foundation of a compelling political case for presidential removal.

The legal aspect of the case is the easy part. That impeachable offenses have been committed is manifest once one grasps the concept of "high crimes and misdemeanors"—which are offenses against the governing fabric by those sworn to uphold it; fraud on the public and its representatives by those entrusted with the highest fiduciary duty. In fact, given that the point of impeachment is to preserve the United States of America, and that the point of the Obama presidency is, as he boldly promised supporters, to "fundamentally transform the United States of America,"[14] how surprised can we really be that the president and the Constitution have been on an impeachment collision course?

Proving "high crimes and misdemeanors" is *necessary* to make the case for presidential removal, but it is not *sufficient*. The politics takes precedence: The public must reach the conclusion that the constitutionally subversive nature of the impeachable offenses renders it intolerable to permit the president to continue in power; and the public must make its representatives understand that failing to act on that conclusion will shorten their cherished Washington careers.

That is the true lesson of the Bill Clinton impeachment controversy. The error to avoid is not the endeavor to remove a rogue president; it is the endeavor to remove a rogue president *without first having convinced the public that his removal is warranted*—that the punishment fits the crime.

On December 19, 1998, the House approved two articles of impeachment against President Clinton, involving misconduct that, while criminal and cringe-inducing, reflected more on his deep character flaws than on his execution of the presidency's core responsibilities.

Earlier, a grand jury had been convened to investigate allegations of corruption. Much of this involved the "Whitewater" real estate venture in Arkansas, which occurred before Clinton became president. Some of it, while certainly within the ambit of his presidential duties, was not central to them—for example, cronyism in the firing of White House travel office personnel. In the course of the investigation, it emerged that the president had conducted a sexual liaison with Monica Lewinsky, a young White House intern. Clinton had also pressured Ms. Lewinsky to lie about the affair to investigators, and had lied about previously perjuring himself in a deposition when another woman, Paula Jones, sued him for sexual harassment.[15]

The two impeachment articles charged President Clinton with perjury and obstruction of justice.[16] The charges satisfied the "high crimes and misdemeanors" threshold, for it is perfectly reasonable to conclude that a president who corruptly impedes the administration of justice is not fit for office. After all, his responsibilities include ensuring the administration of justice and otherwise faithfully executing the laws. Clinton, moreover, was clearly guilty.

Nevertheless, the American people obviously did not want him removed over the charges. Opinion polls illustrated that a majority of the public, while troubled by Clinton's character, approved of his overall job performance; and with impeachment proceedings under way, "approval" was effectively a proxy for rejecting the effort to oust him.[17] In addition, on the eve of the House decision to vote articles of impeachment, the public handed Republicans a historically significant loss in the 1998 midterm elections. With Clinton's misconduct front-and-center in the campaign, Republicans gained no Senate seats and actually lost four seats in the House. That may sound marginal, but it marked the first time in over sixty years that a president's opposition party failed to gain seats in a midterm election, and the first time since 1822 that this happened in the midterm elections of a president's second term.[18] With the public clearly disfavoring impeachment, neither article against Clinton garnered majority support, much less the 67 votes needed for conviction, despite the Republicans' 55-to-45 majority in the Senate.[19]

Lawmakers who have determined that presidential malfeasance merits impeachment have an obligation to try to persuade Americans that this is so. Making the effort is not indecorous partisanship; it is the imperative of preserving the Constitution to the best of one's abilities. Nevertheless, lawmakers must also accept that impeachment is innately political. It is not the final link in a rigorous chain of legal logic. High crimes and misdemeanors do not equal impeachment and removal the way, say, stealing your company's money equals embezzlement.

Law is obliged to be logical; politics is not. Law is about faithfully applying settled principles to current controversies—reason shorn of passion. Politics is about compromise and social cohesion—the art of the possible, not of the rigorously rational. If, after extensively scrutinizing the evidence, Americans decide that their president is a creep but his personal creepiness does not materially compromise his job performance, that is a decision they get to make. Members of Congress should respect that decision even if they believe it is wrong—as long as they have had a full and fair opportunity to make the case that the president should be removed.

Obamacare provides a useful analogy. What so enraged Americans about the health-care overhaul that they subjected Democrats throughout the nation, at both the federal and state levels, to a historic "shellacking" in the 2010 elections?[20] Remember, this was before the fraud that pervaded Obamacare's enactment was well understood, before much of the lawlessness that has attended its implementation, and before the havoc it is now wreaking on American families and businesses. The public's anger was inspired by the arrogance exhibited by Democrats in unilaterally ramming the "Affordable" Care Act through despite the full-throated opposition of a strong majority of Americans. It is extremely foolish for politicians to press ahead with highly volatile measures against the will of the American people.

To gauge the strength of the political case for impeachment, the sensibilities of the public to whom the case must be made are just as important as the gravity of the president's malfeasance. You can have a hundred readily provable articles of impeachment; what really counts, though, is what Americans think of their president. The question is not whether the president has done wrong—that will rarely be in dispute. The question is how convinced the public is that a president's continued hold on power profoundly threatens their safety, prosperity, and sense of what kind of country we should be. Clinton's episodes of illegality did not approach this dimension of threat; by contrast, Obama's systematic lawlessness is the classic case—it is, indeed, a self-proclaimed attempt to remake the country fundamentally.

But even classic cases have to be made. It is prudent for Republicans to take from the Clinton impeachment the lesson that the House should not proceed with impeachment articles unless there is such strong public support for removing the president that the Senate would be under great pressure to convict—that senators who protected the president against the weight of the evidence would draw the public's ire. But that does not mean Republicans should refrain from arguing that impeachment is the Constitution's answer to presidential lawlessness.

Republicans, as well as Democrats committed to our constitutional framework, should fearlessly marshal the administration's frauds, obstructions, and violations of law. They should demand transparency and accountability for the lies, the broken oaths, the betrayal of the rule of law, and the damage wrought—including lives not only devastated but lost due to the administration's recklessness. They should forcefully condemn the president's imperial designs. They should unapologetically persuade Americans that the accumulated wreckage coupled with the president's stubborn determination to continue on his course—indeed, to increase the pace and scope of his diktats—cries out for serious consideration of his removal from office. They should make presidential lawlessness the central issue in the upcoming election cycle. *Lawlessness*, faithless execution, is the theme that illuminates Obamacare, the IRS scandal, the Benghazi massacre, Fast and Furious, the campaign to erode our constitutional liberties, and the growing instability that threatens our prosperity and security.

Of course, the ability to prove grave impeachable offenses that threaten the constitutional framework will not count for much unless the American people are actually invested in preserving the limitations on presidential authority that safeguard their liberties. Do Americans still broadly believe that a president's gradual assumption of dictatorial power must be halted? That the constitutional equilibrium of divided authorities balancing and checking each other must be preserved? That their liberty hinges on the separation of powers? That their liberty is what defines and empowers them?

President Obama has not just "pushed the legal envelope," opined Tom McClintock, a Republican congressman from California, but has "shredded the legal envelope." Yet this does not seem to trouble many younger Americans, he lamented, and with

Obama having been reelected despite violating the laws, Representative McClintock could not see impeachment on the horizon. "Ultimately," he concluded, "it will come down to whether the owners of the Constitution insist that it be enforced with the votes they cast at the ballot box. So far this generation has been rather lax."[21] True enough. But these same young Americans are now coming of age and beginning to experience the wages of lawlessness in very personal and painful ways. To borrow an ironic refrain from a president who doesn't seem to learn much, perhaps we have arrived at "a teachable moment."

All presidential lawlessness is not the same, and thus all impeachable offenses are not created equal. Real impeachment will never happen unless the people are convinced, by the nature of the president's lawlessness, that it must be stopped and that it will not be stopped unless he is removed from office. Are we talking about a Clintonesque episode that casts grave doubt on the fitness and judgment of the incumbent but, on balance, does not appear to threaten our governing framework and thus our freedom and security? Or is it a systematic, remorseless attack on that governing framework with the precise purpose of supplanting it—not because the president is necessarily a badly flawed character, but because he has a different vision of the just society and an ideological fervor to impose it?

President Obama's lawlessness falls into the latter category, and therefore the political case for impeachment should by all means be made. The objective must be removal, not just formal articles of impeachment—to purge the lawlessness, not merely document it. Historians may catalogue Obama's derelictions of duty; Congress's job is to check those derelictions *effectively*.

CHAPTER FOUR

THE POINT
IS REMOVAL

While Republican leaders seem terrified by the mere mention of the "i-word," conservatives are divided on the subject—which at least means they're talking about it. David Catron, a writer for the *American Spectator* whose work I admire, passionately argues for impeachment *now*, contrary to my assessment that a public case has to be built before the House considers actually filing articles of impeachment. In Catron's view,

> It is the *duty* of the House of Representatives to impeach Obama. Every member of Congress takes an oath to defend the Constitution and the President has declared war on that foundational document. Barack Obama is systematically destroying the checks and balances the framers put in place to limit the power of the office he holds.[1] [Emphasis in original.]

Mr. Catron reasons that Ted Cruz is "evidently confused" when he observes that there are not enough votes in the Senate for impeachment—as if the senator, a graduate of Princeton and Harvard Law School who has argued several cases before the U.S. Supreme Court as solicitor general of Texas, must have missed class the day they taught the difference between impeachment and removal. According to Catron, the need for a two-thirds Senate majority for removal is "irrelevant" because impeachment, the House allegation of high crimes and misdemeanors, is a "separate step—roughly analogous to an indictment in a criminal court." As Catron's theory unfolds, the House morphs from grand jury to street cop:

> If a policeman sees a thief picking your pocket, should he stand by and ponder the very real possibility that some clever defense attorney might help the criminal escape justice? Of course not. It's his job to arrest the pickpocket and make sure that he faces trial for his crime. Then, even if a corrupt judge or a simple-minded jury lets the crook off, at least he has done his job. In the case under discussion here, Obama is the crook and the House of Representatives is the policeman.

On health care, a subject in which he is well versed, Mr. Catron is a stellar analyst.[2] He appears unfamiliar, though, with the way police and grand juries actually work.

The police do not make an arrest every time they witness a crime. They exercise judgment, which constitutes the investigative side of the prosecutorial-discretion coin. For example, in the disco era of high urban crime, the term "revolving door justice" gained currency, describing a situation where the due process pendulum had swung so far in the direction of the crooks that an arrestee was back out on the street committing more crimes before the cops could finish the paperwork. The police responded rationally, by making fewer arrests.

This was not a dereliction of duty. To the contrary, the cop on the beat understood better than most that a clearly guilty criminal who was cited but not effectively prosecuted—meaning, not convicted and incapacitated by a jail sentence—was emboldened, not chastened. The arrest and its documented description of the charge, which barely slowed down the pace of the arrestee's serial criminality, stood as a testament to the system's lack of resolve to confront his lawlessness in a meaningful way. To maintain their own credibility, which was essential to preserve what remained of law and order, the police did their best to discourage crime by their presence on patrol, though of course they could not be everyplace, or even most places. They often intervened in criminal situations without apprehending anyone, reserving their power to arrest and commence the formal criminal-justice process for those offenses that were too serious for the system to ignore. It was not until the political environment changed—until the public demanded a restoration of domestic tranquility and elected responsive public officials—that the legal environment changed, encouraging police to make more arrests because they knew the cases would be prosecuted through to completion.

There are similar flaws in the comparison of impeachment by the House to indictment by a grand jury. Although it is considerably easier to indict than to convict a defendant, prosecutors generally do not indict cases unless a conviction is highly likely.

It is not without some justification that people say a prosecutor "could indict a ham sandwich," so low is the bar to satisfying a grand jury. There is no defense counsel in the grand jury, and the government's lawyer is, practically speaking, both prosecutor and judge. The prosecution is not obliged to disclose any exculpatory evidence it may have. The prospective defendant's side of the story is rarely presented. The proof standard for approving an indictment is merely "probable cause," not the more exacting "beyond a reasonable doubt." And the grand jury's decision, unlike a trial jury's, need not be unanimous.

It sounds terribly unfair. Remember, however, that the principal purpose of the grand jury is not to try the case or establish guilt; it is to establish that *there is a case*. Moreover, a grand jury requires testimony under oath, thus theoretically protecting the citizen against charges that are trumped up, based on grossly inadequate evidence, or disproportionate to the conduct involved. An indicted case is not necessarily a persuasive case, just one deemed worthy of graduating to a trial court, where the allegations will be scrutinized with much more rigor.

All that said, a good prosecutor has no more interest in pursuing a fatally flawed case than a good police officer has in making a pointless arrest. Prosecutors generally bring to the grand jury only those cases they've already decided are worthy of an eventual trial—meaning, they've made the ethical calculation that the expenditure of public resources to process the case through to verdict is warranted because the case is sufficiently serious, the defendant is worth prosecuting (because of his prior history and/or the gravity of the alleged offense), and the evidence is such that a rational jury would convict. Many cases do not make the cut. Thus, a prosecutor does not indict them, even though, as a matter of law, he easily could.

If a case is terminated without further prosecution, that does not mean the underlying arrests were invalid. It means that even though the police established probable cause of some crime, either (a) there is not enough evidence to prove guilt beyond a reasonable doubt, or (b) the criminal conduct is too petty to warrant further processing when finite law enforcement and judicial resources are better allocated to more serious cases. In the prosecution's discretion, such cases are dismissed outright or on "deferred prosecution" arrangements (i.e., the charges will be expunged if the arrestee keeps his nose clean for an agreed-upon period of time).

For the cases deemed worthy of being pursued, the grand jury serves a very useful public function. Yes, it is rare that grand juries return a "no true bill," a formal refusal to indict, but often the prosecutor decides not to ask for a true bill because the presentation to the grand jury does not go well. The grand jury's questions for the witnesses or colloquies with the prosecutor may have convinced the government that the case has severe weaknesses, and the result may be a plea bargain to lesser charges. Prosecutors may conclude that the case should never have been pursued in the first place and cut their losses with an outright dismissal. Most importantly, the grand jury's vetting serves the purpose of moving forward only with cases worthy of being prosecuted—cases in which there is *a strong chance of convicting the defendant* on charges that reflect the conduct's seriousness.

Special grand juries are often convened for long-term investigations involving major criminality such as racketeering enterprises or multimillion-dollar fraud schemes. The grand jury's investigative tools—subpoenas for testimony and physical evidence, or compulsion orders that confer immunity from prosecution on accomplices in exchange for truthful testimony—enable the prosecutor to amass evidence and build a solid, prosecutable case. The process can be painstaking, sometimes lasting well over a year, while the case is strategically built and the grand jury is gradually persuaded to indict. The time is worth taking because it increases the chance that serious, highly insulated criminals will be convicted.

The point of this mini tutorial is to demonstrate that, *pace* Mr. Catron, the objective of the criminal justice process is most certainly not merely to accuse someone of a crime. The objective is to do justice: Press the cases that merit being pressed, and convict the guilty in those cases. The pickpocket is not always arrested—the police may decide it is a higher priority to catch the armed robber they are chasing than to stop for the pickpocket. If the pickpocket is arrested, he may never be indicted, much less brought to trial—the police and the prosecutor may decide that he is a first offender and all he managed to take was your handkerchief; or that the backlog of violent felonies counsels letting him plead guilty to trespass and moving on. We can be confident, though, that he will be arrested and indicted only if the government believes it can convict him of a crime worth the expense of the process. Otherwise, either the arrest will not happen or the matter will be dismissed without further ado.

There is a patent flaw in the logic of Obama critics who want the president impeached right now despite the certainty that he would be acquitted. Mr. Catron declaims that, given the sizable Republican majority in the House, "one or more articles of impeachment could be passed against Obama . . . without a single Democrat vote." Catron elsewhere acknowledges, however, that the impeachment power—or, as he puts it, the impeachment *"duty"*—is vested in the *full House*, not just the House Republicans. Democratic representatives have no less a duty than their GOP counterparts to rein in the president's lawlessness. But Catron would not be calling for impeachment if Republicans were in the minority, because he knows it would be a waste of time—indeed, a counterproductive waste of time, since the defeat of an impeachment initiative would be construed as a congressional endorsement of Obama's outlaw methods. Of course, it would not *legally* qualify as an endorsement, but that would be the *political* fallout, the fallout that matters.

If the public is ever persuaded to support impeachment, it will be because the American people want the president removed from office; they will not be content with mere articles of impeachment. As things currently stand, the public does not support impeachment—no surprise, given that no substantial argument for impeachment has been attempted. Nor is it rational to demand that the Republican-controlled House impeach the president *now*, when the Democratic-controlled Senate would surely acquit him.

The only thing that would change this calculus is politics. To demonstrate why, it is more useful to compare impeachment to repealing Obamacare than to a grand jury indictment. Unlike the political case for impeachment, the case against the perversely titled Patient Protection and Affordable Care Act has been built. The law, always unpopular, is increasingly abhorrent. It thus makes perfect sense for the GOP-controlled House to keep passing repeal bills and forcing Senate Democrats either to cast accountable votes against repeal or to engage in parliamentary gamesmanship to prevent repeal from coming to the floor. It is a win-win, improving the chances of both defeating Obamacare supporters at the ballot box and ultimately repealing Obamacare (though I'm not holding my breath on that one).[3] Similarly, if a persuasive political case for removing President Obama were built, it would make sense for the House to pass articles of impeachment. At that ripe point, doing so would force Senate Democrats (and perhaps some of their moderate Republican colleagues) to confront the unpalatable but unavoidable choice of enabling an unpopular president's continued lawlessness or bowing to the public's will.

But to move on impeachment before political support is built, no matter how honorably intended, would look like partisan hackery. It would also be worse than futile.

Unlike President Obama, Attorney General Eric Holder—who came to the Obama administration tainted by his complicity in Clinton administration scandals like the pardons of Marc Rich and Puerto Rican FALN terrorists[4]—has never been broadly popular. By mid-2012, following revelations of his Justice Department's misrepresentations to Congress about the Fast and Furious investigation,[5] topped off by his defiance of lawful subpoenas for relevant DOJ documents, opinion polls showed increasing public support for Holder's resignation.[6]

House Republicans would have been wise to begin impeachment proceedings against Holder at that point, with the political wind at their backs. Congressional Democrats who had ferociously harassed Alberto Gonzales, the Bush attorney general, into resignation over comparative trifles[7] would have been boxed into a dreaded political corner, facing the choice of hypocritically rallying behind the unpopular Holder while he was still defying congressional subpoenas, or joining Republicans in removing him from office. To escape the dilemma, they would have pressured the White House and the attorney general himself for Holder's resignation—much as top Republicans pressured Richard Nixon to resign when supporting him became politically untenable in 1974. In the process, a bright public spotlight would have been fixed on the execrable Fast and Furious tactics; the resulting (and predictable) murder of a brave Border Patrol agent, Brian Terry; Holder's politicized and racially discriminatory stewardship of the Justice Department; and Obama administration lawlessness in general.[8]

Instead, with the 2012 election looming, Beltway Republicans convinced themselves that dealing responsibly with Holder would be more damaging for them than carrying Holder would be for the president. Fearful of being slandered as bigots over removing an African American Democratic attorney general (which for some strange reason does not seem to occur when Democrats chase a Hispanic Republican attorney general out of town), the GOP-controlled House cravenly settled on a toothless option: Holder was held in contempt for defying the Judiciary Committee's subpoenas. While Republicans congratulated themselves on this "unprecedented" species of rebuke, they made no effort to remove the attorney general from office. Ludicrously, they rationalized that the imagined gravity of this contempt citation would make Holder mend his ways.

To the contrary, down here on Planet Earth, Holder felt invincible. The contempt citation was laughed off as a partisan tactic—even though the lopsided 255–67 vote (with 17 Democrats in favor) illustrated that a serious attempt to remove Holder would have put Democrats on the defensive.[9] In theory, the congressional citation established the predicate for a criminal contempt prosecution; but of course, only the Obama Justice Department led by Holder could pursue such a case, and you'll be shocked to learn that there has been no indictment.[10] In the interim, the attorney general has merrily continued to defy the subpoena and to bury Fast and Furious as a public issue.[11] He has, in addition, provided Congress with more misleading testimony,[12] stonewalled more investigations, and appointed an Obama campaign donor to "investigate" the Obama administration's use of the IRS to harass Obama's political opponents,[13] while the department he leads files more vexatious lawsuits against states in defiance of Supreme Court precedent[14] and selectively prosecutes a conservative Obama critic.[15]

That is to say: the House's vaunted contempt citation became a license to mutilate—a formal proclamation of grave misconduct coupled with a convincing exhibition of the lack of will to do anything about it. As one would expect, it encouraged a bad actor to continue acting badly, and he has not disappointed.

Passing articles of impeachment against President Obama in the House at this premature point would have the same effect. There is no public will to remove the president and therefore no prospect of convicting him—or even of making Democrats nervous about protecting him—in the Senate. A good many fair-minded Americans would see the futile exercise as a partisan stunt and the president would be confirmed in his conceit that he can violate our laws with impunity.

Could things change? Of course they could. Richard Nixon won a landslide reelection in November 1972, prevailing by 503 electoral votes and 18 million popular votes. Only 21 months later, he resigned to avoid certain impeachment and removal. Obama is not nearly as popular now as Nixon was in late 1972. He won a fairly close reelection in 2012, his popular-vote tally plummeting by about 4 million from his initial election—making him the first incumbent president ever to win despite losing support. It is now clear that he won a second term on false premises: people will not be able to keep their health-care plans and doctors, al-Qaeda is not decimated, debt is higher, the percentage of Americans in the workforce is lower, and as the world grows more dangerous his response is to slash the military down to pre–World War II size. Obama's approval ratings have tanked, yet he remains firmly committed to his agenda. The president is causing pain, and pain has a way of changing people's minds.

Still, to recall the wisdom of Prime Minister Margaret Thatcher, you have to win the argument before you can hope to win the vote. An argument cannot be won if it's never made.

CHAPTER FIVE

POLITICS, NOT LAW

There are deep flaws in the contention that the House of Representatives should impeach whenever there are high crimes and misdemeanors just as a grand jury could indict whenever a crime is committed. We have seen that grand juries, in fact, are not asked to indict in every case where a crime is committed; they do not indict every case that is brought before them; and often their role is more investigative than accusatory—more to build a case worth pursuing than to issue a formal allegation of wrongs done. But this does not begin to capture the extent to which a presidential impeachment differs from a court case.

Good lawyers grasp the distinction. They know something that is not really a legal process when they see it. That is why, when asked about impeachment, Ted Cruz did not give the questioner a dissertation on the common law roots of "high crimes and misdemeanors." He cut to the chase: we don't have the votes. He also did not bring up impeachment; he addressed lawlessness in an effective manner, which naturally *led the audience* to bring up impeachment, the Constitution's remedy for executive lawlessness. The public is moved by the marshaling of facts, and when the facts are shown to be clear and damning, people will not shrink from grave words like "impeachment." To speak of impeaching Richard Nixon the day after he was reelected in 1972 would have been laughable; a little over a year later, once public attention had been riveted to his administration's lawlessness, only the weather was a more common topic of conversation.

That, of course, is why Senator Cruz was courting so much anger from the legacy media. To that shriveling adjunct of the White House press office, the story is not why Americans would think it worth asking whether their president should be impeached. It is instead what they perceive as the horrifying development that some prominent Americans are beginning to dignify the question with serious answers.

Unlike Cruz, Senator Tom Coburn is a medical doctor, not a constitutional lawyer. He is also more of a Washington fixture. After six years in the House, Coburn is now well into his second (and what he says is his last) term in the Senate. It was there that he became chummy with Senator Barack Obama during the latter's pit stop on the way to the Oval Office.

The friendship, like the country, is fraying thanks to Obama's imperious and profligate presidency. At a town hall meeting with constituents in Oklahoma, Coburn listened as a voter groused about the "lawless" administration and then posed this exasperated question: "Who is responsible for enforcing [the president's] constitutional responsibilities?"

That would be Congress. Typically, when someone brings up the subject of our Constitution's Article I branch performing its core responsibility of reining in the excesses of the Article II branch, the default mode of most lawmakers is evasion. To his credit, Coburn did not duck. "I don't have the legal background to know" whether the "serious things" raised by the voter "rise[] to high crimes and misdemeanors," he pensively said. "But I think you're getting perilously close."[1]

Indeed, our survey of how the Framers adopted the impeachment remedy and the "high crimes and misdemeanors" standard should leave no doubt that a president's systematic lawlessness and abdication of his constitutional responsibilities take us a good deal beyond "perilously close." Yet, on cue, Obama's media cried foul.

And it really is Obama's media: The main pushback came from David Axelrod, Obama's longtime political guru and formerly the top spinmeister on his White House staff. Through the familiar Beltway alchemy that transforms lefty political operatives into lefty media operatives, Axelrod is now—*what else?*—a political commentator for NBC News and its all-but-officially-certified Obama Permanent Campaign division, MSNBC.

He belittled Coburn's "considered legal opinion as an obstetrician"—which is the thanks the self-deprecating senator gets for conceding his lack of legal training. Obama's left-hand man proceeded to accuse the senator of spreading "a kind of virus that has infected our politics"[2]—which, I suppose, is Axelrod's considered medical opinion as a windbag.

As it happens, both Coburn and Axelrod were wrong. To repeat, impeachment is not a legal matter. It is a *political* remedy: the stripping of political authority due to the president's gross abuse of power or commission of offenses so grave he must be regarded as unfit for the presidency's unparalleled public trust. The distinction between law and politics is a point worth emphasizing and reemphasizing because the conflation of the two is not just an understandable error; it is an insidious strategy.

Law is how the left strangles politics. Recall how Clinton supporters were not content to argue that his offenses did not involve core presidential duties. They lawyered the misconduct down to the grain, to the absurd point that we were debating whether the president's false testimony was "material," as if weighing the significance of a *president's* lying to a grand jury for purposes of assessing his fitness for office were no different from analyzing the sufficiency of the evidence against a garden-variety perjury defendant. The ubiquity of the litigator's trick bag suffocates the political vitality of a self-determining culture, in much the same way that the left's vast administrative state enervates a democratic society, as Alexis de Tocqueville foresaw.

There was a time, not so long ago, when we understood that not every great public question can be anticipated and controlled by antecedent law. We relied, instead, on the discretion of political officials, who would calculate America's vital interests and act accordingly—not because they were good guys, although we hoped they were, but because they answered to voters and to other political actors whose duty it was to check their excesses.

Now, we put our faith in law and process, not political judgment and accountability. The law becomes a readymade excuse for inaction while the lawyers temporize. You start with a president who obstructs justice and uses the Oval Office for sexual trysts with an intern less than half his age. Common sense tells you one thing about it, but the lawyers and pundits lecture that your judgment must turn on "what the definition of 'is' is." Flash forward two decades, to a presidency that, unlike Clinton's, threatens to explode our system of governance, and you find Tom Coburn—a very good, very conscientious senator—thinking he is not competent to say whether systematic lawlessness constitutes "high crimes and misdemeanors" because he lacks a law degree.

And he is not alone in confusing a political matter with a legal process. Congressman Lamar Smith, a Texas Republican who used to head the Judiciary Committee and still sits on it, claims, "I can't answer any impeachment questions . . . because any impeachment actions go through the Judiciary Committee, and I don't want to have to recuse myself."[3] But why on earth would he have to do that? He is not a juror or a judge in a court case; he is a legislator with a duty to protect the Constitution and act as a check against presidential malfeasance. Does he suppose the Democrats who carry President Obama's water day in and day out while administration officials stiff-arm committee investigations would recuse themselves?

Similarly, Darrell Issa, the California Republican and non-lawyer who chairs the House Oversight and Government Reform Committee (a body the administration is stonewalling in several investigations), says he is unsure whether the administration's withholding of information from Congress—about the activities of agencies created and funded by Congress—rises to the level of "high crimes and misdemeanors." Chairman Issa, who has gone to court in an effort to enforce the committee's subpoenas, expressed astonishment at the Justice Department's counterargument that Congress's proper remedy is its own impeachment power, not resort to the judicial power.[4] The Justice Department is actually right about this—but note that Attorney General Holder puts forward this explosive "I dare you" argument because he knows that Republicans are scared to death of the "i-word." Getting bogged down in the legal weeds has become a convenient way of not dealing with it.

It is a common error to think of impeachment in legal terms because there is a legal process for it—just as there is a legal process attendant to many essentially political activities (e.g., the convening of electors to formalize the result of a presidential election). To underscore the gravity of impeachment, moreover, the Framers designed it to resemble a criminal proceeding. In fact, before adopting Gouverneur Morris's proposal that impeachments be tried by the newly created Senate, they considered suggestions by Edmund Randolph and Alexander Hamilton, respectively, that impeachment trials be conducted before "national" (what today are called "federal") or state judges. In addition, the Philadelphia convention's "Committee of Detail" at one point recommended giving jurisdiction over impeachments to the new Supreme Court.[5]

Ultimately, as we've seen, the House was given "the sole Power of Impeachment"—meaning the plenary authority to lodge the formal accusation. Taking the form of "articles of impeachment," that accusation is roughly analogous to a grand jury indictment. Though very different in nature and procedure, felony indictments and impeachment articles similarly serve the function of placing the accused on notice of the charges against him. An impeachment by the House leads to a trial in the Senate, presided over by a federal judge, the chief justice of the Supreme Court—a simulacrum of a regular criminal trial, with senators ostensibly sitting as petit jurors determining the defendant's fate.

Nevertheless, there are salient distinctions between impeachment proceedings and criminal trials—differences of kind, not just degree. The House is a political body, the elected and accountable representatives of the people. It is not a legal buffer between the people and the prosecutor, which is the constitutional role of the grand jury. Because grand juries are generally concerned with private infractions of the law investigated by police agencies, they deliberate in secret. By contrast, hearings in a House impeachment investigation probe wrongdoing by public officials and are conducted on the public record, as, of course, is the Senate's eventual impeachment trial. House members considering impeachment and senators deciding on removal deliberate openly and cast public votes, ensuring their accountability to voters for that momentous decision.

That is night-and-day different from a legal trial. The law demands that trial jurors be impartial, so they are thoroughly vetted to weed out potential bias. Once seated, jurors are instructed throughout the proceedings to avoid prejudicial influences like press reports and the opinions of their family members about the case. The law mandates that they deliberate without fear or favor, basing their verdict solely on whether the evidence presented is sufficient to prove the allegations in the indictment.

Lawmakers who participate in impeachment proceedings, on the other hand, are partisans. Some will be ardent presidential detractors, others loyalists, and all of them are apt to have a political stake in the outcome of a presidential impeachment controversy. The highly charged political nature of the process inescapably encourages these elected representatives—who of course want to be reelected—to consider whether their constituents support or oppose the president's removal. That practical consideration weighs far heavier in the politicians' deliberations than whether, technically speaking, impeachable offenses have been proved. At the Clinton impeachment trial, Chief Justice William Rehnquist admonished the House "managers," who presented the case for impeachment, not to refer to senators as "jurors." This was done at the Senate's insistence, on the rationale that the senators' role was not merely to evaluate the evidence like jurors but to judge the effect the president's removal might have on the nation.[6] Juries are expected to return unpopular verdicts if that is what the law and the evidence dictate; to the contrary, the Senate's impeachment role is powerfully influenced—perhaps even dominated—by the public will.

In criminal proceedings, grand jurors are expected to take legal guidance from the prosecutor, and trial jurors from the judge. That guidance must be firmly rooted in the penal statutes and relevant judicial precedents defining the crimes charged and the analytical principles that apply. By contrast, members of Congress judge for themselves what rises to the level of "high crimes and misdemeanors." They are not beholden to statutory law or jurisprudence. At a criminal trial, the judge is every bit the presiding government official, whereas the chief justice at a Senate impeachment trial performs the essentially ministerial role of keeping the proceedings moving along. It is the senators who decide how to proceed, what evidence merits consideration, whether witnesses should be called, and whether the articles of impeachment have been proved to their satisfaction. Their calculations are political, not legal—as seen to a fare-thee-well in the Clinton impeachment trial, in which senators permitted no live testimony, and then conveniently found the case had not been proved.

The double-jeopardy doctrine provides yet another telling constitutional distinction between legal cases and the political impeachment process. The Fifth Amendment, applicable to all federal criminal proceedings, protects Americans from being made "subject for the same offense to be twice put in jeopardy of life or limb." This protection does not apply to impeachment. Instead, the Constitution expressly provides that "the party convicted shall nevertheless be liable and subject to indictment, trial, judgment and punishment, according to law."[7] That is, once the politics is done and the decision is made whether to disqualify the president from holding public office, the law is free to take over and impose its distinct processes and penalties.

The tendency of nonlawyer politicians to view impeachment as a legal process beyond their ken is insidious. It is of a piece with the disturbing proclivity of modern lawmakers to abdicate to staff counsel their basic responsibility to read and understand the bills they enact. It subverts republican democracy. Elected officials are supposed to actuate the will of their self-determining constituents, not delegate to attorneys whatever powers they have not already transferred to the sprawling bureaucracy. The Framers did not believe that free people needed lawyers to figure out how to govern themselves. The standard they gave us for impeachment and removal from high public office is so simple that even obstetricians and windbags should have no trouble grasping it.

The legal grounds for impeachment are vital; without them, the political case for impeachment cannot be built. The primary question, however, is whether the president's conduct is so egregious that continuing to repose in him the chief executive's awesome powers would be intolerable and could permanently damage if not destroy the nation. An understanding of the nature and extent of impeachable offenses will shed necessary light on that question, but cannot answer it.

President Obama's popularity has plummeted, but he still has passionate supporters. Like him, they see the Constitution as an impediment to their ideological agenda. For them, his violations are cause for celebration not impeachment. Many other Americans, though they object to the president's lawlessness, are not convinced it so threatens the nation that impeachment is warranted; or they fear, thanks to the toxic climate created by Obama's most demagogic supporters, that calls for his removal would brand them as racists. These considerations, which have little to do with whether impeachable offenses can be proved, are not trivial. The decision to impeach a president is a political judgment that the peril posed by a corrupt man wielding enormous power outweighs the national trauma that ousting him would necessarily entail.

71

Let's not kid ourselves: the trauma would be profound. Class warfare and sowing us-versus-them resentments are the stock-in-trade of Obama's hard-left political base. Many of these supporters adhere to the community-organizing methodology of Saul Alinsky, with its unapologetic resort to bare-knuckles tactics of "direct action" (less euphemistically known as extortion).[8] Any meaningful effort to remove President Obama from power would put those activists in overdrive.

On the other side of the coin, the public's perception that Obama's imperial presidency endangers the nation is tough to assess. American progressives have spent over a century promoting the conceits that the Constitution is obsolete (at least as originally understood); that deference to individual liberty undermines social justice; and that power should be centralized in the executive branch and the administrative bureaucracy so that government experts can steer us through the complexities of modern life. This campaign has largely succeeded, which is why most of President Obama's unconstitutional usurpations are happening in broad daylight. He and his backers argue, for example, that his controversial Obamacare "waivers"—his unilateral presidential rewriting, repealing, and nonenforcement of the Patient Protection and Affordable Care Act's congressionally enacted provisions—show him to be farseeing and pragmatic, not lawless. That, of course, is the standard dictatorial self-image. It makes Obama the answer to the self-described "fantasy" of *New York Times* columnist Tom Friedman in which the U.S. government becomes an authoritarian "China for a Day"—no longer straitjacketed by republican democracy's constraints on power.[9] Is a nation inured to big government any longer alarmed by the prospect of officials who blithely slough off the Constitution's limits on government?

More to the point, is the nation alarmed by this president? Not just perturbed—are Americans generally open to the possibility that Obama is too dangerous to be trusted with power?

There may be some legitimate surprise at the president's extremism and the harm he is causing. After all, candidate Obama and his supporters, beginning in 2007, sedulously hid his history of radicalism.[10] And while Obama is abominable at policy, he is adept (with a helping media hand) at stage-managing the resulting catastrophes—Obamacare's time-bombs and debacles like Benghazi have been carefully choreographed so their worst features would not become manifest until after elections. Nevertheless, that Obama was a movement leftist with ambitions to be a transformative president was information available, without great effort, to anyone who wanted to be informed. His statist policy preferences, his class warfare tactics, and the disconnect between his rhetoric and our reality have long been readily apparent. Yet he was elected and, after four years of his governance, reelected (albeit by a much narrower margin and with markedly diminished support). This may tell us as much about contemporary America as it does about the president.

President Obama continues to provide an abundance of cause for his removal—one might say, a *determined* abundance generated by a willful purpose to dismantle the governing framework that the impeachment remedy exists to preserve. At the moment, though, the popular will to remove him is lacking. Absent that political imperative for action, the legal sufficiency of the case makes little difference.

The nature of President Obama's high crimes and misdemeanors is only the *second* most important factor in establishing the political imperative for impeachment. The factor of greatest importance is ourselves. On that, the jury is out.

CHAPTER SIX

THE 'PROSECUTORIAL DISCRETION' CANARD

In June 2012, as his reelection bid spun into high gear, President Obama took pandering to a new orbit. Courting Hispanic voters, he endeavored to impose by executive order what Congress had declined to enact by lawful statute: an immigration amnesty for illegal aliens who had come to the United States before they were sixteen years old. Consistent with the Obama administration's politicization of law enforcement, this transparent campaign gambit—the moribund "DREAM Act" revived by presidential ukase—was announced by the Homeland Security secretary, Janet Napolitano. She rationalized the radical new policy as a simple matter of "exercising prosecutorial discretion."[1]

In explaining his usurpation of legislative prerogative, President Obama claimed that these illegal aliens are "Americans . . . in every single way but one—on paper."[2] Of course that was untrue. They are not Americans under the only thing that matters, the thing Obama officials have cynically chanted like a mantra since the president's very first day in power: the rule of law.

The Constitution and congressional statutes are written on parchment. That is the only relevance of "paper" in this equation: it serves as the "hard copy" of our social contract and of the laws enacted pursuant to it. The Constitution vests Congress, not the president, with lawmaking power, in this instance, the power "To establish a uniform Rule of Naturalization."[3] Congress exercises this power by passing laws. Under the Constitution, which Obama took an oath to preserve, protect and defend, and under the laws it is his duty to execute *faithfully*, illegal aliens are not citizens of the United States— no matter how sympathetic their plight, no matter how blameless they may be for their outlaw status. They are not Americans. Period. It is not "paper" that separates them from our body politic. It is the law, of which Obama's office makes him a servant, not the master.

In addition to conferring effective immunity from prosecution, the president further presumed the authority to craft positive government benefits. The administration announced it would begin offering and processing "work permits" for the lucky DREAMers.[4] Of course, only Congress is constitutionally empowered to grant and fund federal benefits. You'd think our Harvard Law–educated chief executive would know that. And you'd be right. Just a year earlier, he told a throng of Latino activists at a rally held by his friends at La Raza (The Race), "The idea of doing things on my own is very tempting, I promise you, not just on immigration reform. But that's not how our system works. . . . That's not how our democracy functions." Faced with complaints about deportations, Obama had countered, "I swore an oath to uphold the laws on the books."[5] But that was then. Now, he claims the power to rewrite the books.

As it happens, the deportation complaints were wildly inflated. It would be hard to fault La Raza, though, since it was no doubt relying on Obama administration figures. Senator Jeff Sessions, the intrepid Alabama Republican who has studiously tracked what he calls the president's "non-enforcement of federal immigration law," notes that Homeland Security's Immigration and Customs Enforcement agency (ICE) has significantly "padded its deportation statistics," including "19,422 removals in fiscal year 2010 that were really from the previous fiscal year," and "adding 6,500 to the final removal numbers" by a bookkeeping trick involving a Mexican repatriation program.[6]

While immigration is critically important, the real gravity here lies not in the subject matter of Obama's edict but in the authoritarian assumptions of its issuance. They transcend mere arrogance: Beneath the "prosecutorial discretion" camouflage, the president is striking at our constitutional foundation.

Take with a grain of salt his periodic rhetorical nods to Congress, like the ones at the La Raza rally. They are not so much admissions of limits on his authority as tropes for stringing along restive constituencies. It is Obama's *actions* that matter. They proclaim nothing less than the power to pronounce what the law is. This usurpation, moreover, complements the dictatorial powers he has claimed—for example, to enforce only the laws of his choosing, and to deprive the states and their citizens of their sovereign prerogatives and constitutional rights.[7]

To be sure, a president has not only the authority but the duty to refrain from enforcing congressional statutes that violate the Constitution. Presidents are no less duty-bound in this regard than the federal courts, which are obliged to hold that such enactments are null and void when the question arises in litigation. That, however, is not what Obama is doing. As John Yoo, a Berkeley law professor and former Bush Justice Department official, observes, there is no conceivable argument that the federal immigration laws are constitutionally suspect.[8] Obama simply rejects them as a matter of policy preference.

That itself is a blatant violation of his constitutional oath. So is what the president pulled in Arizona after the state enacted a new immigration enforcement law in 2010. The law enabled police to inquire about a detained suspect's immigration status—a prospect that had the left shrieking and the president portraying Arizona as East Germany, though in reality it was something even the Obama Justice Department had conceded to be constitutionally permissible before Arizona ever passed its statute.[9] Now the administration claimed that the state law was barred by the legal doctrine of "preemption." The contention seemed frivolous. As Arizona pointed out, courts had long recognized the state interest in immigration enforcement, and the preemption doctrine only bars state laws that *undercut* federal statutes, whereas Arizona was *strengthening* Congress's immigration enforcement provisions. The Obama administration, however, had a new doctrine in mind: States were to be preempted not by *federal law* (i.e., congressional statutes) but by *Obama administration policy*. Thus, even if Arizona was in perfect harmony with Congress's immigration enforcement principles, its laws should be struck down if they interfered with Obama's nonenforcement practices.[10] In the imperial presidency, Congress's laws are irrelevant.

The Supreme Court, not persuaded by the Obama preemption doctrine, upheld the disputed provision of Arizona's law. Before the ink on the ruling was dry, the vindictive administration announced that it was suspending immigration cooperation with Arizona police.[11] In effect, they told the state to "drop dead," as Governor Jan Brewer put it.

The president of the United States, as we've seen, is the only federal official required by the Constitution to swear, as a condition precedent to assuming the vast powers of his office, that he will "faithfully execute" this office and, "to the best of my ability, preserve, protect and defend the Constitution of the United States." It is his constitutional duty to "take care that the Laws be faithfully executed," which includes the laws with which he disagrees on policy grounds. Nor ought we forget that nominees to the federal bench and top Justice Department posts are routinely grilled by the Senate—particularly by Senate Democrats on the matter of the right to abortion manufactured by *Roe* v. *Wade*—about their willingness to honor even those laws and precedents they believe to be wrongheaded. It is a bedrock principle that once the people's representatives enact a law to which there is no plausible constitutional objection, government officials must honor that law—regardless of their personal views about it—unless and until it is repealed or amended *through the process prescribed by the Constitution*.

Obama's distortion of the prosecutorial discretion doctrine cannot justify his indefensible evasions and usurpations.

Prosecutorial discretion is a commonsense resource-allocation principle related to criminal law enforcement. It is not a generalized license to ignore congressional statutes, let alone effectively amend them. It is a legal concept, so leave it to the clerisy—just as we saw with "high crimes and misdemeanors"—to intimate that only smart lawyers like Barack Obama and Janet Napolitano, not *hoi polloi*, can grasp its nuances. But it is really very simple. Resources are finite. Practicality demands that the Justice Department and other agencies of the executive branch make good-faith judgments about which law violations are enforcement priorities and which may go unaddressed. They cannot prosecute every transgression— and, given the modern proliferation of laws, few Americans would want them to try.

Narcotics enforcement is illustrative. The federal and state governments have concurrent jurisdiction over drug offenses.

Federal agencies have interstate and international jurisdiction but comparatively few investigative agents. State and municipal police have limited geographic jurisdiction but cover it with more police officers. It therefore makes sense for the feds to concentrate primarily on felonies committed by large-scale, international and interstate drug importation and distribution networks, leaving to state and county district attorneys the prosecution of less serious intrastate offenses, including those involving simple possession of illegal controlled substances. But notice: When the DEA and the FBI ignore minor federal crimes like drug possession (as opposed to distribution), they are not implying that what Congress has prohibited should no longer be deemed criminal, as Obama does in his "prosecutorial discretion" gambits. They are merely apportioning resources rationally; minor offenses like simple possession are still crimes, and federal agents reserve the right to make simple possession arrests in appropriate cases.[12]

To take another example, let's say that five people sit in a circle and pass a marijuana cigarette to each other, or that a street dealer sells five-dollar vials of crack to thirty different customers in a half hour. Each separate handoff of the weed and each hand-to-hand crack sale is a felony. In theory, a prosecutor could charge every single one as a separate crime—and at twenty years a pop, the offenders would soon be looking at centuries of jail time. That, however, would be ridiculous and thus it never happens. In all likelihood, the feds would not charge the marijuana case at all, and the crack dealer would probably be looking at one distribution count (lumping all the sales together) and limited jail time. Again, this discretionary approach does not effectively amend or repeal congressional statutes; it rationally adjusts investigative priorities and fits the punishment to the crime.

That is *real* prosecutorial discretion: faithfully executing the law in a manner that allocates police and prosecutorial budgets and energy in accordance with the crime problems that most harm the public. What Obama is doing is a perversion of prosecutorial discretion. It is an effort to delegitimize and effectively reverse laws he opposes on philosophical grounds. He is not saying the executive branch *lacks the resources* to enforce the immigration statutes and other federal law he finds uncongenial. He is proclaiming that *they should not be laws and he chooses not to execute them as such.*

Moreover, Obama's power grab goes way beyond refusing to execute the laws. In rationalizing his imperious issuance of work permits to illegal aliens, the president claimed, as he now frequently does in other contexts, that he cannot just sit around and wait for Congress to act on what he perceives to be pressing problems. But as he well knows, on the DREAM Act, lawmakers *have* acted: They said *no.*

When people disagree, as most Americans do with Obama's brand of progressive authoritarianism, the answer frequently is "no." That is a choice, not an omission—and even if it were the latter, presidents do not get to fill the lacunae with their own decrees and call it "prosecutorial discretion."

Another abuse of the concept involves the Yucca Mountain project in Utah. Congress designated the site in 1987 as a repository for spent commercial nuclear fuel, of which the nation has 70,000 metric tons that must be disposed of safely. Well over $15 billion in taxpayer funds has been expended on studying and preparing the site.[13] Finally, in June 2008, the Department of Energy (DOE) submitted an application for the Yucca Mountain nuclear-waste storage facility. Governing law on the matter could not be clearer: the 1983 Nuclear Waste Policy Act requires the U.S. Nuclear Regulatory

Commission to issue a final decision approving or disapproving DOE license applications within three years.

Much of the left adamantly opposes nuclear power—except, evidently, for Iranians. For all the legitimate concern about security against accidents and meltdowns, the most formidable impediment to exploiting the promise of nuclear energy is, as Adam White explains, "the difficult problem of where to dispose of its radioactive byproducts."[14] If projects like Yucca Mountain are the solution, nuclear power becomes a viable answer to our huge energy demands. Naturally, then, frustrating the enterprise is crucial to the political survival of a Nevada leftist like Senator Harry Reid. For an anti-nuke ideologue like President Obama, throwing the muscle of the Oval Office behind the effort to thwart Yucca is both a philosophical imperative and a source of considerable suasion over the powerful Senate majority leader. Together, Obama and Reid have worked to derail the project—by blatantly violating the law.[15]

Gregory Jaczko is a hard-charging progressive physicist and former Reid staffer. In a "maybe if we're nice to them they'll be nice to us" move out of the Beltway GOP playbook, President Bush appeased Senator Reid by appointing Jaczko to the Nuclear Regulatory Commission (NRC) in 2005. Upon taking office in 2009, President Obama promptly tapped him to run the commission. As night follows day, Jaczko issued a directive that halted work on the NRC's processing of the Energy Department's Yucca application. Because federal law (the aforementioned 1983 nuclear waste statute) did not permit the NRC to halt the application, Jaczko needed a fig leaf to cover his noncompliance and sell it to his four fellow commissioners. Thus, even though there was plenty of funding to process the application, he rationalized that Congress's failure to pass a budget for the federal government invited the NRC to rely on President Obama's nonbinding (and largely symbolic) budget request. Of course, that request called for zeroing out funding in order to kill the project. Later, the NRC's inspector general would issue a scathing report, finding that Jaczko had "strategically" withheld information from his fellow commissioners—homing in on his failure to be "forthcoming" about his intention to use Obama budget guidance to halt legally mandatory work on the application.[16]

Jaczko left the NRC in 2012, but Obama has now appointed all five NRC commissioners.[17] You'll no doubt be stunned to learn that work on the DOE's Yucca application has remained lawlessly halted. The Obama administration has sought to justify the NRC's intransigence by invoking prosecutorial discretion.

One of the nation's most influential federal courts, the U.S. Court of Appeals for the D.C. Circuit, has not been sparing in its condemnation of this legerdemain. Late last year, the court found that the NRC had illegally shut down its review of the DOE application, willfully ignoring the statutory three-year deadline.[18] Indeed, the commission and the Obama administration told the court, in essence, that they did not care what the law says—they have no intention of complying with the controlling statute and they assume no one has the power to force their hand. The appeals court was thus compelled to issue a writ of mandamus directing the NRC to comply with the statute and resume processing the application.

A year earlier, upon similarly ruling that the NRC was in violation of federal law, the same court had ruled that the commission's intransigence could be excused only if Congress enacted new legislation amending or repealing the 1983 law.[19] In the court's latest decision, Judge Brett M. Kavanaugh returned to this theme, providing a lapidary exposition of Obama administration lawlessness. It is, the court observed, among the "bedrock principles of constitutional law" that

Under Article II of the Constitution and relevant Supreme Court precedents, the President must follow statutory *mandates* so long as there is appropriated money available and the President has no constitutional objection to the statute. So, too, the President must abide by statutory *prohibitions* unless the President has a constitutional objection to the prohibition. If the President has a constitutional objection to a statutory mandate or prohibition, the President may decline to follow the law unless and until a final Court order dictates otherwise. But the President may not decline to follow a statutory mandate or prohibition simply because of policy objections. [Emphasis in original.]

In our pantheon of law, the Constitution has pride of place. Consequently, it is the first consideration in the president's duty to execute the laws faithfully. Thus, the court readily acknowledged, the president has broad inherent powers (under Article II) to refuse to enforce congressional statutes he believes in good faith to be unconstitutional. As we saw with the immigration laws, however, there is no plausible argument that the nuclear waste statute is infirm. Yucca, like most of the Obama administration's lawlessness, involves an ideological policy dispute, not a question of constitutionality.

And when the dispute is about policy, particularly outside the realm of criminal law enforcement, "prosecutorial discretion" has nothing to do with it. As Judge Kavanaugh explained, the president (and thus the Justice Department) has unreviewable authority to decline prosecution and to issue pardons for criminal wrongdoing, based on his policy preferences as well as his constitutional concerns. Saliently, the court noted that prosecutorial discretion is an aspect of the preservation of individual liberty through separation of powers:

One of the greatest *unilateral* powers a President possesses under the Constitution, at least in the domestic sphere, is the power to protect individual liberty by essentially under-enforcing federal statutes regulating private behavior—more precisely, the power either not to seek charges against violators of a federal law or to pardon violators of a federal law. The Framers saw the separation of the power to prosecute from the power to legislate as essential to preserving individual liberty.

Tellingly, the court brought us right back to the Philadelphia convention of 1787, to James Madison's trenchant warning—as true today as it was over two centuries ago—that "the accumulation of all powers, legislative, executive, and judiciary, in the same hands . . . may justly be pronounced the very definition of tyranny."[20] Notably, Judge Kavanaugh recalled, Madison and the other Framers had been profoundly influenced by Montesquieu, the great political philosopher of the Enlightenment, who warned that "When the legislative and executive powers are united in the same person, or in the same body of magistrates, there can be no liberty; because apprehensions may arise, lest the same monarch or senate should enact tyrannical laws, to execute them in a tyrannical manner."[21]

The very same safeguards against tyranny that prohibit Congress from dictating whom the president must prosecute reciprocally compel the president to honor Congress's valid legislative authority. Prosecutorial discretion has no bearing on that constitutional requirement, as the appeals court explained:

> Prosecutorial discretion encompasses the Executive's power to decide whether to initiate charges for legal wrongdoing and to seek punishment, penalties, or sanctions against individuals or entities who violate federal law. Prosecutorial discretion does not

include the power to disregard other statutory obligations that apply to the Executive Branch, such as statutory requirements to issue rules, . . . or to pay benefits, or to implement or administer statutory projects or programs. Put another way, prosecutorial discretion encompasses the discretion not to *enforce* a law against private parties; it does not encompass the discretion not to *follow* a law imposing a mandate or prohibition on the Executive Branch.

It was patently obvious, then, that thwarting the Yucca Mountain project by stubborn noncompliance was "simply flouting the law." The court took pains to reiterate that "the President and federal agencies may not ignore statutory mandates or prohibitions merely because of policy disagreement with Congress."

On this, a final point bears making. The people's representatives in Congress make laws for *the United States*. These laws are not just advice that the administration and the rest of us are free to ignore. They are binding, conferring benefits and imposing obligations on every one of us. These rights and duties are not the president's to alter or cancel; the president's job is to execute the laws. Thus his alterations and cancellations are not just lawless, they are invalid—they do not change our statutory benefits and obligations.

When, for example, Congress enacts a mandate requiring that businesses failing to offer health insurance to employees must pay a penalty, that money belongs to the nation, not to President Obama. He can purport to "waive" the penalty, but that does not change a corporation's obligation under federal law to pay it. Similarly, as he panics over revelations that Obamacare's burdensome coverage demands on insurers are eliminating the health plans he fraudulently promised we could keep, the president can purport to "waive" the coverage demands; but insurers are bound by federal law to adhere to them. Only at their legal peril do they flout Congress's statute in reliance on the say-so of the president, who actually has no say in the matter.[22]

"Independent" regulatory commissions and insurers and illegal aliens and doctors and private corporations and all Americans are bound by the law, not by President Obama's whims. When he imperiously purports to waive federal statutes, he does not merely violate the law and flout his constitutional obligations. He subjects Americans to the intolerable dilemma of abiding by the law or bending to his extortionate abuse of raw power. He renders us vulnerable to legal action for ignoring our statutory duties.

That is no exercise of prosecutorial discretion, a doctrine designed to protect our liberties from overbearing law, not to subject us to legal jeopardy by overbearing executive aggression. We are imperiled more than we may realize by a president who scoffs at his duty to execute the laws faithfully. His lawlessness does not erase our duty to follow the laws faithfully.

PART II

PREFACE

MAKING THE CASE

In many years as a federal prosecutor, I learned that the best way to make a case is . . . to make a case. That is, you sit down and figure out what you've really got. You get a grip on what the law is, then you assess the facts you are in a position to prove with an eye toward those legal requirements. The question is: Can you establish the "essential elements" of the penal statutes applicable to the conduct?

An impeachment case is significantly different from a legal case, as we've seen. It is more about political persuasion than legal sufficiency. Nevertheless, legal sufficiency has its place. It remains critical to any demonstration that the political case for impeachment deserves to be heard. The more convincing the proof of high crimes and misdemeanors, the more systematic the malfeasance, the more faithless the execution of a president's sworn duties—the more compelling becomes the political case for the president's removal. And the more realistic is the opportunity to sway the public will.

I do not presume to know whether the public will can be swayed to favor the impeachment and removal of President Obama. Four decades ago, it was swayed dramatically, and over a remarkably short period of time, to favor the impeachment and removal of President Nixon. Obama's lawlessness leaves Nixon's in the dust—which is only natural when Obama is trying to overhaul our constitutional system, while Nixon was mainly trying to save himself.

But there is a huge difference in the atmospherics. The mainstream media detested Nixon, bashing him day after day, powerfully influencing the public's perception; but the mainstream media is one of Obama's core constituencies, shielding him day after day from the onslaught of fact. It is true that the legacy press is not as imposing as it was in the 1970s. The rise of alternative media— especially conservative talk radio, websites, and social networking— has seen to that. Still, the mainstream press remains a force to be reckoned with, and for the current White House incumbent it is manning the barricades, not storming them.

In any event, the best way to make a case is still to make a case—to state it clearly and convincingly. The overarching case is straightforward: In the constitutional framework we have been bequeathed, impeachment is the ultimate check on executive lawlessness; the other potential check, Congress's power of the purse, has proved ineffective. The failure to execute the laws faithfully is a high crime and misdemeanor. Systematic faithlessness in this regard imperils our system and our liberties. If the process of impeachment and removal is not seen as a viable option, we are effectively resigning ourselves to the loss of what has made our nation prosperous and free.

That's all logical. But a political case takes more than logic. It requires a concrete demonstration of what you've really got. Not a lot of heated talk about impeachment, but a hardheaded, exacting assessment of whether the case is compelling.

Here, then, is a presentation of what articles of impeachment against President Obama would actually look like.

They'd look overwhelming.

THE ARTICLES OF IMPEACHMENT

Resolved, That Barack Hussein Obama, President of the United States, is impeached for high crimes and misdemeanors and that the following articles of impeachment be exhibited to the United States Senate:

Articles of impeachment exhibited by the House of Representatives of the United States of America in the name of itself and of the people of the United States of America, against Barack Hussein Obama, President of the United States of America, in maintenance and support of its impeachment against him for high crimes and misdemeanors.

ARTICLE I

THE PRESIDENT'S WILLFUL REFUSAL TO EXECUTE THE LAWS FAITHFULLY AND USURPATION OF THE LEGISLATIVE AUTHORITY OF CONGRESS

Using the powers of the office of President of the United States, Barack Hussein Obama, in violation of his constitutional oath faithfully to execute the office of President of the United States and, to the best of his ability, preserve, protect and defend the Constitution of the United States, and in violation of his constitutional duty to take care that the laws be faithfully executed, has willfully usurped the constitutional authority of Congress to write, amend, and repeal federal law. He has, moreover, willfully refused to execute indisputably constitutional and valid laws of the United States.

This conduct has included one or more of the following:

Unilateral Amendments of the Patient Protection and Affordable Care Act

Without constitutionally required congressional authorization, he has unilaterally amended the Patient Protection and Affordable Care Act (the "PPACA," which, due to his aggressive championing of it, is commonly referred to as "Obamacare"). He has, moreover, unilaterally usurped the constitutional power of Congress to legislate public duties and benefits, and he has denied the American people equal protection of the laws by favoring some over others in his unilateral decrees and in his often haphazard maladministration of the PPACA. He has refused to seek congressional amendment, as the Constitution requires, for the changes he has imposed. He has, in fact, threatened to veto congressional attempts to amend the PPACA—even amendments that could codify his lawless rewriting of the law. Furthermore, many of his unilateral amendments have been strategically timed for political purposes, in particular, to prevent the most financially and emotionally painful provisions of the PPACA from taking effect in the weeks and months before federal elections, as the statute required.

Moreover, because his unilateral decrees have not been codified by statute, and because the American people, like presidents, are bound by constitutionally enacted law, he has rendered Americans who follow his unilateral decrees vulnerable to eventual enforcement actions and private civil lawsuits based on the lawfully enacted terms of the PPACA.[1]

This conduct has included one or more of the following:

- He has unilaterally imposed the PPACA regime of subsidies and taxes on states that lawfully declined to establish state health-care exchanges under the PPACA, the express terms of which permit this regime of subsidies and taxes only in states that establish health-care exchanges.[2]
- He has unilaterally "waived" the PPACA employer mandate that, effective January 14, 2014, requires all businesses with 50 or more full-time employees to provide health insurance to their employees or pay a penalty. He has further "waived" the reporting requirements related to the employer mandate and subsidy determinations.[3] This latter "waiver" made verification of employee income for subsidy-qualification purposes impractical, a problem the president and his subordinates responded to by announcing that the applicants' "self-attestation" of income would be permitted —inviting massive fraud.[4]
- In his first unilateral "waiver" of the PPACA employer mandate (in July 2013), he applied the "waiver" through 2015 to all businesses with 50 or more full-time employees. He subsequently (in February 2014) unilaterally "waived" the employer mandate a

second time for an additional year, through 2016. In this second "waiver," he unilaterally and arbitrarily decreed separate categories of "waiver" beneficiaries: a category of businesses with between 50 and 99 employees would enjoy a total "waiver" of the mandate to provide health insurance; a category of businesses with 100 or more employees would be required to provide coverage to only 70 percent of their full-time employees in 2015, and to only 95 percent of their employees in 2016 and thereafter.[5]

- He has unilaterally imposed a requirement that employers, in order to qualify for the employer "waiver" he unilaterally prescribed, must certify to the IRS, under penalties applicable to false statements, that the "waiver" was not a motivating factor in hiring or firing decisions. Given that the "waiver" is valuable and encourages employers to employ fewer than 100 full-time employees, it is both financially sensible and lawful to fire or refuse to hire employees in order to be below 100 employees. In effect, the president has unilaterally prescribed a criminal offense—namely, false statements to conceal lawful, rational conduct—that is punishable by up to five years in prison and a substantial fine, in connection with a "waiver" he had no authority to issue.[6]

- He has "waived," first until 2015 and then through October 2017, the PPACA mandate that, effective January 1, 2014, insurers must comply with the very coverage standards that he endorsed in the enactment of the PPACA. The "waiver" followed public outcry over the apparent and knowing falsity of his oft-repeated promise that Americans would be allowed to keep their health insurance plans if they liked them.[7]

- Rather than seek congressional amendment, as the Constitution requires, he reacted to the PPACA problem created by his policies and maladministration—namely, millions of Americans losing their health insurance plans yet unable to seek new ones because his subordinates failed to construct a working website—by promulgating regulations that threatened punitive action against insurers that failed to provide coverage without payment.[8]

- He has unilaterally "waived" until 2015, under the rubric of a "hardship exemption," the PPACA individual mandate (requiring all Americans to purchase health insurance or pay a penalty), which was required to take effect on January 1, 2014, for millions of Americans who have had their health insurance policies canceled due to the failure of those policies to meet the very coverage standards he endorsed in the enactment of the PPACA. That is, the president has unilaterally determined that the "hardship" justifying a mass exemption from the PPACA is the PPACA itself—in particular, the manner in which it drives up the cost of health insurance for millions of Americans.[9] The "waiver" followed public outcry over the apparent and knowing falsity of his oft-repeated promises that Americans would be allowed to keep their health insurance plans if they liked them.
- He has "waived" until 2015 the PPACA caps on out-of-pocket medical costs (including deductibles and copayments) that were required to go into effect on January 1, 2014, after it became clear that the caps, which he endorsed in the enactment of the PPACA, were causing premiums to rise.[10]
- He has unilaterally and selectively "waived" PPACA coverage requirements and mandates for thousands of companies, including many employing low-wage employees covered by low-cost "mini-med" health insurance plans, after it became obvious that enforcing the PPACA coverage requirements that he endorsed would induce the companies to drop insurance for millions of Americans.[11] At the same time, other companies and individuals are forced to comply with PPACA requirements, which violates the constitutional principle of equal protection under the law.
- He has unilaterally and selectively exempted members of Congress and members of congressional staffs from the full financial burden of purchasing health insurance on a PPACA

exchange by unilaterally prescribing subsidies that are not permitted under applicable congressional statutes.[12]

- He has unilaterally "waived" payment of a PPACA-required reinsurance fee by certain labor-union-run health insurance plans, which will increase fees for plans not receiving the "waiver," and thus increase premiums and deductibles for consumers of the nonwaived plans, violating the constitutional principle of equal protection under the law.[13]

- He has unilaterally "waived" the PPACA prohibition against the provision of better health benefits to top executives than to other employees in employer-sponsored health-care plans, which was to take effect in October 2010.[14]

- He has unilaterally cut off enrollment in the high-risk insurance pools created by the PPACA, citing a lack of funds, although close to half the funds allocated were still available (some of which the administration instead used for media promoting enrollment in the PPACA exchanges).[15]

- He has unilaterally delayed until 2015 the establishment of federal exchanges for small businesses, which was to take effect by January 1, 2014, and has similarly unilaterally postponed until 2015 the requirement, under the Small Employer Health Option Program (SHOP), that these small-business exchanges offer qualified health insurance plans.[16]

Unilateral Amendments of the WARN Act

He has unilaterally "waived" the statutory requirement of the Worker Adjustment and Retraining Notification (WARN) Act that employers must give notice to workers sixty days in advance of plant closings and other actions that will cause mass layoffs. On at least one occasion, the WARN Act "waiver" was timed to prevent layoff notifications from being sent out prior to the 2012 presidential election. The president's subordinates at the White House Office of Management and Budget have announced that the government would subsidize companies sued by employees for failure to comply with the WARN Act—in effect, the president is using public funds to encourage and underwrite the violation of federal law.[17]

Unilateral Amendment of Welfare-Reform
Work Requirements

He has unilaterally "waived" the provisions of the 1996 welfare reform law (the Personal Responsibility and Work Opportunity Act) that directed states participating in the Temporary Assistance for Needy Families program to require able-bodied adults to work or prepare for work—reforms that resulted in significant decreases in both welfare rolls and child poverty.[18]

Unilateral Amendments of Immigration Law

Without constitutionally required congressional authorization, and by diverting resources that Congress has allocated for other public purposes, he has unilaterally "waived" provisions of the Immigration and Nationality Act (INA). He has, moreover, usurped the constitutional power of Congress to legislate public duties and benefits, and he has denied the American people equal protection of the laws by favoring some over others, and by favoring non-Americans unlawfully present in our country over American citizens and lawful immigrants, in his unilateral decrees and in his often haphazard maladministration of federal immigration law. Furthermore, many of his unilateral amendments have been strategically timed for political purposes.

This conduct has included one or more of the following:

- He has decreed an amnesty for a category of illegal aliens he has unilaterally defined, namely, illegal aliens who came to the United States before they were sixteen years old. Furthermore, he has unilaterally instituted an unauthorized federal benefits program for these aliens, including the unlawful issuance of permits enabling them to obtain employment in violation of federal law. He has engaged in these actions not merely in the absence of congressional authorization but in defiance of Congress, which had considered and declined to pass the DREAM Act.

- He has unilaterally "waived" provisions of the Immigration and Nationality Act and decreed an amnesty for a category of illegal aliens he has unilaterally defined, namely, illegal aliens who have United States citizen relatives, allowing them "unlawful presence waivers" in lieu of the statutory mandate that requires seeking permission to enter the United States lawfully. Furthermore, he and his subordinates have unlawfully legislated qualifications for this unlawful "waiver," instructing United States Citizenship and Immigration Services (USCIS) officers that applicants with histories of criminal offenses are eligible for the "waiver" under conditions unilaterally determined by the executive branch.[19]

- He has unilaterally "waived" provisions of the Immigration and Nationality Act and decreed an amnesty for a category of illegal aliens he has unilaterally defined, namely, illegal aliens who are parents, guardians, or primary caretakers of children who are United States citizens or lawful permanent resident aliens.[20]

- He has unilaterally "waived" provisions of the Immigration and Nationality Act and decreed an amnesty "parole in place" for a category of illegal aliens he has unilaterally defined, namely, illegal aliens who are family members of active-duty and some reserve members of the United States Armed Forces.[21]

- Besides being a clear violation of the Constitution's vesting of law-making power in Congress, including plenary power to establish naturalization standards, his maladministration in failing to execute the immigration laws faithfully and in unilaterally conferring federal benefits has undermined the Constitution's legislative process, frustrating the capacity of Congress to engage in the negotiations and compromise necessary to resolve difficult national problems within the rule of law.

Unilateral Amendment and Maladministration of the Clean Air Act
He and his subordinates have engaged in reckless maladministration
by applying the Clean Air Act of 1970, which pertains to emissions of
pollutants, to carbon dioxide, which is never mentioned in the Clean
Air Act or its amendments.[22] Applying the Clean Air Act to carbon
dioxide is impractical because carbon dioxide is ubiquitous and naturally occurring, and thus is released into the atmosphere in quantities
that dwarf the emission of pollutants. If the Clean Air Act were applied
as intended by Congress, it would not be applied to carbon dioxide. To
apply the Clean Air Act as written by Congress to carbon dioxide, he
and his subordinates must sweep millions of structures—including
homes, schools, houses of worship, hospitals, farms, and other businesses—into the act's regulatory sphere.

To address this problem of their own making, rather than abandon
their regulatory malfeasance, he and his subordinates have unilaterally
"waived" the Clean Air Act's prescribed regulation standards while
unilaterally and unlawfully imposing new regulation standards, drasti-
cally different from those enacted by law.[23]

**Undermining of the Processing of the Yucca Mountain Nuclear
Waste Application Mandated by Law**
He, his subordinates, and his appointees have willfully undermined
the execution of the 1983 Nuclear Waste Policy Act and willfully defied
lawful orders of the United States court that directed compliance with
the act, by unlawfully halting and delaying the Nuclear Regulatory
Commission's processing of the Department of Energy's application
regarding the nuclear waste project at Yucca Mountain, Nevada.

**Ignoring the Duty, Mandated by Law, to Propose a Plan to Address
Impending Insolvency of the Medicare Program**
He has willfully ignored and failed to execute the requirement of federal
law—specifically of the Medicare Prescription Drug, Improvement, and

Modernization Act of 2003—that requires the president to propose to Congress a plan to address the impending insolvency of the Medicare program when the program's trustees issue a Medicare funding warning. The trustees have issued a warning in each year of his presidency. Moreover, the Secretary of Health and Human Services has acknowledged that the Medicare program, as currently structured, "is unsustainable." Yet he has refused to submit the proposal mandated by statute.[24]

ARTICLE II

USURPING THE CONSTITUTIONAL AUTHORITY AND PREROGATIVES OF CONGRESS

Using the powers of the office of President of the United States, Barack Hussein Obama, in violation of his constitutional oath faithfully to execute the office of President of the United States and, to the best of his ability, preserve, protect and defend the Constitution of the United States, and in violation of his constitutional duty to take care that the laws be faithfully executed, has willfully usurped and undermined the constitutional authority and prerogatives of Congress.

Beyond the usurpation of Congress's legislative authority described in Article I, above, this conduct has included one or more of the following:

Usurping the War Powers of Congress

He has willfully usurped the constitutional power of Congress to declare war and to authorize combat operations by instigating an undeclared, unauthorized and unprovoked war and military invasion of Libya, a nation with which the United States was at peace and a regime the United States government—including the president and his administration—publicly regarded as a key counterterrorism ally of the United States which was thus being supported by American taxpayer dollars. He instigated this undeclared, unauthorized and unprovoked war in the absence of any threat to American national security and any vital American interests.[1] Moreover, he instigated military operations at great risk and expense to the American people in consultation with foreign and international institutions unelected by, and often hostile to, the American people—including the United Nations and the Arab

105

League—while refusing to seek the constitutionally required authorization from the elected representatives of the American people, whom he nevertheless expected to pay for these military operations.

His unprovoked and unconstitutional resort to military force had the foreseeable result of empowering and strengthening terrorist organizations affiliated with al-Qaeda, an international terrorist network that has killed thousands of Americans and with which the United States was (and is now) at war pursuant to congressional authorizations of the use of military force. This empowerment and strengthening of anti-American jihadists, particularly in Benghazi and other parts of eastern Libya, gravely endangered American national security and international stability, foreseeably resulting in several terrorist operations against American and Western targets and, ultimately, the murders of the United States ambassador and three other American officials, as well as the wounding of several other American officials.

Making "Recess Appointments" When the Senate Is Not in Recess
He has willfully purported to make "recess" appointments when the Senate was not in recess, thus usurping the constitutional power of each house of Congress to determine the rules of its proceedings and the times during which its sessions are in recess, and the constitutional power of the Senate to provide advice and consent before his nominees may fill high government offices. He has, moreover, abused and failed faithfully to execute his constitutional authority to fill vacancies in high government office unilaterally only when the Senate is in recess. To wit, in January 2012, while the Senate was formally in session and thus not in recess, he purported to appoint by recess appointment a director to the Consumer Financial Protection Bureau and three members to the National Labor Relations Board (NLRB).[2] Despite the patently unconstitutional manner of these appointments, and the resulting protest from the American people and members of Congress over the denial of their constitutional protections and prerogatives, he enabled these invalid appointees to take the appointed positions, work on public business, and thus prejudice the legal rights and protections

of Americans. The United States Circuit Court of Appeals for the District of Columbia later ruled that the appointments to the NLRB (the only ones before the court in the case at bar) were unconstitutional.[3]

Undermining and Exhibiting Contempt for the Constitutional Duty of Congress to Conduct Oversight of Executive Branch Agencies Created by Congress and Funded by the American People

He and his subordinates have repeatedly, systematically and willfully withheld from Congress and from the American people information to which they are entitled, despite numerous congressional requests, the issuance of congressional subpoenas, and the filing of Freedom of Information Act demands. In addition, he and his subordinates have repeatedly, systematically and willfully provided Congress and the American people with false information about matters of grave public concern. Furthermore, he and his subordinates have exhibited contempt for the constitutional duty of Congress, on behalf of the American people and in furtherance of the Constitution's checks and balances, to conduct oversight of executive branch agencies created by Congress and funded by the American people.

This conduct is further described in the Articles of Impeachment that follow.

ARTICLE III

DERELICTION OF DUTY AS PRESIDENT AND COMMANDER IN CHIEF OF THE UNITED STATES ARMED FORCES

He has been derelict in his duties as President of the United States and Commander in Chief of the United States Armed Forces to protect American troops and personnel serving in hostile foreign nations and territories.

This conduct has included one or more of the following:

Combat Rules of Engagement

He has imposed on American armed forces serving the United States in congressionally authorized combat missions, in Afghanistan and elsewhere, unconscionable rules of engagement. In a war against terrorists who hide among civilians, and who strategically use civilians to shield themselves when plotting and launching attacks, he and his subordinates have imposed rules-of-engagement restrictions that prioritize the safety of Afghan and other civilians over the lives of Americans troops. U.S. forces under threat on the battlefield have thus been admonished not to fire unless they are certain the target is not only an enemy operative but also armed. They have been forbidden in all but the most dire circumstances to enter civilian homes—the places where the enemy notoriously hides in a war zone—absent "extraordinary circumstances involving urgent risk to life and limb." And they have been denied air cover while under attack due to fear of potential civilian casualties. Of the more than 2,300 U.S. combat deaths in and around Afghanistan, twice as many—nearly 1,700—have occurred during his five years as commander in chief than during the first seven years of the war.[1]

The Benghazi Massacre

The unprovoked and unauthorized military attack that the president launched against Libya (described in Article II, above) left anti-American and anti-Western jihadist organizations, including some affiliated with al-Qaeda, strengthened in eastern Libya. In fact, the presence of these elements there, and the fact that they used eastern Libya as a platform for infiltrating jihadists into Iraq to conduct terrorist operations against American forces there, were among the main reasons the United States had provided support to the Libyan regime of Muammar Qaddafi, which had been providing the United States with intelligence on these jihadist organizations.[2]

After Qaddafi was overthrown because of the president's unprovoked and unauthorized military incursion, jihadist groups in eastern Libya conducted numerous terrorist operations against American and Western targets. For example, in May 2012, an al-Qaeda affiliate bombed the offices of the International Red Cross in Benghazi; on June 5, 2012, terrorists detonated an explosive outside a State Department facility that the Obama administration maintained in Benghazi despite the obvious danger and lack of adequate security; and a week later, terrorists attacked the British ambassador's convoy as it moved through Benghazi.[3] The attacks and the perilous environment induced the British government to pull its personnel out of Benghazi; but the president and his subordinates kept American personnel in place.[4]

Meantime, al-Qaeda's leader, Ayman al-Zawahiri, was calling on jihadists, particularly in Libya, to attack Americans, including in retaliation for the killing (by a U.S. drone attack on June 4, 2012) of al-Qaeda's Libyan leader, Hassan Mohammed Qaed, better known by his *nom de guerre*, Abu Yahya al-Libi. "His blood urges you and incites you to fight and kill the crusaders," Zawahiri said. The recorded exhortation, released on the morning of September 11, 2012, intimated that a revenge strike would be the most fitting way for Libyans to mark the day when, eleven years earlier, al-Qaeda killed nearly 3,000 Americans.[5]

The president and his subordinates have never explained why the administration was maintaining a diplomatic facility and a nearby CIA facility in Benghazi, one of the most dangerous places in the world for Americans. Consular and other diplomatic functions of the United States in Libya are handled at the U.S. embassy in Tripoli. It is clear that security in Benghazi was appallingly inadequate—for the most part, contracted out to local militias without on-sight security support from U.S. military components. Despite the obviously heightening security threat, and the pleas for enhanced security from State Department personnel in Libya, the president and his subordinates declined to enhance security.[6] At the time, the president was in the stretch run of a reelection campaign during which he claimed that his policies had left al-Qaeda "decimated" and "on the run," that the war on terror was thus nearing an end, and that his Middle East policy of cooperation with Islamists in places like Egypt and Libya was stabilizing the region and fostering the birth of real democracy.[7]

As the eleventh anniversary of the September 11 atrocities beckoned, there was a significant uptick in threatening activity by jihadist groups in the Middle East. Outside the American embassy in Cairo, there had long been continuous demonstrations calling for the release and return to Egypt of Omar Abdel Rahman, the "Blind Sheikh," who has been in U.S. prison since 1993 and is serving a life sentence imposed in 1996 for terrorism offenses. Abdel Rahman is a revered Egyptian jihadist who ran the murderous terrorist organization Gama'at al-Islamia (the Islamic Group), which has had close ties to (and cross-pollinating membership with) al-Qaeda since the 1980s.[8] (As noted in Article V, below, the president and his subordinates issued a visa to a member of Gama'at, in violation of federal laws against material support to terrorism, to come to Washington and consult on Egypt.) Moreover, after the fall of the Mubarak government in Egypt in 2011, as Islamists led by the Muslim Brotherhood gradually took control, a contingent of jihadist leaders strongly tied to al-Qaeda—in fact, led by Mohammed al-Zawahiri, the brother of al-Qaeda's leader, Ayman al-Zawahiri—became active in and around Cairo.[9]

In July 2012, the Blind Shiekh's son, Abdallah Abdel Rahman, threatened to raid the U.S. embassy in Cairo and hold Americans hostage to coerce his father's release.[10] On September 10, 2012, the CIA was warning, based on its monitoring of social media, that there had been calls for a demonstration the next day, September 11, at the U.S. embassy, which jihadists were threatening to raid. Similarly, the Arab press was reporting that jihadist groups, including Gama'at and Egyptian Islamic Jihad (the organization in which Mohammed al-Zawahiri was active, and that Ayman al-Zawahiri had run and merged into al-Qaeda), were threatening to burn the U.S. embassy in Cairo to the ground and take Americans hostage unless the Blind Sheikh and other jihadists detained by the United States were released.[11]

On September 11, 2012, the demonstrations that U.S. intelligence agents had been warning about in Cairo materialized. Although the American embassy was not burned down, it was stormed and fires were set. Protestors scaled the walls and removed the American flag, replacing it with the black jihadist flag commonly flaunted by al-Qaeda and its confederates.[12] The protestors openly celebrated al-Qaeda and its late leader, Osama bin Laden, chanting, "Obama, Obama, there are still a million Osamas!"[13] One of the chief instigators was Mohammed al-Zawahiri. In addition, at least three other senior al-Qaeda-linked jihadists helped spark the protest-turned-assault. One of them, Rifai Ahmed Taha Musa, was a prominent Gama'at leader and confidant of the Blind Sheikh, Osama bin Laden, and Ayman al-Zawahiri, and had signed al-Qaeda's 1998 declaration of war against the United States (an announcement of the formation of a "World Islamic Front Confronting the Jews and Crusaders").[14]

That night in neighboring Libya, there was a terrorist attack against the recklessly unsecured diplomatic facility operated by the Obama administration in Libya. In the course of the attack, J. Christopher Stevens, the American ambassador to Libya, was murdered, as were Sean Smith, a State Department information technology specialist, and two former Navy SEALs, Tyrone Woods and Glen Doherty, who were providing security services to the State Department and who had heroically taken it upon themselves to respond to the terrorist attack, saving numerous American lives before they were finally killed by the enemy. Ambassador Stevens and Mr. Smith appear to have been killed in the early phase of the attack; the two former SEALs were killed toward the end of the siege, which went on for many hours.[15]

Despite being briefed about the ongoing terrorist attack at the Benghazi facility very soon after it began, the president took no meaningful action as president and commander in chief to protect and defend Americans who were fighting for their lives. The president and his subordinates have refused to account to the American people and their representatives in Congress regarding his actions and whereabouts while Americans were under attack.

The president and his subordinates initially denied that he had any contact with military commanders and the relevant cabinet officials on the evening of September 11 as the terrorist attack proceeded. After then–Secretary of State Hillary Clinton testified in a congressional hearing that she spoke with the president by telephone at around 10 p.m. that evening (by which point she knew that Ambassador Stevens had been murdered), the president and his other subordinates changed their story, reporting that the president had spoken with Secretary Clinton but providing few details and acknowledging no other contacts with top administration officials who were futilely responding to the attack.

The next morning, after making a brief public statement as his subordinates dealt with the aftermath of the terrorist attack and accounted for Americans killed and wounded, the president flew to Las Vegas for a political fundraiser.[16] That evening, at a campaign event, he told supporters, "A day after 9/11, we are reminded that a new tower rises above the New York skyline, but al-Qaeda is on the path to defeat and bin Laden is dead."[17]

ARTICLE IV

FRAUD ON THE AMERICAN PEOPLE

The president and his subordinates have willfully engaged in schemes and artifices to defraud the American people in connection with matters of great public importance, in violation of his duty to execute the laws faithfully and his fiduciary duty to be truthful in his statements to the American people. These fraudulent schemes and artifices have included, but are not limited to, fraudulent misrepresentations intended to cover up derelictions of duty and evade accountability for catastrophic policies; fraudulent misrepresentations intended to secure passage of legislation; and fraudulent misrepresentations to improve his prospects for winning reelection in November 2012.

This conduct has included one or more of the following:

The Libya War Fraud

In addition to involving the nation in an unauthorized war in Libya that empowered jihadist enemies of the United States, he and his subordinates falsely represented that the purpose of the war was to protect civilians, pursuant to a United Nations resolution.[1] In fact, the purpose of the war was to overthrow the Libyan regime of Muammar Qaddafi, a government that he and his subordinates had previously portrayed as a key counterterrorism ally of the United States.[2]

Moreover, in a specious attempt to justify unilaterally taking the nation to war without congressional authorization and in the absence of any threat to the United States or vital American interest at stake, he and his subordinates claimed that the war he had launched—the military invasion of a sovereign nation, including the aggressive use of American air power, bombardment of Libyan government forces, and logistical support to NATO, at a cost of over $1 billion to the American people;[3] plus the killing of thousands of people,[4] the killing of Libya's head of state, and the overthrow of that nation's government—did not amount to "hostilities" for purposes either of Congress's constitutional war powers or of the 1973 War Powers Resolution.[5]

The Benghazi Fraud

Despite the severe and foreseeable terrorist threat on the eleventh anniversary of 9/11 against the American embassy in Cairo (further described in Article III, above), State Department personnel there began putting a public non-terrorism spin on the mayhem they knew was coming. Even before the rioting started, they took to Twitter to condemn "religious incitement" and "the continuing efforts by misguided individuals to hurt the religious feelings of Muslims." The object of these condemnations was an obscure video trailer for a film called *Innocence of Muslims* that was derogatory of Islam and its prophet, Mohammed.

The effort to blame the anticipated protests on the video, which had been produced by a California-based Egyptian, was not a complete fabrication. Although extraordinarily few people had actually seen the video, Egypt's Grand Mufti had publicly denounced it on September 9, 2012, inspiring some local Muslims to inveigh against it.[6] Nevertheless, as recounted in Article III, the threats to the embassy in Cairo, which had been intensifying in the weeks and months before anyone ever heard of the video, came primarily from jihadists and organizations long involved in terrorist attacks and plots against the United States, encouraged by the permissive atmosphere created by an Egyptian government now run by members of the Muslim Brotherhood, a notoriously anti-American organization.

Notwithstanding the State Department's choice to emphasize the video to the exclusion of other causes of anti-American violence, it was a small item on the menu compared with threats from al-Qaeda and its jihadist allies. But it was a politically convenient item. The 2012 election was less than two months away, and the president had been campaigning on having put the supposedly "decimated" al-Qaeda "on the path to defeat," so any alternative explanation for anti-American jihadist violence (apparently, no matter how implausible) was preferable to acknowledging the continuing severe threat posed by al-Qaeda and its jihadist allies and offshoots. Moreover (and as further discussed in Article VII, below), the president and his subordinates had been colluding with the Organization of Islamic Cooperation for nearly four years on efforts to render illegal—despite the First Amendment—speech derogatory of Islam. The State Department had been at the forefront of this project. It was useful to this cause to frame free expression—rather than Islamic supremacist ideology—as the cause of Muslim rioting.[7]

The September 11 Benghazi massacre commenced at 9:42 p.m. Libya time, which was late afternoon in Washington. American officials knew from the first minutes that a terrorist attack was underway. General Carter Ham, commander of AFRICOM, who happened to be in Washington, was contacted immediately. He promptly informed then–Defense Secretary Leon Panetta and General Martin Dempsey, chairman of the Joint Chiefs of Staff, that the diplomatic facility was under terrorist siege and that Ambassador Stevens was already missing, as was Sean Smith. Secretary Panetta and General Dempsey were about to attend a scheduled meeting with the president. They immediately proceeded to the White House, where they briefed the president about the ongoing terrorist attack.[8]

Meanwhile at the State Department, then–Secretary of State Clinton first learned of the attack at around 4 p.m. Washington time. From then on, she later recalled, she was "in continuous meetings and conversations, both within the department, with our team in Tripoli, with the interagency and internationally."[9] The leader of "our team in Tripoli" was Gregory Hicks, deputy to Ambassador Stevens and one of the last people ever to speak with him. Shortly before Secretary Clinton began monitoring events, Ambassador Stevens had urgently called Mr. Hicks to alert the State Department that the Benghazi facility and Stevens himself were "under attack." In later congressional testimony, Hicks made clear that all American personnel on the ground in Libya knew that what was happening in Benghazi was a terrorist attack. The anti-Islamic video "was a non-event," he explained.[10]

At approximately 8 p.m. Washington time, Hicks spoke directly with Clinton and some of her top advisors by telephone. Not only was it then apparent that an attack by terrorists was underway; Hicks's two most profound fears at the time he briefed Clinton precisely focused on those terrorists. First, there were reports that Ambassador Stevens might be in the clutches of the terrorists at a hospital they controlled; second, there were rumblings that a similar attack on the embassy in Tripoli could be imminent, convincing Hicks that State Department personnel should evacuate. He naturally conveyed these developments to Clinton, who agreed that evacuation was the right course.[11]

At about 9 p.m. Washington time, Hicks learned from the Libyan prime minister that Stevens was dead. Hicks relayed this information to Secretary Clinton's subordinates in Washington, although he did not speak directly with the secretary again that evening.[12]

Secretary Clinton testified that she spoke with the president at approximately 10 p.m. The president and his subordinates had initially claimed that the president had not spoken with any of his cabinet officials that evening.[13] After Clinton's testimony, though, the White House press secretary amended this account, now saying, "At about 10 p.m., the president called Secretary Clinton to get an update on the situation." Secretary Clinton's summary of their conversation was similarly brief: "I spoke with President Obama later in the evening to, you know, bring him up to date, to hear his perspective."[14] Neither the president nor Secretary Clinton has provided an account of what was discussed in this conversation, said to have occurred about six hours after the start of the attack but while Tyrone Woods and Glen Doherty were still fighting for their lives. Just a few minutes after the time of the phone call, however, the Washington press began reporting that the State Department had issued a statement by Secretary Clinton regarding the Benghazi attack. In it, she endeavored to shape the public's perception of the violence as attributable to the video, not jihadist terror:

> Some have sought to justify this vicious behavior as a response to inflammatory material posted on the Internet. The United States deplores any intentional effort to denigrate the religious beliefs of

others. Our commitment to religious tolerance goes back to the very beginning of our nation.[15]

In the days following the attack, a vigorous effort was made by the president and his subordinates to downplay the role of terrorism and blame the Benghazi attack on the anti-Muslim video. The video was portrayed as having ignited a spontaneous riot that spun out of control, resulting in the violent killings. (Sadly, the depravity that would be necessary to cause people to commit mass murder over a mere video was implicitly assumed in this explanation.)[16]

The CIA prepared draft "talking points" that explicitly referred to "al-Qaeda" and the fact that there had been a terrorist "attack." Yet, in consultation with the State Department and the White House staff, CIA Acting Director Michael Morell edited the talking points, purging references to al-Qaeda and to a terrorist attack.[17] Also purged was the assertion that "The wide availability of weapons and experienced fighters in Libya almost certainly contributed to the lethality of the attacks."[18] As noted in Article III, above, the wide availability of weapons in Libya is a direct result of the chaos and the empowerment of jihadists after Qaddafi's regime was overthrown due to the president's unauthorized military intervention.

The final version of the talking points, completed on Saturday 15, 2012, stated instead that

> The currently available information suggests that the demonstrations in Benghazi were spontaneously inspired by the protests at the U.S. Embassy in Cairo and evolved into a direct assault against the U.S. diplomatic post and subsequently its annex. There are indications that extremists participated in the violent demonstrations.[19]

Of course, the State Department had already dubiously blamed the video for the Cairo "protests," in addition to putting out the late-evening statement from Secretary Clinton on September 11, blaming the video ("inflammatory material posted on the Internet") for the Benghazi "demonstrations."

The completion of the fraudulent talking points on Saturday is significant because they served as the basis for the serial appearances on the network television political talk shows on Sunday by Susan Rice, the American ambassador to the United Nations. It is odd that this should be so, since Ambassador Rice obviously had the security clearance for and access to the classified information that provided the government's most complete and accurate account of then-current knowledge. Ambassador Rice also seemed an unusual choice for the president and his subordinates to offer for network appearances. Her United Nations responsibilities had little if anything to do with the siege in Libya. One might have expected the president and his administration to offer appearances by the secretary of state or a different high-ranking State Department official who had been directly involved in the administration's Benghazi response. But the president and his subordinates chose Rice, the president's longtime advisor and confidante.[20]

Ambassador Rice dutifully repeated for the audiences of five different national telecasts the same yarn she spun on ABC's *This Week*:

> [O]ur current best assessment, based on the information that we have at present, is that, in fact, what this began as, it was a spontaneous—not a premeditated—response to what had transpired in Cairo. In Cairo, as you know, a few hours earlier, there was a violent protest that was undertaken in reaction to this very offensive video that was disseminated.[21]

Rice told *Face the Nation* that "we do not have information at present that leads us to conclude that this was premeditated or pre-planned" and that she could not agree that al-Qaeda or its affiliates had been involved since "we'll have to find that out."[22] She told *Fox News Sunday*:

> The best information and the best assessment we have today is that in fact this was not a preplanned, premeditated attack. That what happened initially was that it was a spontaneous reaction to what had just transpired in Cairo as a consequence of the video.

. . . [W]e don't see at this point signs this was a coordinated plan, premeditated attack. Obviously, we will wait for the results of the investigation and we don't want to jump to conclusions before then. But I do think it's important for the American people to know our best current assessment.[23]

Ambassador Rice did note, repeatedly, the "heavy weapons" that "unfortunately are readily available in post-revolutionary Libya."[24] She made no reference to Obama administration policies responsible for that state of affairs. Besides the video, Rice suggested to CNN's *State of the Union* that "democracy," too, was a culprit:

This is a turbulent time. It's a time of dramatic change. It's a change that the United States has backed because we understand that when democracy takes root, when human rights and people's freedom of expression can be manifested, it may lead to turbulence in the short-term, but over the long-term, that is in the interest of the United States[25]

It quickly became clear to members of Congress with access to the classified information that the version of events being publicized by the president and his subordinates, and the sanitized talking points on which it was based, bore scant resemblance to what Rice called "our best current assessment." Initially, the president's press spokesman and CIA Acting Director Morell falsely denied that the White House staff had collaborated in editing the talking points—Morell "emphatically" testifying, as a Senate Intelligence Committee report recounts, that the talking points were provided to the White House "for their awareness, not for their coordination." This was flatly false: not only does the email paper trail prove White House collaboration; Morell himself wrote an email explicitly stating that "Everyone else has coordinated" on the talking points and noting "tweaks" made by both State Department and White House officials.[26]

The president, through his spokesman, risibly claimed that the changes—erasing references to al-Qaeda and terrorism, changing "attack" to "demonstration"—were merely "stylistic."[27] Meanwhile, Morell and other administration officials stonewalled when Congress pressed for an explanation of who had changed the talking points. On November 27, 2012, Morell accompanied Ambassador Rice to a meeting with three senators, the objective of which was to soften opposition to the president's prospective nomination of Rice to replace the retiring Clinton as secretary of state. The senators asked Morell who changed the talking points. He falsely responded that the FBI had made the changes because "they didn't want to jeopardize their investigation." Upon hearing about Morell's allegation, FBI leadership angrily and unequivocally denied it. Afterwards, CIA officials contacted the senators to say that Morell "misspoke" and to concede that "the CIA" had edited the talking points—though "it" would not say why. As one senator in the Morell/Rice meeting concluded, Morell "knew when he met with us that it wasn't the FBI who had changed the talking points. He lied."[28]

Meanwhile, with the election looming, the president and his subordinates aggressively promoted the story that the video—not the considerably less than "decimated" jihadist network—had ignited the "spontaneous" massacre. After the president agreed with the assessment of a CBS News correspondent that he "went out of [his] way to avoid using the word 'terrorism' in connection with the Libya attack," the president was pointedly asked whether the Benghazi killings had resulted from "a terrorist attack." He replied, "Well, it's too early to know exactly how this came about, what group was involved[.]"[29] As noted in Article III, above, the president then moved on to his Las Vegas fundraiser, where he reasserted the campaign-trail claim that "al-Qaeda is on the path to defeat."

At Andrews Air Force Base just three days after the terrorist attack, when the bodies of Ambassador Stevens, Sean Smith, Tyrone Woods, and Glen Doherty were returned home, Secretary Clinton used the somber occasion to conflate the Benghazi massacre with the Cairo rioting that the State Department was blaming on the video: "We've seen the heavy assault on our post in Benghazi that took the lives of those brave men. We've seen rage and violence directed at American embassies over an awful Internet video that we had nothing to do with."[30] Echoing this theme, the State Department soon released commercial ads, paid for by American tax dollars and aired on Pakistani television (with Urdu captions), that featured the president and Secretary Clinton condemning the video—"We absolutely reject its content and message," declaimed Clinton.[31]

Then, just two weeks after the massacre, in a globally anticipated September 25 speech at the United Nations, the president proclaimed, "The future must not belong to those who slander the prophet of Islam."[32]

At the aforementioned Andrews Air Force Base ceremony for the four fallen Americans on September 14, Secretary Clinton did not merely highlight the video in her remarks; she also made a point of assuring Charles Woods, the father of Tyrone Woods, that the administration was going to "arrest and prosecute" the man responsible for the anti-Muslim video.[33] Sure enough, on September 27, police in Los Angeles showed up at the home of 55-year-old Nakoula Basseley Nakoula, the *Innocence of Muslims* producer, and arrested him on a violation of supervised release—the federal analogy to a parole violation.[34]

In 2010, Nakoula had pleaded guilty to opening bank accounts using fake names and stolen Social Security numbers. The offense was sufficiently minimal that Nakoula spent less than two years in jail before being released under monitoring by a probation officer, like tens of thousands of former prisoners.[35] There was clearly no reason to arrest Nakoula, particularly in the dead of night as if he were a violent criminal. With the president and his subordinates publicly blaming the video and its maker for both the massacre and the violent proclivities of Islamic radicals, Nakoula had voluntarily submitted to an interview, just as he had voluntarily been meeting with his probation officer while on release.[36] The common procedure when a convict is cited for a nonviolent supervised-release violation is to give him a summons to appear in court on a future date.[37]

Nevertheless, even as his family went into hiding because the attention the president and his subordinates were calling to the obscure video made them potential targets of Muslim extremists, Nakoula was made an example of. Although his film production was plainly protected by the First Amendment, federal agents grilled him about it—under the guise of monitoring his computer and Internet use, as permitted by his supervised-release status. They then cited him for violations culled, in part, from what were alleged to be false statements about the production. Although this "crime" was minor and nonviolent, a federal magistrate judge ordered him detained without bail as if he were a severe flight risk and danger to the community.[38] He was subsequently sentenced to a year in prison—nearly as much time as he'd served for the underlying felony fraud conviction. Obviously cognizant of the constitutional impropriety of punishing free expression but not wanting to undercut the administration's fraudulent "Blame the Video" story, Justice Department prosecutors quietly dropped the supervised-release "violations" related to Nakoula's film production (allowing him to admit only the violations related to his use of false identities). That is, the government's real, unconstitutional reason for singling him out for prosecution was made to look as if it had nothing to do with his imprisonment.[39]

This treatment was highly unusual: Absent the commission of a serious new crime, convicts on supervised release are rarely imprisoned for a first violation; normally, judges admonish them to abide henceforth by the terms of release and allow them to remain at liberty. With jails overcrowded, it can often take multiple violation incidents before a court will finally reincarcerate a typical convict.[40] But there was nothing typical about the treatment of Nakoula by the administration of a president pledged to protect constitutional principles like free speech and equal protection under the law.

As for accountability of the government officials actually responsible for derelictions of duty in Benghazi and the energetic cover-up of the terrorist attack, that has proved elusive. The president and his subordinates continue to stonewall Congress, denying access to key witnesses and critical documents. As the addendum that six senators attached to the Senate Intelligence Committee's report surmised, "this lack of forthrightness stems from a desire to protect individual political careers, now and in the future, and the [State] Department's reputation, at the expense of learning all the facts and apportioning responsibility."[41]

The Obamacare Fraud

The president and his subordinates made numerous willful misrepresentations and material omissions of fact in order to (a) discredit opponents of the health insurance legislation commonly known as "Obamacare" (the PPACA), (b) secure political support for the passage of the legislation despite intense public opposition to it, and (c) win his reelection to the presidency by concealing damaging information about the prohibitively high costs and burdens of the PPACA that would have demonstrated that many of his prior representations had been false.

He repeatedly assured Americans, "If you like your health-care plan, you will be able to keep your health-care plan. Period[,]" and similar assertions to that effect. Internal Obama administration analyses, however, estimated that 40 to 67 percent of Americans in the individual insurance market would not be able to keep their health insurance plans. This would amount to several million Americans losing their health insurance plans.[42]

Moreover, as it became clear that millions of Americans were, in fact, losing health plans they wanted to keep despite his fraudulent misrepresentation that this would not happen, he and his subordinates switched gears and fraudulently claimed that the problem of Americans losing health insurance was comparatively small: confined to the individual health insurance market, which, they further claimed, amounted to just 5 percent of the overall health insurance market. Even on its face, this claim was false: the individual market constitutes approximately 8 percent of the overall market. The 3 percent difference amounts to millions of Americans.[43]

That misrepresentation, however, paled in comparison to the overarching fraud: the president and his subordinates well knew that the problem of Americans losing health insurance plans they wanted to keep was not confined to the individual insurance market. In fact, the individual market was a small fraction of the problem. The Obama administration's own projections, explicitly set forth in the Federal Register in mid-2010 (that is, before, during and after the president's repeated claim that Americans would be permitted to keep their health plans), showed that the majority of Americans in the much larger employer-provided health insurance market would also lose their health insurance—most of them by 2013.[44] This fact, and the administration's intimate knowledge of it, was reflected in a legal brief filed in federal court by the Justice Department (in connection with litigation over the PPACA's unconstitutional denial of First Amendment religious liberty, further discussed in Article VII, below):

> The [Affordable Care Act's] grandfathering provision's incremental *transition* does not undermine the government's interests in a significant way. Even under the grandfathering provision, it is projected that more *group health plans* will *transition* to the requirements under the regulations as time goes on. [Officials of the Department of Health and Human Services] have estimated that *a majority of group health plans will have lost their grandfather status by the end of 2013.*[45] [Emphasis added.]

A "group health plan" is employer-provided insurance, the market in which approximately 156 million Americans obtain health insurance for themselves and their families.[46] As the brief states, most of those 156 million Americans will not be able to keep their health-care plans. Indeed, given that a principal purpose of the PPACA is to force insurers to cover a menu of treatments and conditions that (a) has been decreed by the executive branch, and (b) is more extensive than insurers were previously able to offer in accordance with their consumers' choices, the president and his subordinates well knew that it would soon be illegal for insurers to offer many of the health plans they were falsely claiming that consumers could keep. Furthermore, the president and his subordinates well understood, as the Justice Department brief and the Federal Register estimate elucidate, that the "grandfathering" provision they touted as the legal authority exempting pre-PPACA plans so consumers could keep them was exceedingly narrow, readily disqualifying insurance plans from "grandfathering" status. Thus, comparatively few consumers would be able to keep "grandfathered" plans—and even then, for a very limited time.

The president and his subordinates similarly represented, repeatedly, that Americans who liked their doctors would be able to keep their doctors. That, similarly, was willfully false. The loss of health insurance plans that previously covered the doctors Americans wanted to keep, plus the PPACA-enabled regulations that cut many physicians and hospitals out of PPACA-exchange health-care plans, ensured that millions of Americans would lose doctors they wanted to keep.[47]

He and his subordinates similarly represented, repeatedly, that the PPACA would lower annual health insurance premiums by $2,500 for American families.[48] That, too, was willfully false. In fact, Americans are already learning that the PPACA causes staggering increases in premiums, deductibles, and other out-of-pocket costs. It has been estimated that average American families will see premiums spike by 30 percent or more.[49] The president and his subordinates were well aware that health insurance costs would increase dramatically. Indeed, the intent to conceal the inevitable price increases as the PPACA began to be implemented explains the excruciating dysfunction of Healthcare. gov, the government's PPACA website through which Americans shop for insurance.[50]

Since the PPACA went into effect, millions of Americans have lost health insurance plans and doctors they wanted to keep. Their insurance costs are skyrocketing. The pace and intensity of these damaging developments will increase as the PPACA is phased in, as the president knew it would when he was promising otherwise.[51]

Enabling Iran's Nuclear Program while Vowing to Prevent Iran from Acquiring Nuclear Weapons

The president and his subordinates have engaged in diplomatic negotiations that facilitate Iran's pursuit of nuclear weapons despite his oft-repeated public pledge that the United States, under his leadership, would prevent Iran from acquiring nuclear weapons. Furthermore, he and his administration have concealed from the American people an agreement with the Iranian government—a longtime, avowed enemy of the American people—about how a "Plan of Action" enabling Iran to enrich uranium will be implemented.

Having turned a deaf ear to the Iranian people in 2009 when they were being crushed while attempting to rise up against their totalitarian regime—the leading state sponsor of jihadist terror[52]—President Obama reached out in 2013 to the Iranian regime's new front man, President Hassan Rouhani.[53] Despite numerous prior public assurances that the United States, under his leadership, would prevent Iran from acquiring nuclear weapons,[54] the president and his subordinates have entered an "interim" agreement with the Iranian regime that enables Iran to continue enriching uranium. The express concession that Iran may enrich uranium guts years of UN Security Council resolutions against Iran's uranium enrichment activities.[55] It further concedes the Iranian government's claimed right to enrich uranium.[56]

The Iranian government aptly regards this agreement as a "surrender" by the United States. Rouhani publicly boasted in a tweet that "world powers surrendered to Iranian nation's will."[57] Moreover, Iran's foreign minister insists that, contrary to Obama administration claims, the regime "did not agree to dismantle anything" in its nuclear or ballistic program.[58]

In November 2013, the president and his subordinates, and the administrations of five other major nations, struck a "Joint Plan of Action" with Iran, which was released publicly.[59] But the president and his subordinates also agreed to a side deal with Iran regarding how the "Joint Plan of Action" would be implemented. The Iranians maintain that if people want to know what the side deal actually says, they should read the text. The president and his subordinates, however, have refused to publish the text to the American people—releasing only a "summary," which the Iranians maintain is inaccurate.[60] It is known that Iran was required to make no concessions regarding its promotion of revolutionary jihadist terror—the chief reason why its acquiring nuclear weapons is not acceptable.[61]

Fraudulent Misrepresentation of Immigration Enforcement Activity
He and his subordinates have repeatedly provided Congress and the American people with false representations regarding immigration enforcement efforts by the Department of Homeland Security and its component agencies.

For example:

- He and his subordinates publicly claimed that the Immigration and Customs Enforcement agency (ICE) had increased by 47 percent the annual rate of removal of illegal aliens from the United States during the president's first term in office. In fact, this figure was significantly inflated by adding thousands of illegal aliens who had not been removed—those who had voluntarily departed. The actual increase in removals was 13 percent, and in overall departures (removals plus voluntary departures) was 5 percent.[62]
- In response to negative criticism of its lack of adequate immigration enforcement, and in an effort to entice support for comprehensive immigration reform legislation that would provide amnesty for millions of illegal aliens,[63] the president and his subordinates undertook in 2010 to top the previous year's number of deportations. It ostensibly accomplished this objective[64]—claiming to have set a record high for deportations of illegal aliens—by improperly inflating its figures by 25,000.[65]
- By contrast, in later soft-pedaling deportation during a 2011 meeting with advocates of amnesty for illegal aliens, the president explained that the administration's deportation statistics "are actually a little deceptive." He elaborated that he and his subordinates actually "have not been more aggressive" in dealing with certain categories of illegal aliens—including, he said, "DREAM Act kids," although, as noted in Article I, there is no DREAM Act. Nevertheless, he added, the statistics seem high because "what we've been doing is . . . apprehending folks at the border and sending them back. That is counted as a deportation."[66]

- A few weeks later, ICE not surprisingly proclaimed that its fiscal-year-end statistics showed the "largest number of deportations in the agency's history." Yet, the Department of Homeland Security's annual statistics demonstrated that ICE is actually *detaining* fewer illegal aliens than at any time in its history.[67]

Moreover, as noted in Article V, below, the president and his subordinates have embarked on an administrative amnesty of thousands of illegal aliens under the cloak of "prosecutorial discretion." This has been carried out through directives issued from high-ranking DHS officials to field offices handling immigration cases.[68] In August 2010, pursuant to these directives, ICE's chief counsel in Houston issued a memorandum ordering his subordinates to review all new and pending cases and dismiss any that did not meet the agency's "top priorities."[69] The memo was issued only after the chief counsel was encouraged by superiors to, as he put it in an email, "publish an office policy on prosecutorial discretion" and meet regularly with his staff "to discuss low and non-priority cases to be terminated."[70]

Hundreds of cases were thus dismissed. On August 25, 2010, the *Houston Chronicle* broke the story about the dismissals. Although they had clearly encouraged the dismissals, ICE quietly rescinded the chief counsel's order the day the newspaper story appeared, suggesting he had perhaps misunderstood their guidance.[71]

Afterwards, several senators on the Judiciary Committee wrote to DHS demanding an explanation of the dismissals in Houston and contending that DHS officials were "selectively enforcing the laws against only those aliens it considers a priority." In response, a top DHS official wrote the senators a letter assuring them that "the directive you cited in your letter instructing ICE attorneys to seek the dismissals of immigration proceedings involving certain classes of criminal aliens does not exist." In fact, the directive clearly existed and was later touted by DHS Secretary Janet Napolitano. Meanwhile, a recent study by the Center for Immigration Studies, based on ICE's own recordkeeping, found that in 2013 alone, ICE released approximately 68,000 aliens with criminal convictions back into the community. In fact, in 772,000 encounters with potentially deportable aliens, ICE chose to file charges against only 195,000 (about one-fourth of the total).[72]

The Solyndra Fraud

The president and his subordinates willfully defrauded the American people, including investors in the public securities exchanges, in connection with Solyndra, a solar energy enterprise that he and his subordinates subsidized with over half a billion taxpayer dollars despite obvious indication that the venture was not viable and would collapse. Moreover, when the inevitable collapse occurred, the public learned that the president and his subordinates, for the benefit of the company that was backed by a major Obama campaign bundler, had agreed to an invalid restructuring; specifically, the president and his subordinates "waived" enforcement of a federal law that protects taxpayers when a subsidized company goes bankrupt, resulting in American taxpayers' absorption of millions of dollars in losses that should have been borne by Solyndra's backers.[73]

The Energy Policy Act of 2005 empowers the government to use public funds to invest in private energy-sector ventures.[74] It requires, however, that in the event the investments go bust, taxpayers be prioritized over stakeholders when the bankrupt company's remaining assets are sold.

Solyndra was denied Energy Policy Act funding before the president entered office.[75] This is because it was, as one analyst put it, "an absolute complete disaster," with operating expenses, including supply costs, that nearly doubled its revenue in 2009—and that does not factor in high capital expenditures and other costs in what is a low-profit-margin industry.[76] The chance that Solyndra would ever become profitable was essentially nonexistent, particularly given that solar panel competitors backed by China produce energy at much lower prices.[77]

Yet, Solyndra pushed again for public funding from the Obama administration. The president is an ardent proponent of renewable energy experiments. Moreover, the company's major stakeholders included the George Kaiser Family Foundation. Mr. Kaiser, an Oklahoma oil magnate, was a major Obama campaign fundraiser. Solyndra officers and investors reportedly visited the White House no fewer than twenty times while the loan guarantee was being considered and, later, revised. Within six days of the president's assumption of office, an Energy Department official acknowledged that the Solyndra "approval process" was suddenly being considered anew. Eventually, the administration made Solyndra the very first recipient of a public loan guarantee when the Energy Policy Act program was beefed up in 2009, as part of the "stimulus" spending.[78]

The public loans were extended despite the qualms of officials in the Energy Department and the Office of Management and Budget. They realized that the company was hemorrhaging money and, even with the loan, would lack the necessary working capital to turn that equation around. Yet, with Vice President Joe Biden scheduled to announce the loan in connection with a ballyhooed September 2009 speech on "renewable energy," it was approved. An OMB email laments that the timing of the loan approval was driven by the politics of the announcement "rather than the other way around."[79]

Although Solyndra was a private company, it was using its government loans as a springboard to go public. Securities and Exchange Commission rules for an initial public offering of stock require the disclosure of a company's financial condition. In Solyndra's case, outside auditors from PricewaterhouseCoopers (PWC) found that condition to be dire. "The company has suffered recurring losses from operations, negative cash flows since inception, and has a net stockholders' deficit," the PWC accountants concluded. Even with the gigantic loan, Solyndra was such a basket case that PWC found "substantial doubt about its ability to continue as a going concern."[80] "Going concern" is a term of art to which auditors resort when there is an extraordinary need to protect themselves and the company from legal liability because a company is likely to fail.[81]

With no alternative if they wanted to make a play for market financing, Solyndra's backers disclosed the auditors' bleak diagnosis in March 2010. The government had thus been aware of it for two months when the president came to Solyndra on May 26—the company was to be the backdrop to a speech on the administration's energy initiatives.

Federal law severely criminalizes schemes to defraud the United States.[82] Our law also extensively regulates the sale of securities. "In connection with the purchase or sale of any security," it similarly criminalizes fraudulent schemes, false statements of material fact, and—significantly for present purposes—statements that *omit any "material fact necessary in order to make the statements made . . . not misleading."*[83] Quite apart from statutory and regulatory law, moreover, the president, duty-bound to execute the laws faithfully, has a fiduciary responsibility to be forthright with the American people, an obligation that certainly applies when he speaks to investors who are about to be solicited for funding by a business into which the president has poured millions of public dollars.

In his May 26 speech, however, the president averred that when it came to channeling public funds into private hands, "We can see the positive impacts right here at Solyndra." He bragged that the $535 billion loan had enabled the company to build the state-of-the-art factory in which he was then speaking. He said nothing about how Solyndra was continuing to lose money—public money—at a catastrophic rate. Instead, he painted the brightest of pictures: 3,000 construction workers to build the thriving plant; manufacturers in 22 states building an endless stream of supplies; technicians in a dozen states constructing the advanced equipment that would make the factory hum; and Solyndra fully "expect[ing] to hire a thousand workers to manufacture solar panels and sell them across America and around the world." Not content with that rosy portrait, the president further predicted a "ripple effect": Solyndra would "generate business for companies throughout our country who will create jobs supplying this factory with parts and materials."[84]

In sum, auditors had scrutinized Solyndra and found it to have, from its inception, a fatally flawed business model that was hurtling toward collapse. Yet, the president touted it as a success story that would be spurring jobs, growth, and spectacular success for the foreseeable future.

Taxpayers were stuck with the president's investment decisions once he became president, but private investors get to choose where their money goes. They were more influenced by the PWC auditors than by the president's speech. Solyndra had to pull its initial public offering due to lack of interest. As the IPO failed and the company inevitably sank in a sea of red ink, Solyndra's panicked backers pleaded with the administration to restructure the loan terms—to insulate them from their poor business judgment, allowing them to recoup some of their investment.[85]

This is where the Energy Policy Act's protection of taxpayers is supposed to come in. As is standard and consistent with the law, the original government loan put the public first in line for proceeds on the sale of Solyndra's assets if it collapsed. OMB officials fully understood that there was no economic sense in restructuring: Solyndra was heading for bankruptcy anyway, and an immediate liquidation would net the government a better deal—about $170 million better. The case for leaving things as they were was so compelling that OMB feared "questions will be asked" if the Department of Energy proceeded with an unjustifiable restructuring. But the president and his subordinates at DOE permitted the Solyndra stakeholders to renegotiate the terms anyway. They absurdly rationalized that the restructuring was necessary "to create a situation whereby investors felt there was a value in their investment."[86] Of course, the *value* in an investment is the value created by the business in which the investment is made. Here, Solyndra had no value. Investors could be enticed only by an invalid arrangement to recoup some of their losses—the kind of scheme from which the Energy Policy Act and the public officials enforcing it are supposed to protect the public.

In exchange for lending some of their own money and thus buying more time, Solyndra officials were given priority over taxpayers with respect to the first $75 million in the event of a bankruptcy.[87]

That event came to pass in short order.

ARTICLE V

FAILURE TO EXECUTE THE IMMIGRATION LAWS FAITHFULLY

Using the powers of the office of President of the United States, Barack Hussein Obama, in violation of his constitutional oath faithfully to execute the office of President of the United States and, to the best of his ability, preserve, protect and defend the Constitution of the United States, and in violation of his constitutional duty to take care that the laws be faithfully executed, has willfully undermined the federal immigration laws; he has willfully refused to execute indisputably constitutional and valid laws of the United States; and he has engaged in gross maladministration by punishing states that seek to enforce federal immigration law, and denying them the sovereign right to defend themselves from the economic and security harms caused by illegal immigration, while rewarding states that flout federal immigration law.

This conduct has included one or more of the following:

Immigration Amnesty by Executive Edict

As alleged in Article I, he has unilaterally and in violation of the Constitution conferred amnesty on several categories of illegal aliens, which categories he has unilaterally defined, and he has instituted unauthorized federal benefits for those aliens, without congressional authorization and in defiance of Congress.

Administrative Amnesty

He has abused his authority over the Department of Homeland Security, and its component agencies charged with enforcement of the immigration laws, to confer an administrative amnesty on categories of illegal immigrants, which categories he has unilaterally defined, in order to undermine federal immigration laws and the constitutional authority of Congress to enact immigration law.

This conduct has included one or more of the following:

He and his subordinates have conspired to use executive orders, administrative regulations, and claims of prosecutorial discretion to supplant the plenary constitutional authority of Congress to make immigration law. Internal Department of Homeland Security memoranda have described contemplated "administrative alternatives" to congressional immigration legislation, by which the president and his subordinates have planned to "reduce the threat of removal for certain individuals present in the United States without authorization" and "extend benefits and/or protections to many individuals and groups" of illegal aliens.[1]

Such memoranda have further detailed a plan to proceed "in the absence of legislation" by way of deferred enforcement action, deferred enforced departure from the United States, waivers of enforcement against certain categories of illegal aliens, and "parole in place" for certain categories of illegal aliens.[2] Demonstrating the Obama administration's awareness of both the lawlessness of its actions and the fact that they were certain to undermine legislative efforts to reform immigration law in a manner consistent with the Constitution, one DHS memorandum observed:

> Even many who have supported a legislated legalization program may question the legitimacy of trying to accomplish the same end via administrative action, particularly after five years where the two parties have treated this as a matter to be decided in Congress.[3]

Underscoring the politicization of law enforcement activities that has been a hallmark of the Obama administration, the same memorandum states:

> Done right, a combination of benefit and enforcement-related administrative measures could provide the Administration with a clear-cut

political win. If the Administration loses control of the message, however, an aggressive administrative proposal carries significant political risk.

. . . .

More ambitious measures would have to be carefully timed. We would need to give the legislative process enough time to play out to deflect against charges of usurping congressional authority. . . . This is likely to mean that the right time for administrative action will be late summer or fall [2010]—when the midterm election is in full-swing.[4]

He and his subordinates have directed the use of "prosecutorial discretion" to dismiss thousands of pending cases against illegal immigrants and to prevent the arrest and prosecution of thousands of illegal immigrants. Pursuant to these directives, he and his subordinates have barred immigration enforcement agents from detaining illegal aliens unless they have committed crimes independent of their violation of the immigration laws. Far from faithfully executing the laws, he and his subordinates are undermining the laws in granting administratively the amnesty Congress has declined to grant by statute. Indeed, as noted in Article IV, above, in 2013 alone, the administration released approximately 68,000 deportable aliens with criminal convictions back into American communities, and filed charges only against approximately one-fourth of the 772,000 deportable aliens it encountered—many of whom were brought to its attention after being arrested by local police. As a federal district court in Texas recently ruled, federal law "mandates the initiation of immigration removal proceedings whenever an immigration officer encounters an illegal alien who is not 'clearly and beyond a doubt entitled to be admitted.'" Moreover, the court explained, the Department of Homeland Security does not have "prosecutorial discretion" to ignore this requirement; Congress, not the president, has the plenary power to make immigration law; and the executive branch may not "implement measures that are incompatible with Congressional intent."[5]

USCIS officials have pressured employees to approve immigration applications that should have been denied, and have pressured employees to process such applications despite the lack of adequate time to complete applicant interviews.[6]

He and his subordinates have instituted a policy whereby American immigration agents assist human traffickers in assisting aliens with relatives in the United States to enter the United States illegally. A federal district judge in Texas has issued a court order noting "the apparent policy of the Department of Homeland Security of completing the criminal mission of individuals who are violating the border security of the United States."[7]

He and his subordinates have issued a visa to a self-proclaimed member of a formally designated Egyptian terrorist organization in order to enable that member of the terrorist organization to consult with administration officials at the White House, in violation of the federal laws that prohibit material support to terrorism.[8]

He and his subordinates have undermined a congressional statute, Section 287(g) of the Immigration and Nationality Act, that enables state and local law enforcement officers to enforce the federal immigration laws within their jurisdictions.[9]

In any controversial matter involving humanitarian, national security, and rule-of-law concerns, Congress's capacity to legislate depends on whether lawmakers and the public have confidence that the president and his subordinates will faithfully execute the laws that are enacted and genuinely cooperate with Congress's fact-finding and oversight responsibilities. The president's maladministration, which erodes public confidence in the government's commitment to enforce immigration law and to provide Congress and the public with complete and accurate information, has undermined the capability of Congress to negotiate and enact immigration legislation.[10]

Punishing States That Enforce Immigration Law

The president and his subordinates have compelled citizens of the state of Arizona and other citizens of the United States to expend public funds on an extensive litigation over a Justice Department lawsuit seeking to prohibit Arizona from enforcing state and federal laws against illegal immigration.

During the course of the litigation against the State of Arizona, the president and his subordinates announced that the Immigration and Customs Enforcement agency would not process or accept illegal immigrants that the State of Arizona's police agencies sought to transfer to federal custody.[11]

Immediately after the U.S. Supreme Court ruled against the Obama administration on a provision of Arizona law authorizing police to take investigative steps to determine the immigration status of lawfully detained persons, the administration announced that ICE was suspending immigration enforcement cooperation with Arizona's state police agencies.

The president and his subordinates have compelled citizens of the states of Florida and Arizona, and other citizens of the United States, to expend public funds on extensive litigation over Justice Department lawsuits seeking to prohibit those states from preventing illegal aliens from voting in elections.[12]

Rewarding States That Refuse to Enforce Immigration Law

The Obama administration's stated justification, in court and in public statements, for suing the State of Arizona was the policy of compelling states to adhere to federal immigration law and the immigration enforcement practices established by the administration. Yet the president and his subordinates announced that the administration would take no legal or administrative action against "sanctuary cities" that refuse to facilitate the enforcement of federal immigration law, and have in fact taken no meaningful action against such cities.[13]

ARTICLE VI

FAILURE TO EXECUTE THE LAWS FAITHFULLY: THE DEPARTMENT OF JUSTICE

Using the powers of the office of President of the United States, Barack Hussein Obama, in violation of his constitutional oath faithfully to execute the office of President of the United States and, to the best of his ability, preserve, protect and defend the Constitution of the United States, and in violation of his constitutional duty to take care that the laws be faithfully executed, has willfully undermined the rule of law by engaging, in conjunction with his subordinates, in the gross maladministration of the Department of Justice, the federal government's chief law enforcement arm.

He and his subordinates have willfully abused their investigative authority, politicizing the enforcement of the laws; recklessly creating dangerous conditions that resulted in violent crimes, including the murder of a United States Border Patrol agent; enforcing the civil rights laws in a racially discriminatory manner, in violation of the constitutional principle of equal protection under the law; violating the constitutional rights and prerogatives of citizens and sovereign states; undertaking selective and vindictive investigations and prosecutions of perceived political opponents and in retaliation for policy disputes; encouraging state law enforcement authorities to violate state law under the guise of "prosecutorial discretion"; providing false testimony to Congress; and systematically obstructing the constitutional authority of Congress to monitor and conduct oversight of the activities of the Department of Justice, a government department created by congressional statute and underwritten by Congress with billions of dollars in public funds.

This conduct has included one and more of the following:

Fast and Furious

The president and his subordinates at the Department of Justice and its component agencies, including the Bureau of Alcohol, Tobacco, Firearms and Explosives (ATF), concocted a reckless investigation internally known as "Fast and Furious." The operation involved allowing thousands of firearms and ammunition purchased from American firearms dealers to be transferred illegally to unauthorized recipients, including violent criminals and criminal organizations in Mexico. This investigative tactic, known as "gun-walking," was undertaken without controls that would enable law enforcement agents to make arrests at or near the point of illegal transfer and seize the firearms. Consequently and foreseeably, thousands of firearms fell into the hands of violent criminals—setting up a scenario, politically useful to opponents of the constitutional right to keep and bear arms, in which it could be argued that American gun rights were responsible for violent crime in Mexico and elsewhere. Predictably, the firearms illegally transferred have resulted in—and will inevitably continue to result in—numerous crimes of violence, including the murder of at least one federal law enforcement agent, U.S. Border Patrol agent Brian Terry, on December 14, 2010.[1]

The president and his subordinates at the Justice Department have made false representations to Congress about the tactics of the Fast and Furious investigation and their awareness of the investigation. For example, on February 4, 2011, nearly two months after Agent Terry was murdered, the Justice Department sent Congress a letter flatly denying that it had facilitated the illegal transfer of weapons to Mexico and insisting that its agencies always make "every effort to interdict weapons that have been purchased illegally and prevent their transportation to Mexico." Those assertions were false. Furthermore, to conceal information about the investigation from Congress and the public, the attorney general has given misleading testimony and refused to comply with lawful congressional subpoenas and requests.[2] As a result, the attorney general has been held in contempt of Congress. Notwithstanding his duty to take care that the laws be faithfully executed, the president, rather than correcting his attorney general's contemptuous stonewalling, has aided and abetted it by frivolously invoking executive privilege in order to obstruct Congress and the public from access to information about Fast and Furious.[3]

Racially Discriminatory Enforcement of the Civil Rights Laws

The president and his subordinates at the Department of Justice have willfully denied Americans the Constitution's guarantee of equal protection under the law by practicing racial discrimination in the enforcement of the federal civil rights laws. As written by Congress and enacted into law, the civil rights laws are race-neutral, as the Constitution requires. Nevertheless, he and his subordinates have adopted a policy holding that these laws are for the protection of racial minorities only; therefore, they will not be enforced when the victims of civil rights offenses are white and the suspects are members of a minority group. This policy has resulted in the Justice Department's dismissal of a voter-intimidation case in Philadelphia, despite the fact that the government had already prevailed in the case—a case in which the defendants, caught on videotape intimidating voters, contemptuously defaulted by ignoring the Justice Department's complaint. One prominent Democrat and longtime civil rights activist on the scene that day described the defendants' menacing behavior as "the most blatant form of voter intimidation I have encountered in my life in political campaigns in many states, even going back to the work I did in Mississippi in the 1960s." Moreover, career prosecutors regarded the case as overwhelmingly strong. Yet the president's subordinates, in consultation with organizations that are vigorous political supporters of the president, dismissed the case just as the court was about to enter judgment in favor of the United States.[4]

Politicization of Hiring

The president and his subordinates at the Department of Justice have politicized the hiring and, in some instances, the assignment of prosecutors.

Ensuring the public integrity of law enforcement is one of the federal government's most important responsibilities. Thus, the recruitment of prosecutors and the day-to-day administration of justice must not be unduly influenced by political ideology and partisanship.[5] Yet the president and his subordinates at the Justice Department have clearly used progressive ideology and activism as a hiring litmus test, systematically filling the Justice Department, particularly the Civil Rights Division, with political activists. Indeed, it has been reported that the president's appointed acting assistant attorney general for civil rights, at the outset of the president's administration, ordered the résumés of highly qualified applicants to be rejected if they lacked experience working with left-wing activist organizations. And an extensive analysis of hiring during the administration strongly indicates that this preference became a practice.[6]

Moreover, upon revelations that the Internal Revenue Service, under the president and his subordinates, had invidiously targeted conservative organizations for harassment and disparate treatment in the awarding of tax-exempt status (as further described in Article VII, below), the president's subordinates at the Justice Department handpicked to run the investigation a prosecutor from the Civil Rights Division who is a partisan Democrat and a donor to both the president's political campaigns and the Democratic National Committee.[7]

Politicization of Investigation and Prosecution

The president and his subordinates at the Department of Justice have invidiously selected prosecution targets, and otherwise used the investigative powers of the executive branch, for political purposes. They have pursued investigations and prosecutions against perceived political opponents of the president, in retaliation for policy decisions opposed by the president, and to satisfy groups and factions that support the president politically.

This conduct has included one or more of the following:

- The Justice Department, under the president and his subordinates, has filed a civil lawsuit against the rating agency Standard & Poor. The indictment was filed after S&P downgraded the credit rating of the United States below triple-A for the first time in history, embarrassing and causing practical governance problems for the Obama administration. Following the downgrade, the president's treasury secretary angrily warned S&P's chairman that there would be "a response from the government." The Justice Department thereafter filed a civil lawsuit seeking $5 billion in damages against S&P. The suit involved conduct arising not out of the downgrade but out of the 2008 financial meltdown triggered by the collapse of mortgage-backed securities. Similarly situated rating agencies have not been prosecuted.[8]
- The Justice Department, under the president and his subordinates, has filed a criminal indictment against Dinesh D'Souza, a well-known conservative commentator, author and film producer, who wrote a best-selling book and co-produced a popular movie that covered the president's background and were negatively critical of the president's governance. The indictment charges a campaign finance violation in a paltry amount, $15,000. The Justice Department routinely declines prosecution on such offenses of that scope, permitting them to be handled by administrative fine. For example, the Justice Department has declined to prosecute anyone involved in the president's 2008 campaign, notwithstanding campaign finance violations involving millions of dollars (i.e., more than 100 times the amount alleged against D'Souza); the case against the Obama campaign was administratively disposed by a fine of $375,000. Furthermore, in the statute under which D'Souza was indicted, Congress prescribed a maximum sentence of only two years' imprisonment. In filing its indictment, however, the Justice

Department added a second felony charge of causing false statements. As a practical matter, it is not possible to commit the campaign finance offense (involving misrepresentation of the source of donations) without causing false statements to be made. By gratuitously adding the second felony count, however, the Justice Department increased D'Souza's potential exposure to seven years' imprisonment, rather than the two prescribed by Congress. Moreover, though D'Souza posed no flight risk or danger to the community, and was thus suited for pretrial release on his own recognizance or, at most, a small bail package, prosecutors argued for the setting of bail at $500,000. (For comparison purposes, the bail in D'Souza's case is significantly higher than the fine the Obama campaign was required to pay in lieu of prosecution for underlying offenses that dwarf the D'Souza allegation.) As one prominent legal commentator has observed, D'Souza's "is clearly a case of selective prosecution."[9]

- As further detailed in Article IV, above, the Justice Department prosecuted Nakoula Basseley Nakoula for a violation of supervised release after the president and his subordinates fraudulently claimed that a video trailer for a film he produced, *Innocence of Muslims*, was responsible for the killings of the U.S. ambassador to Libya and three other Americans in Benghazi on September 11, 2012. The prosecution was commenced after the secretary of state told the father of one of the Benghazi victims that the Obama administration would arrest and prosecute the man responsible for the film it was scapegoating as the cause of the massacre. Though the making of the film was constitutionally protected activity under the First Amendment, Nakoula was interrogated about it and cited for violations of his supervised-release conditions arising out of it. Those violations were quietly dismissed when Nakoula admitted to the violations involving the use of aliases.
- The Justice Department, under the president and his subordinates, pressured the State of Florida to file murder charges against George Zimmerman, who shot to death Trayvon Martin,

a seventeen-year-old African American, in the course of an altercation on February 26, 2012. While the killing was tragic, it was readily apparent to competent lawyers that there was insufficient evidence, particularly of criminal intent, to support a murder charge—which was why the law enforcement professionals in Florida who initially investigated the case declined to file charges. The president, however, made inappropriate and politically charged comments about the case. The attorney general proceeded to pressure Florida to bring charges, including by means of a joint appearance with Al Sharpton, who threatened that his "action network" would "move to the next level" unless Zimmerman was arrested. The attorney general strongly suggested that the Justice Department would bring a civil rights prosecution against Zimmerman if Florida failed to act. It was readily apparent to competent lawyers, however, that there was even less evidentiary basis for a federal civil rights case than for a state murder case. Nevertheless, Florida prosecutors bent under the pressure and filed a murder charge. As expected, Zimmerman was swiftly acquitted at trial. Subsequently, having raised expectations of a federal civil rights prosecution, the attorney general was forced to acknowledge that there was no legal basis to bring one.[10]

• The Justice Department, under the president and his subordinates, reopened an investigation of the CIA and some of its officers who had carried out controversial interrogations against high-value terrorist detainees under guidance from the George W. Bush Justice Department. The investigation had been thoroughly and professionally pursued by career prosecutors, not political appointees, before being closed without charges. Nevertheless, during the 2008 presidential campaign, the current attorney general, who was then an Obama campaign spokesman, had promised a "reckoning" for Bush war-on-terror policies he claimed violated constitutional and international law (many of which policies have been maintained by the Obama administration).[11] The reopening of the investigation in the absence of just cause paralyzed the intelligence community and extended the anxiety of national security agents who had been cleared. The politicized decision discourages national security agents from following directives and taking action in defense of the United States due to fears that they will be prosecuted for doing so when a new political administration is elected. After three years, the reopened investigation was quietly closed with no new charges brought.[12]

Investigation of the Press

The president and his subordinates at the Department of Justice have abused their power in conducting unduly aggressive surveillance and other investigation of members of the press, and then in providing Congress with misleading information about their investigative activities.

Under the guise of investigating leaks, the Justice Department issued sweeping subpoenas for the telephone usage records of numerous media reporters, notwithstanding the department's venerable guidelines, which direct that subpoenas and requests for information from members of the media should be narrowly tailored and resorted to only when other potential avenues of obtaining the information either are impractical or have been exhausted.[13]

Furthermore, after the Justice Department targeted a Fox News reporter for a criminal investigation under the Espionage Act, in a matter involving unauthorized disclosure of classified information, the attorney general provided Congress with misleading information about his knowledge and approval of the investigation. Specifically, he testified:

> With regard to the potential prosecution of the press for the disclosure of [classified] material, that is not something I've ever been involved in, heard of, or would think would be wise policy.[14]

It subsequently emerged, however, that the attorney general had actually approved a search warrant for the reporter's private emails.

The warrant was governed by the Privacy Protection Act, which safeguards First Amendment free-press rights by limiting such searches to situations in which there is probable cause to believe the reporter is guilty of a crime. The attorney general and his subordinates thus represented to the court—in apparent contradiction of what the attorney general told Congress—that they were investigating the reporter, and that there was probable cause to believe the reporter had violated the Espionage Act. That is, they were investigating the reporter for committing a crime that could be prosecuted in federal court.[15]

The attorney general later told Congress that just because the Justice Department was *investigating* a reporter for commission of a crime did not mean the Justice Department was actually considering *prosecuting* the reporter for committing the crime.[16] This dubious rationalization of the attorney general's conflicting positions was apparently not made known to the federal judge who was asked to sign the search warrant. In fact, the judge was told that the Justice Department needed a search warrant because requesting voluntary disclosure of the information sought from the reporter was not practical due to "the Reporter's own potential criminal liability in this matter."[17]

Using Law Enforcement Power to Coerce States

The president and his subordinates at the Department of Justice have used the executive's awesome law enforcement power, including its access to vast sums of public money for conducting investigations and filing lawsuits, to intimidate the states into complying with Obama administration policies, including when those policies conflict with the states' lawful powers, prerogatives and obligations under the Constitution and state law.

The Justice Department and the attorney general, under the president, have encouraged state attorneys general to follow the Obama administration's practice of declining, under the guise of "prosecutorial discretion," to enforce and defend laws—in particular, state marriage laws that conflict with Obama administration support for gay marriage, notwithstanding the Supreme Court's reaffirmation that marriage regulation is a state law matter.[18]

The Justice Department and the attorney general contend that voter identification laws, which promote the integrity of elections and ensure that the citizen's right to vote is not eviscerated by ineligible voters, are vehicles for "suppressing voting rights." Consequently, aware that defending against even a meritless lawsuit filed by the federal government is a prohibitively expensive proposition, the Justice Department has filed vexatious lawsuits to discourage states from enforcing voter identification laws.[19]

At the same time, the Justice Department, under the president, has dropped lawsuits vindicating federal law that requires states to remove ineligible voters from their rolls. Moreover, it has filed lawsuits in order to prevent states from undertaking this legal obligation to remove ineligible voters from their rolls.[20]

As further described in Article V, above, the Justice Department has filed lawsuits to prevent states from enforcing the immigration laws. The effort puts the states in an impossible security bind: They may not legislate or act in their own defense against illegal immigration because they have been preempted by federal action, and yet the federal government will not meaningfully enforce the immigration law—leaving the defenseless states to bear the immense security and financial burdens of illegal immigration.

Stonewalling Congress

As further detailed above, the president and his subordinates at the Justice Department and its component agencies have assiduously undermined the capacity of Congress to perform its lawful oversight functions. They have impeded Congress's investigations and fact-finding efforts on behalf of the American people in connection with the Fast and Furious investigation, the Benghazi massacre and the cover-up in its aftermath, the IRS's harassment and selective targeting of conservative groups (further described in Article VII, below), and an array of government actions in matters of great public interest.

ARTICLE VII

WILLFULLY UNDERMINING THE CONSTITUTIONAL RIGHTS OF THE AMERICAN PEOPLE THAT HE IS SWORN TO PRESERVE, PROTECT AND DEFEND

Using the powers of the office of President of the United States, Barack Hussein Obama, in violation of his constitutional oath faithfully to execute the office of President of the United States and, to the best of his ability, preserve, protect and defend the Constitution of the United States, and in disregard of his constitutional duty to take care that the laws be faithfully executed, has willfully and repeatedly engaged in conduct violating the constitutional rights of citizens.

This conduct has included one or more of the following:

Selective Targeting of Political Opponents for Harassment and Abuse by the Internal Revenue Service

The president and his subordinates have willfully undermined and prejudiced the rights of the American people to equal protection under the law and to engage in free political speech and association. He and his subordinates have employed the awesome powers of the Internal Revenue Service (IRS) in the interest of partisan politics, selectively harassing conservative groups opposed to the president's policies and denying them the Constitution's guarantee of equal protection under the law. Specifically, he and his subordinates targeted conservative groups for heightened scrutiny in order to delay and deny them tax-exempt status, under Section 501(c)(4) of the Internal Revenue Code, as "social welfare" organizations.

Section 501(c)(4) prescribes a tax exemption for organizations principally engaged in "social welfare." They are permitted to engage in "political activities" without disqualifying themselves from exempt status provided that these are not the organization's "primary activity."[1]

The Supreme Court's 2010 *Citizens United* ruling,[2] which affirmed the right of corporations to engage in political speech and campaign activity, was unpopular on the political left. Indeed, a week after it was decided, the president audaciously scolded the justices over the case as they sat before him during his 2011 State of the Union Address.[3] Between the Court's ruling, the shellacking that Democrats took in the 2010 midterm elections, and the Obama campaign's gear-up for a reelection run, prominent Democrats began calling for more scrutiny of tax exemptions for conservative groups, especially Tea Party groups.[4]

The Exempt Organizations division of the IRS was run by Lois Lerner, a partisan Democrat who, in a previous stint at the Federal Election Commission, had subjected Republican and conservative groups to heightened scrutiny.[5] Ms. Lerner enthusiastically took on the role of selecting conservative groups for enhanced IRS examinations—directing that they be isolated for a higher level of inspection and subjected to a "multi-tier" review system that quite intentionally slowed the review process to barely a crawl. The additional scrutiny achieved its immediate purpose: without their tax-exempt status clarified, many conservative groups were sidelined from participating in the 2012 election cycle.[6]

In May 2013, the Treasury inspector general for tax administration reported that the IRS had inappropriately targeted Tea Party and other conservative groups, subjecting them to heightened scrutiny.[7] The president and his subordinates attempted to shift blame for this blatant violation of constitutional rights onto a single IRS field office in Cincinnati. But it became clear that the IRS Exempt Organizations group in Cincinnati were acting under the direction of their superiors in Washington, overseen by Lerner. Called to testify before Congress, Lerner obstructed the investigation of the House Committee on Oversight and Government Reform by making sweeping testimonial claims of innocence and then refusing to answer questions—despite the fact that she was a public official who would be expected to cooperate in a congressional probe.[8]

The president, though in charge of the executive branch and obliged to see that the laws are faithfully executed, took no meaningful action to encourage Lerner's cooperation with Congress. To the contrary, while she was now claiming the Fifth Amendment not to testify on the ground that truthful answers could incriminate her, the president was simultaneously making the public claim that there had been "not even a smidgeon of corruption" in the IRS's invidious targeting of his political opponents.[9]

The president's subordinates and their supporters have claimed that Section 501(c)(4) and its enforcement guidance are ambiguous and difficult to apply. In fact, the provision has stood unchanged in the Internal Revenue Code for over half a century, with the guidance well developed by experience and practice over that time. The IRS, for example, had no evident difficulty according exempt status to MoveOn. org—a left-wing organization the IRS decided was not overly "political" notwithstanding its history of aggressive, hardball political activism and its website's proclamation of a mission "to lead, participate in, and win campaigns for progressive change."[10]

When the scandal first broke publicly, the president and the attorney general affected indignation, calling the targeting of Americans for political reasons "intolerable," "inexcusable," "outrageous," and "unacceptable." Thereafter, the president and his subordinates proposed new IRS rules that would codify and implement the very tactics they had condemned.[11]

As previously observed, the administration has stonewalled Congress's probe, and the attorney general selected as the prosecutor to oversee the Justice Department's investigation a partisan Democrat from the Civil Rights Division who has donated to the president's campaigns and the Democratic National Committee.[12] No charges have been filed and, according to an attorney for several of the victims, investigators went months without interviewing them.[13]

Abridging Free Speech in Appeasement
of Islamic Supremacism

The president and his subordinates, in executing an ill-conceived policy of appeasing Islamists who adhere to a supremacist interpretation of Islamic law (sharia), have abridged the right of the American people to free expression, in violation of the First Amendment to the Constitution.

Under an interpretation of Islam that is mainstream and influential in the Middle East and elsewhere, blasphemy is an offense punishable by death, and one as to which individual Muslims often take the law into their own hands. Problematically, this interpretation also construes blasphemy very broadly, to the point that it is said to include any negative criticism of Islam, from trifling slights to scholarly critiques to condemnatory speech of the kind that, though offensive, must be tolerated peacefully by citizens in a free society as the cost of promoting the free exchange of ideas.[14]

The president and his subordinates have adopted a reckless and unconstitutional policy of accommodating the sharia-supremacist interpretation of anti-Islamic blasphemy. The effect of this policy, in the promulgation of law and in the execution of law enforcement, is the denial of First Amendment free expression.

This conduct has included one or more of the following:

- As further detailed in Articles IV and VI, above, the president and his subordinates prosecuted Nakoula Basseley Nakoula for a violation of supervised release after they fraudulently claimed that *Innocence of Muslims*, a video trailer for a film he produced consistent with First Amendment free-speech principles, was responsible for the killings of the U.S. ambassador to Libya and three other Americans in Benghazi on September 11, 2012.
- He and his subordinates have colluded with the Organization of Islamic Cooperation (OIC)—a bloc of 57 governments of nations with substantial Muslim populations plus the Pales-

tinian territories—to restrict the constitutional right of the American people to free expression. Specifically, they have collaborated with the OIC on United Nations Human Rights Council Resolution 16/18, which requires nations to adopt legislation outlawing speech that is negatively critical of Islam, in violation of the First Amendment to the United States Constitution.[15]

- He and his subordinates, in consultation with advisors from Islamist organizations, have purged training materials used to instruct national security agents of information deemed to be unflattering to Islam.[16]

Furthermore, he and his subordinates have refused to acknowledge that the Fort Hood massacre on November 5, 2009, in which thirteen Americans, mostly military personnel, were killed and dozens more wounded in the worst domestic jihadist attack since 9/11, was an act of Islamist terrorism. The jihadist gunman, Nidal Hasan, who screamed *"Allahu Akbar!"* (Allah is greater!)[17] as he fired again and again, was a psychiatrist and commissioned officer in the U.S. Army. He had been exchanging international emails with Anwar al-Awlaki, a top al-Qaeda terrorist who had ministered to the 9/11 suicide-hijackers, for a year before the mass-murder attack. Awlaki was eventually killed in 2011 by a U.S. airstrike in Yemen, an attack the administration justified by its finding that Awlaki was a major operative of the terror network with which our nation is at war—an operative whose main role was to incite the commission of terrorist atrocities.[18]

Just six months before his Fort Hood shooting spree, Hasan, who in previous emails had lauded Hamas suicide bombings against "the Zionist enemy," had written Awlaki in praise of a hypothetical soldier who conducts a sneak attack to prevent "enemy" soldiers from attacking Muslims. Hasan was also on an Awlaki email list and thus a recipient of his incitements condemning Muslims who fight on behalf of the United States and lionizing the *shuhuda* (martyrs) who fight Americans and are killed by them in battle.[19] More recent investigative journalism has uncovered that Hasan made suspicious transfers amounting to nearly $200,000 to the Arab Bank of Palestine while he was working for the army at Walter Reed Medical Center in Bethesda, Maryland, in 2007.[20]

Because of the president's policy of accommodating Islamic supremacists, and of refusing to acknowledge the causal connection between Muslim doctrine as construed by Islamic supremacists and acts of terrorism, government investigators who knew about the Hasan-Awlaki emails—and who were aware of lectures in which the psychiatrist spewed anti-American jihadist rhetoric—dismissed this information as "academic research" and concluded that Hasan "was not involved in terrorist activity." In October 2009, Hasan was told he would be deployed to Afghanistan—where, he believed, Americans were conducting a "war on Islam."[21] The massacre soon followed. Nevertheless, the administration fraudulently labeled the Fort Hood shooting spree against U.S. troops who were about to deploy to a war zone as "workplace violence." The refusal by the president and his subordinates to acknowledge the Fort Hood attack as the product of international terrorism (which obviously must include terrorist acts incited and abetted by al-Qaeda operatives and their foreign supremacist ideology) has resulted in the denial of Purple Heart medals to the soldiers killed and wounded in the attack.[22]

Abridging Free Speech: Malicious Prosecution of a Critic of the President

As detailed in Article VI, above, the president and his subordinates abused the executive's power to enforce federal law in order selectively and vindictively to prosecute an author and film producer who had been negatively critical of the president in a book and a movie, in violation of the First Amendment's core guarantee of free political speech.

Denying Religious Liberty: The Obamacare Abortifacient Mandate

The president and his subordinates have violated the First Amendment's guarantees of religious liberty and freedom of conscience. The president and his subordinates at the Department of Health and

Human Services have promulgated a regulatory mandate, under the PPACA, requiring that the insurance policies that Americans are now compelled to purchase must cover FDA-approved forms of contraception, including abortifacients. The HHS rule blatantly denies the breadth of First Amendment protection, and violates the Religious Freedom Restoration Act, under which Congress promotes First Amendment liberty by prohibiting government from unduly burdening religious freedom.

The HHS merely permits exemptions for "religious employers" (defined as businesses whose main purpose is "the inculcation of religious values" and that both employ and serve primarily persons who "share the religious tenets of the organization").[23] But the law *requires* (not just permits) such an exemption, and it requires a *broader* exemption. The HHS rule unlawfully excludes most religious believers, including most religious believers who conscientiously believe, consistent with venerable religious doctrine, that abetting abortion and contraception is sinful.[24]

The mandate oozes hostility to religion (the sort of thing that, as detailed above, the president and his subordinates propose to ban when the religion in question is Islam). Contraceptives and abortifacients are inexpensive and widely available; exempting religious objectors from this obnoxious mandate would not meaningfully burden any American who wants access to these substances. The mandate is thus gratuitously burdensome.[25]

The president and his subordinates have also taken the position that the federal government has a veto over a church's choice of its ministers and employees. The Supreme Court rejected this offensive claim in a 9–0 ruling that even included the two justices appointed to the high court by the president.[26]

Abridging American Second Amendment Rights
through International Bureaucracies

The president and his subordinates have colluded with officials of foreign governments and international tribunals to restrict the constitutional rights of Americans to keep and bear arms, in violation of the Second Amendment. He and his subordinates have made the United States government a signatory to a multilateral pact, the United Nations Arms Trade Treaty (ATT), that would restrict Second Amendment rights by imposing regulations on firearms transfers and brokers.[27]

Moreover, the text of the ATT is regarded by the president and his subordinates as a stepping stone to more intrusive regulation. For example, Vann Van Diepen, principal deputy assistant secretary in the State Department's Bureau of International Security and Nonproliferation, has argued that it is incumbent upon treaty signatories to take measures not specifically required by the treaty in order to "help achieve [its] ideals."[28] The secretary of state, under the president's direction, signed the treaty despite being alerted to widespread congressional opposition that demonstrated there is no chance for Senate ratification—even as the president and his subordinates contend that our government must not only comply with the treaty's terms but strive to meet its aspirations. The aspirations of international bureaucrats include bringing the United States into a global gun-control regime.

Wherefore Barack Hussein Obama, President of the United States, by such conduct, warrants impeachment and trial, and removal from office.

NOTES

INTRODUCTION—THE RULER OF LAW

1. This introduction is adapted from Andrew C. McCarthy, "The Ruler of Law: On 'justice' in the age of Obama," *The New Criterion*, September 2011.

CHAPTER ONE—WE DON'T HAVE THE VOTES

1. United States Constitution, art. I, sec. 2.

2. Glenn Kessler, "Are there 91 million Americans 'on the sidelines' looking for work?" *Washington Post*, Jan. 30, 2014, http://www.washingtonpost.com/blogs/fact-checker/wp/2014/01/30/are-there-91-million-americans-on-the-sidelines-looking-for-work/. The *Post*'s "Fact Checker" accuses Republicans of distorting the record-high 92 million Americans who lack full-time work into a campaign talking point that implies all such people are looking for work but unable to find it. But even the *Post*'s analysis concedes that there may be 21 million people looking for work, more than double the Obama administration estimate of 10.3 million. Moreover, the *Post*'s figure is a patent lowball. To the administration's absurdly low estimate, it adds only people who (a) "want a job but can't find work"—6 million; (b) "did not actively search for work"—2.4 million; (c) are students or left the job market for "family reasons," illness, or what the *Post* elusively describes as "some other factor"—1.5 million; and (d) "are discouraged and think no job

is available"—0.9 million. The *Post* thus assumes, for example, that all Baby Boomers (the generation born between 1946 and 1964) who hit minimum retirement age and are without work have freely chosen to retire—rather than that, despite having many more potentially productive years, they have reluctantly been driven into early retirement by stagnant economic conditions. Furthermore, the Bureau of Labor Statistics defines U6, the more realistic measure of unemployment, as "total unemployed, plus all marginally attached workers plus total employed part time for economic reasons, as a percent of all civilian labor force plus all marginally attached workers." The *Post* does not count the underemployed. Thanks to Obamacare, there are increasing millions of them because their once full-time jobs have been converted to part-time due to the law's onerous taxes on employers.

3. The Obama administration lauded the announcement in February 2014 that the "unemployment rate" had dropped to 6.6 percent. Yet the real unemployment measure—what the Bureau of Labor Statistics calls U6—was nearly double that amount, 12.7 percent, and has hovered close to 15 percent throughout the past year. See "Chart: What's the real unemployment rate?" CNBC, Feb. 7, 2014, http://www.cnbc.com/id/101398855.

4. See, e.g., Jon Hilsenrath and Victoria McGrane, "Rate Decision to Drive Yellen's Early Agenda," *Wall Street Journal*, Feb. 2, 2014, http://online.wsj.com/news/articles/SB10001424052702304851104579358981469239914; "90 Million Americans Not Working: Another unfortunate milestone for the labor market," *Wall Street Journal*, Oct. 23, 2013, http://online.wsj.com/news/articles/SB10001424052702303902404579151843080376798.

5. See "Whopping 932,000 Americans Drop Out of Labor Force in October; Participation Rate Drops to Fresh 35 Year Low," *Zero Hedge*, Nov. 8, 2013, http://www.zerohedge.com/news/2013-11-08/whopping-932000-americans-drop-out-labor-force-october-labor-participation-rate-drop.

6. Professor Turley has also observed that Obama's "usurpation of authority" is "very dangerous" and unprecedented in American history. See "Liberal Attorney Jonathan Turley: Expansion of Obama's presiden-

tial powers threatens liberty," Fox News, March 6, 2014, http://nation.
foxnews.com/2014/02/13/liberal-attorney-jonathan-turley-expansion-
obamas-presidential-powers-threatens-liberty; Andrew C. McCarthy,
"Impeachment Lessons: The Nineties taught us it's not guilt that matters;
it's political will," *National Review Online*, Dec. 7, 2013, http://www.nation-
alreview.com/article/365742/impeachment-lessons-andrew-c-mccarthy;
Chris Conover, "Progressive Fascism: Obamacare's Lawless Rollout
Cements Case against Single Payer Health Care," *Forbes*, March 6, 2014,
http://www.forbes.com/sites/theapothecary/2014/03/06/progressive-
fascism-obamacares-lawless-rollout-cements-case-against-single-payer-
health-care/; Elizabeth Harrington, "The Imperial Presidency: House
holds hearing on executive overreach," *Washington Free Beacon*, Feb. 26,
2014, http://freebeacon.com/the-imperial-presidency/.

7. Jennifer G. Hickey and John Gizzi, "Dershowitz, Law Enforcement Experts Slam D'Souza Targeting," *Newsmax*, Jan. 29, 2014,
http://www.newsmax.com/Newsfront/DSouza-Dershowitz-targeting-
selective/2014/01/29/id/549845; see also Jacob Gershman, "Dershowitz Says D'Souza Case 'Smacks of Selective Prosecution,'" *Wall
Street Journal*, Jan. 31, 2014, http://blogs.wsj.com/law/2014/01/31/
dershowitz-says-dsouza-case-smacks-of-selective-prosecution/.

8. U.S. Const., art. II, sec. 3.

9. U.S. Const., art. II, sec. 1.

10. See, e.g., Fred Lucas, "Obama Has Touted Al Qaeda's Demise
32 Times Since Benghazi Attack," CNS News, Nov. 1, 2012, http://
cnsnews.com/news/article/obama-touts-al-qaeda-s-demise-32-times-
benghazi-attack-0.

11. Andrew C. McCarthy, "Friendly 'Moderate' Rouhani Boasts
of Obama's 'Surrender to the Iranian Nation's Will,'" *National Review
Online*, Jan. 14, 2014, http://www.nationalreview.com/corner/368434/
friendly-moderate-rouhani-boasts-obamas-surrender-iranian-nations-
will-andrew-c; Michael Wilner, "Rouhani boasts of West's 'surrender'
to Iran in nuclear talks," *Jerusalem Post*, Jan. 14, 2014, http://www.
jpost.com/Iranian-Threat/News/Rouhani-boasts-of-Wests-surrender-
to-Iran-in-nuclear-talks-338135; Tom Cohen, "Iranian official on nuke

deal: We did not agree to dismantle anything," CNN, Jan. 23, 2014, http://edition.cnn.com/2014/01/22/politics/iran-us-nuclear/.

12. Katrina Trinko, "Cruz Calls 'Why Don't We Impeach' Obama 'Good Question'" (audio embedded), *National Review Online*, Aug. 20, 2013, http://www.nationalreview.com/corner/356237/cruz-calls-why-dont-we-impeach-obama-good-question-katrina-trinko; see also Andrew C. McCarthy, "It's Not Crazy to Talk about Impeachment: The Framers did not see impeachment as outlandish," *National Review Online*, Aug. 20, 2013, http://www.nationalreview.com/article/356666/its-not-crazy-talk-about-impeachment-andrew-c-mccarthy.

13. Alexis de Tocqueville, *Democracy in America* (1835, 1840; Penguin Classics, 2003). The French political philosopher and admirer of the American spirit feared that "the manly and lawful passion for equality" would turn into "the depraved taste for equality which impels the weak to attempt to lower the powerful to their own level and reduces men to prefer equality in slavery to inequality with freedom," and that the result would be the devolution of democracy into a suffocating administrative state that

> covers the surface of society with a network of small complicated rules, minute and uniform, through which the most original minds and the most energetic characters cannot penetrate, to rise above the crowd. The will of man is not shattered but softened, bent, and guided; men are seldom forced by it to act, but they are constantly restrained from acting. Such a power does not destroy, but prevents existence; it does not tyrannize, but it compresses, enervates, extinguishes, and stupefies a people, till each nation is reduced to nothing better than a flock of timid and industrious animals, of which the government is the shepherd.

See also Mark R. Levin, *Ameritopia: The Unmaking of America* (Threshold Editions, 2012), p. 161 & ff.

14. Andrew C. McCarthy, "Ron Johnson's Frivolous Obamacare Lawsuit: It is not constitutionally proper or practical for a legislator to sue the president over a public-policy dispute," *National Review Online*, Jan. 8, 2014, http://www.nationalreview.com/article/367823/

ron-johnsons-frivolous-obamacare-lawsuit-andrew-c-mccarthy; see also Andrew C. McCarthy, "Fiction or Faction: Iowa judges have imposed gay marriage on a state that voted against it," *National Review Online*, April 7, 2009, http://www.nationalreview.com/articles/227242/fiction-and-faction/andrew-c-mccarthy.

15. Alexander Hamilton, *The Federalist No. 78* (1788):
Whoever attentively considers the different departments of power must perceive, that, in a government in which they are separated from each other, the judiciary, from the nature of its functions, will always be the least dangerous to the political rights of the Constitution; because it will be least in a capacity to annoy or injure them. The Executive not only dispenses the honors, but holds the sword of the community. The legislature not only commands the purse, but prescribes the rules by which the duties and rights of every citizen are to be regulated. The judiciary, on the contrary, has no influence over either the sword or the purse; no direction either of the strength or of the wealth of the society; and can take no active resolution whatever. It may truly be said to have neither force nor will, but merely judgment; and must ultimately depend upon the aid of the executive arm even for the efficacy of its judgments.

16. "Obama Ignores SCOTUS Ruling, Sues State over Voter ID Law," Judicial Watch Blog, Aug. 26, 2013, http://www.judicialwatch.org/blog/2013/08/obama-ignores-scotus-ruling-sues-state-over-voter-id-law/; "Obama's Union-Controlled NLRB Thumbs Nose at Court Ruling, Chairman Vows to March Onward," *RedState*, Jan. 25, 2013, http://www.redstate.com/2013/01/25/obamas-union-controlled-nlrb-thumbs-nose-at-court-ruling-chairman-vows-to-march-onward/.

17. Laurel Brubaker Calkins, "U.S. in Contempt over Gulf Drill Ban, Judge Rules," *Bloomberg*, Feb. 3, 2011, http://www.bloomberg.com/news/2011-02-03/u-s-administration-in-contempt-over-gulf-drill-ban-judge-rules.html; Michelle Malkin, "Culture of Contempt: Interior Department spanked yet again," *Michelle Malkin*, Feb. 18, 2011, http://michellemalkin.com/2011/02/18/culture-of-contempt-interior-department-spanked-yet-again/.

18. U.S. Const., art. I, sec. 2 & 3; art. II, sec. 4.

CHAPTER TWO—THE MISCONDUCT OF PUBLIC MEN

1. James Madison, "Notes on the Debates in the Federal Convention of 1787," in *The Records of the Federal Convention of 1787*, ed. Max Farrand (1911), http://memory.loc.gov/ammem/amlaw/lwfr.html; see also The Avalon Project, Yale Law School, http://avalon.law.yale.edu/subject_menus/debcont.asp. Madison's convention notes are heavily relied on in this chapter, as is the House Judiciary Committee report prepared and released in connection with articles of impeachment approved in the Watergate investigation, "Constitutional Grounds for Presidential Impeachment," House Judiciary Committee, 1974 (hereafter "House Judiciary Committee Report"), http://www.washingtonpost.com/wp-srv/politics/special/clinton/stories/watergatedoc_3.htm#TOP.

2. *Morrison v. Olson*, 487 U.S. 654, 705 (1988) (Scalia, J., *dissenting*); see also John Yoo, *The Powers of War and Peace: The Constitution and Foreign Affairs After 9/11* (University of Chicago Press, 2005).

3. Alexander Hamilton, *The Federalist No. 70* (1788).

4. Raoul Berger, *Impeachment: The Constitutional Problems* (Harvard University Press, 1974), http://books.google.com/books/about/Impeachment.html?id=UT0_MCzwRW4C; see also House Judiciary Committee Report, *supra*.

5. Jonathan Elliot, *The Debates in the Several State Conventions on the Adoption of the Federal Constitution*, vol. 1 (1827), Liberty Fund, Online Library of Liberty, http://oll.libertyfund.org/?option=com_staticxt&staticfile=show.php%3Ftitle=1905&Itemid=27; see also House Judiciary Committee Report, *supra*.

6. U.S. Const., art. I, sec. 3.

7. Articles of impeachment against President Nixon were approved by the House Judiciary Committee in late July 1974, and a vote by the full House to approve them was imminent. A contingent of Republican senators led by Barry Goldwater of Arizona visited the White House on August 7, 1974, to inform Nixon that they were unwilling and unable to prevent his impeachment and conviction. Nixon resigned the following day. See, e.g., Richard Lyons and William Chapman, "Judiciary Committee approves article to impeach President

Nixon, 27 to 11," *Washington Post*, July 28, 1974, http://www.washing-tonpost.com/wp-srv/national/longterm/watergate/articles/072874-1.htm; Bart Barnes, "Barry Goldwater, GOP hero, dies," *Washington Post*, May 30, 1998, http://www.washingtonpost.com/wp-srv/politics/daily/may98/goldwater30.htm.

8.   For a thorough explication of the relevant history and sympathetic treatment of Burke's campaign against Hastings, see Conor Cruise O'Brien, *The Great Melody: A Thematic Biography of Edmund Burke* (University of Chicago Press, 1992). For a treatment more sympathetic to Hastings, see, e.g., Chris Monaghan, "In Defence of Intrinsic Human Rights: Edmund Burke's Controversial Prosecution of Warren Hastings, Governor-General of Bengal," *Law, Crime and History*, 2011(2): 58–107, http://www.academia.edu/1818643/IN_DEFENCE_OF_INTRINSIC_HUMAN_RIGHTS_EDMUND_BURKES_CONTROVERSIAL_PROSECUTION_OF_WARREN_HASTINGS_GOVERNOR-GENERAL_OF_.

9.   Alexander Hamilton, *The Federalist No. 65* (1788); see also Berger, *Impeachment: The Constitutional Problems, supra*, Chapter II.

10.   4 Blackstone's Commentaries 121 (cited in House Judiciary Committee Report, n.55).

11.   See House Judiciary Committee Report, *supra*:

"High Crimes and Misdemeanors" has traditionally been considered a "term of art," like such other constitutional phrases as "levying war" and "due process." The Supreme Court has held that such phrases must be construed, not according to modern usage, but according to what the framers meant when they adopted them.[56] Chief Justice Marshall [in *United States* v. *Burr*, 25 Fed. Cas. 1, 159 (No 14, 693) (C.C.D. Va 1807)] wrote of another such phrase:

It is a technical term. It is used in a very old statute of that country whose language is our language, and whose laws form the substratum of our laws. It is scarcely conceivable that the term was not employed by the framers of our constitution in the sense which had been affixed to it by those from whom we borrowed it.

12.   U.S. Const., art. II, sec. 4.

13. Constitutional Rights Foundation, "High Crimes and Misdemeanors" (accessed Aug. 23, 2013), http://www.crf-usa.org/impeachment/high-crimes-and-misdemeanors.html.

14. Alexander Hamilton, *The Federalist No. 65* (1788).

15. Jon Roland, "Meaning of 'High Crimes and Misdemeanors,'" Constitution Society, Jan. 16, 1990, http://www.constitution.org/cmt/high_crimes.htm.

16. 1 J. Story, *Commentaries on the Constitution of the United States*, 764, at 559 (5th ed., 1905) (cited in House Judiciary Committee Report, n.83).

17. See, e.g., Berger, *Impeachment: The Constitutional Problems*, *supra*, p. 56 n.1.

18. McCarthy, "It's Not Crazy to Talk about Impeachment," *supra*; see also McCarthy, "Impeachment Lessons," *supra*.

CHAPTER THREE—THE I-WORD

1. Jonathan Strong, "The I-Word: Seeking ways to limit the president's executive overreach, Republicans still shy away from impeachment," *National Review Online*, Dec. 5, 2013, http://www.nationalreview.com/article/365566/i-word-jonathan-strong.

2. McCarthy, "Impeachment Lessons," *supra*.

3. William C. Kimberling, Deputy Director, Federal Election Commission, Office of Election Administration, "The Electoral College," rev. ed., May 1992, http://www.fec.gov/pdf/eleccoll.pdf.

4. See, e.g., James Madison, *The Federalist No. 10* (1787), http://www.constitution.org/fed/federa10.htm; see also McCarthy, "Fiction and Faction," *supra*.

5. Andrew C. McCarthy, "How to Constitutionally Fund the Government: It's the House's prerogative to supply funds, or not, for Obamacare," *National Review Online*, Sep. 28, 2013, http://www.nationalreview.com/article/359767/how-constitutionally-fund-government-andrew-c-mccarthy/page/0/1.

6. See, e.g., Andrew C. McCarthy, "Against the Boehner Plan: Nothing can justify adding $2.5 trillion to the government's credit card," *National Review Online*, July 29, 2011, http://www.nationalreview.com/

articles/273130/against-boehner-plan-andrew-c-mccarthy; McCarthy, "How to Constitutionally Fund the Government," *supra*; McCarthy, "The Art of the Impossible: The strategy to repeal Obamacare by winning serial elections is not even a Hail Mary pass," *National Review Online*, Oct. 19, 2013, http://www.nationalreview.com/article/361655/art-impossible-andrew-c-mccarthy.

7.   McCarthy, "Against the Boehner Plan," *supra*.

8.   Andrew C. McCarthy, "The GOP Should Use the Power of the Purse: The way to cure the rogue behavior of Obama's agencies is not to pay for it," *National Review Online*, Feb. 8, 2104, http://www.nationalreview.com/article/370652/gop-should-use-power-purse-andrew-c-mccarthy; "Obama's IRS 'Confusion': New evidence undercuts White House claims about IRS motivation," Review & Outlook, *Wall Street Journal*, Feb. 7, 2014, http://online.wsj.com/news/articles/SB10001424052702304181204579365161576171176?mod=WSJ_Opinion_LEADTop.

9.   Aaron B. Wildavsky, *The New Politics of the Budgetary Process*, 3rd ed. (Addison-Wesley Educational Publishers, 1997); Patrick Louis Knudsen, "Why Congress Needs a New Budget Process," Heritage Foundation, Center for Policy Innovation, Discussion Paper no. 14 (Dec. 5, 2013), p. 2 n.1 (quoting and citing Aaron B. Wildavsky), http://thf_media.s3.amazonaws.com/2013/pdf/CPI_DP_14.pdf.

10.   Strong, "The I-Word," *supra*.

11.   U.S. Const., art. I, sec. 3.

12.   Strong, "The I-Word," *supra*.

13.   See Andrew C. McCarthy, "Debt-Ceiling Surrender: Republicans use Senate rules to play a con game on the folks back home," *National Review Online*, Feb. 22, 2014, http://www.nationalreview.com/article/371716/debt-ceiling-surrender-andrew-c-mccarthy (describing Senate GOP tactic of voting against Obama's agenda only after ensuring that Democratic majority will be able to pass it, then using the deliberately futile "nay" vote to claim they are aggressively fighting Obama's agenda).

14.   Victor Davis Hanson, "Obama: Transforming America: from energy to foreign policy to the presidency itself, Obama's agenda rolls along," *National Review Online*, Oct. 1, 2013, http://www.nationalreview.

com/article/359967/obama-transforming-america-victor-davis-hanson (noting President Obama's assertion, just before being elected in 2008, that "We are five days away from fundamentally transforming the United States of America," and the similar declaration of Michelle Obama, on May 14, 2008, that "We are going to have to change our conversation; we're going to have to change our traditions, our history; we're going to have to move into a different place as a nation.").

15. See generally Rich Lowry, *Legacy: Paying the Price for the Clinton Years* (Regnery, 2003); see also Peter Baker, "Clinton Settles Paula Jones Lawsuit for $850,000," *Washington Post*, Nov. 14, 1998, http://www.washingtonpost.com/wp-srv/politics/special/clinton/stories/jones111498.htm.

16. "Approved Articles of Impeachment," *Washington Post*, Dec. 20, 1998, http://www.washingtonpost.com/wp-srv/politics/special/clinton/stories/articles122098.htm.

17. See, e.g., Gallup, "Presidential Approval Ratings: Bill Clinton," http://www.gallup.com/poll/116584/presidential-approval-ratings-bill-clinton.aspx; Robert E. Denton Jr. and Rachel L. Holloway, eds., *Images, Scandal, and Communication Strategies of the Clinton Presidency* (Praeger, 2003), pp. 178–79.

18. Henry J. Enten, "Can the Democrats really win back the House in the 2014 midterms?" *Guardian*, July 11, 2013, http://www.theguardian.com/commentisfree/2013/jul/11/democrats-win-house-2014-midterms; Sean Sullivan, "Can Obama defy history in second midterm election?" *Washington Post*, March 4, 2013, http://www.washingtonpost.com/blogs/the-fix/wp/2013/03/04/can-obama-defy-history-in-second-midterm-election/; Nancy Gibbs and Michael Duffy, "Fall of the house of Newt," *Time* and CNN, Nov. 9, 1998, http://www.cnn.com/ALLPOLITICS/time/1998/11/09/gingrich.html.

19. Peter Baker and Helen Dewar, "The Senate acquits President Clinton," *Washington Post*, Feb. 13, 1999, http://www.washington-post.com/wp-srv/politics/special/clinton/stories/impeach021399.htm; Andrew Glass, "Bill Clinton's impeachment trial ends, Feb. 12, 1999," *Politico*, Feb. 12, 2009, http://www.politico.com/news/stories/0209/18734.html.

20. Kara Rowland, "Obama concedes 'shellacking': Blames process, not his policies, for Democrats' setback," *Washington Times*, Nov. 3, 2010, http://www.washingtontimes.com/news/2010/nov/3/obama-concedes-shellacking/?page=all.

21. Strong, "The I-Word," *supra*; see also Andrew C. McCarthy, "The Voters Who Stayed Home: They need better choices," *National Review Online*, Nov. 10, 2012, http://www.nationalreview.com/articles/333135/voters-who-stayed-home-andrew-c-mccarthy (even with a noticeable decline in support from voters under the age of thirty, President Obama still captured 60 percent of this demographic in 2012, and due to the steep overall decline in voter participation, young voters increased slightly as a percentage of the electorate despite the fact that their participation level was down slightly from 2008).

CHAPTER FOUR—THE POINT IS REMOVAL

1. Daniel Catron, "Of Course He Should Be Impeached: Do we have a Congress or a coffle of slaves?" *American Spectator*, Feb. 17, 2014, http://spectator.org/articles/57838/course-he-should-be-impeached.

2. See Mr. Catron's blog, "Health Care BS: Cleaning the Augean Stables of the Health Care Debate," http://www.healthcarebs.com; see also, e.g., David Catron, "A Serious GOP Alternative to Obamacare," *American Spectator*, Feb. 3, 2014, http://spectator.org/articles/57631/serious-gop-alternative-obamacare.

3. Andrew C. McCarthy, "The Art of the Impossible," *supra*.

4. See Andrew C. McCarthy, "A Rich Vein for Holder Questions: Will the Senate Judiciary Committee ask them?" *National Review Online*, Jan. 15, 2009, http://www.nationalreview.com/articles/226697/rich-vein-holder-questions/andrew-c-mccarthy; see also Andrew C. McCarthy, "Unpardonable: Holder's Marc Rich Shuffle: The AG nominee's 1995 lawsuit refutes claims of ignorance about the fugitive," *National Review Online*, Jan. 21, 1995, http://www.nationalreview.com/articles/226728/unpardonable-holders-marc-rich-shuffle/andrew-c-mccarthy; Andrew C. McCarthy, "'The Right Man' to Protect Us from Terror? At least, that's what some of Eric Holder's surprising supporters say," *National Review Online*, Jan. 13, 2009, http://m.nationalreview.

com/articles/226682/right-man-protect-us-terror/andrew-c-mccarthy; Andrew C. McCarthy, "Opposed to Holder Without Apology: The shameful pardons are disqualifying," *National Review Online*, Nov. 25, 2008, http://www.nationalreview.com/articles/226388/opposed-holder-without-apology/andrew-c-mccarthy; Andrew C. McCarthy, *How the Obama Administration Has Politicized Justice*, Broadside Series no. 7 (Encounter Books, 2010).

5.   Andrew C. McCarthy, "Holder's Dubious History: The AG's Fast & Furious amnesia is reminiscent of his Marc Rich amnesia," *National Review Online*, Oct. 5, 2011, http://www.nationalreview.com/articles/279201/holder-s-dubious-history-andrew-c-mccarthy.

6.   Matthew Boyle, "New poll finds bipartisan support for Eric Holder's resignation," *Daily Caller*, June 15, 2012, http://dailycaller.com/2012/06/15/new-poll-bipartisan-popular-support-for-eric-holders-resignation-40-percent-of-americans-want-it-only-27-percent-oppose/.

7.   Andrew C. McCarthy, "Politicizing Justice: How would Holder fare under the Democrats' Gonzales standards?" *National Review Online*, Jan. 27, 2009, http://m.nationalreview.com/articles/226758/politicizing-justice/andrew-c-mccarthy; see also McCarthy, "Holder Continues to Claim That He Knew Nothing about Rich," *National Review Online*, Jan. 25, 2009, http://m.nationalreview.com/corner/176207/holder-continues-claim-he-knew-nothing-about-rich-andrew-c-mccarthy.

8.   See, e.g., Andrew C. McCarthy, "Fast and Furious and OCDETF: Whom is executive privilege protecting?" *National Review Online*, June 23, 2012, http://www.nationalreview.com/articles/303808/fast-and-furious-and-ocdetf-andrew-c-mccarthy; Andrew C. McCarthy, "Investigate Racism in the Obama Justice Department: Racial animus is not the stuff of policy disagreement; it's a constitutional travesty," *National Review Online*, Sept. 28, 2010, http://www.nationalreview.com/articles/247956/investigate-racism-obama-justice-department-andrew-c-mccarthy/page/0/1; J. Christian Adams, Hans von Spakovsky and Richard Pollock, "'Every Single One': *PJ Media*'s Investigation of Justice Department Hiring Practices," *PJ Media*, 2011 (collecting links to 11-part series), http://pjmedia.com/every-single-one-pj-medias-investigation-of-justice-department-hiring-practices/.

9. Portraying the contempt vote as naked partisanship, 108 Democrats walked off the floor in protest—which, of course, spared them the dilemma of condemning Holder's contempt for their institution or casting an embarrassing vote to support him. See Betsy Woodruff, "Holder's Contempt Vote Moves Forward," *National Review Online*, June 28, 2012, http://www.nationalreview.com/corner/304320/holders-contempt-vote-moves-forward-betsy-woodruff; see also McCarthy, "Fast and Furious and OCDETF," *supra*; "House votes to hold Attorney General Holder in Contempt of Congress," Fox News, June 29, 2012, http://www.foxnews.com/politics/2012/06/28/house-holds-holder-contempt/.

10. Robert Beckhusen, "Holder Held in Contempt of Congress, Which Means Almost Nothing," *Wired*, June 28, 2012, http://www.wired.com/dangerroom/2012/06/holder/.

11. See, e.g., Josh Gerstein, "Fresh DOJ loss in 'Fast and Furious' docs fight," *Politico*, Sep. 30, 2013, http://www.politico.com/story/2013/09/fast-and-furious-doj-documents-97604.html (federal district court denies Justice Department's motion to dismiss lawsuit brought by House committee—DOJ motion relied on President Obama's assertion of executive privilege); "JW Sues over Fast and Furious Stonewall: Seeks Docs about DOJ's Legal Fight over Holder Contempt of Congress Citation," Judicial Watch, Sep. 17, 2013, http://www.judicialwatch.org/press-room/press-releases/judicial-watch-sues-over-fast-and-furious-stonewall-seeks-documents-about-dojs-legal-fight-over-holder-contempt-of-congress-citation/.

12. Jim Hoft, "Breaking: Holder Lied to Congress on His Role in Investigating News Reporters," *Gateway Pundit*, May 23, 2013, http://www.thegatewaypundit.com/2013/05/breaking-holder-caught-lying-to-congress-on-phone-records-investigation-video/; Jonathan Easley, "House Judiciary investigating whether Attorney General Holder lied under oath," *The Hill*, May 28, 2013, http://thehill.com/blogs/blog-briefing-room/news/302131-house-judiciary-investigating-whether-holder-lied-under-oath; Katie Pavlich, "Did Eric Holder lie under oath?" *Townhall.com*, May 24, 2013, http://townhall.com/tipsheet/katiepavlich/2013/05/24/did-eric-holder-lie-under-oath-n1605570; Karl Rove, "Did Holder mislead Congress about targeting reporters

like James Rosen?" Fox News, May 24, 2013, http://www.foxnews.com/
opinion/2013/05/24/did-holder-mislead-congress-about-targeting-
reporters-like-james-rosen/.

13. At a Senate Judiciary hearing in early February 2014, Senator Ted Cruz got no meaningful response from Attorney General
Holder upon asking, "Is it your position that of the 117,000 employees
at the Department of Justice, the only lawyer available to head this
[IRS targeting of conservatives] investigation was a major Obama
donor?" Eliana Johnson, "Renewed GOP Focus on the IRS Scandal,"
National Review Online, Feb. 5, 2014, http://www.nationalreview.com/
article/370370/renewed-gop-focus-irs-scandal-eliana-johnson; see
also Andrew C. McCarthy, "Cruz to Holder: Appoint an Independent
Prosecutor in IRS Scandal," *National Review Online*, Jan. 22, 2014,
http://www.nationalreview.com/corner/369222/cruz-holder-appoint-
independent-prosecutor-irs-scandal-andrew-c-mccarthy; Eliana Johnson
and Josh Hicks, "Obama political donor leading Justice Department's
IRS investigation," *Washington Post*, Jan. 9, 2014, http://www.washing-
tonpost.com/blogs/federal-eye/wp/2014/01/09/obama-political-donor-
leading-justice-departments-irs-investigation/.

14. Hans von Spakovsky, "Eric Holder's Mounting War against
Texas," Heritage Foundation, *The Foundry*, Aug. 22, 2013, http://blog.
heritage.org/2013/08/22/eric-holders-mounting-war-against-texas/
(Justice Department sues Texas over voter identification law—Holder
claims such laws are intended to "suppress voting rights"—despite
2008 Supreme Court ruling that such voter identification laws do not
violate Constitution); see also "Justice Department to sue Texas over
voter ID law," Fox News, Aug. 22, 2013, http://www.foxnews.com/
politics/2013/08/22/justice-department-to-sue-texas-over-voter-id-law/
(noting that Attorney General Holder claimed Supreme Court's June
2013 Voting Rights Act ruling in *Shelby County* v. *Holder* was flawed
and vowed to challenge the ruling); Hans von Spakovsky and Michael
Carvin, "The 'Voting Rights' Partisan Power Play: An attempt to cir-
cumvent a recent Supreme Court case isn't about redressing wrongs.
It's about winning elections," *Wall Street Journal*, Feb. 10, 2014, http://
online.wsj.com/news/articles/SB10001424052702303519404579351

331174088064 (subscription req'd) (observing that "many past court decisions castigat[e] the Justice Department for filing unwarranted objections under Section 5 [of the Voting Rights Act]. In 2012, a federal court overturned Attorney General Eric Holder's objection to South Carolina's voter ID law—but it cost the state $3.5 million to beat the Justice Department. Most jurisdictions don't have the resources to fight the department.").

15. Andrew C. McCarthy, "Amnesty, but not for D'Souza: For Obama's Justice Department, campaign-finance law is a partisan club," *National Review Online*, Feb. 1, 2014, http://www.nationalreview.com/article/370097/amnesty-not-dsouza-andrew-c-mccarthy.

CHAPTER FIVE—POLITICS, NOT LAW

1. "Coburn raises possibility of impeachment at town hall," NBC News, Aug. 22, 2013, http://www.nbcnews.com/politics/first-read/coburn-raises-possibility-impeachment-town-hall-v20142926.

2. Andrew Johnson, "Axelrod: Talk of Impeachment 'Virus That Needs to Be Curbed,'" *National Review Online*, Aug. 23, 2010, http://www.nationalreview.com/corner/356566/axelrod-talk-impeachment-virus-needs-be-curbed-andrew-johnson.

3. Jonathan Strong, "The I-Word: Seeking ways to limit the president's executive overreach, Republicans still shy away from impeachment," *National Review Online*, Dec. 5, 2013, http://www.nationalreview.com/article/365566/i-word-jonathan-strong.

4. Ibid.

5. Michael J. Gerhardt, *The Federal Impeachment Process: A Constitutional and Historical Analysis* (University of Chicago Press, 2000).

6. Douglas O. Linder, "The Impeachment Trial of President William Clinton," University of Missouri at Kansas City, 2005, http://law2.umkc.edu/faculty/projects/ftrials/clinton/clintontrialaccount.html.

7. U.S. Const., art. I, sec. 3. Also note that the Fifth Amendment requires that "no person shall be held to answer for . . . [an] infamous crime, unless on presentment of indictment of a Grand Jury" (except in matters involving the armed forces that are inapposite for

our purposes). As noted, articles of impeachment *resemble* a grand jury indictment but they are not the functional equivalent. If impeachment were a legal rather than a political proceeding, an indictment would be mandatory.

8.   On aggressive tactics of community organizing, see, e.g., Stanley Kurtz, *Radical-in-Chief: Barack Obama and the Untold Story of American Socialism* (Threshold Editions, 2010), pp. 116–23; Andrew C. McCarthy, *The Grand Jihad: How Islam and the Left Sabotage America* (Encounter Books, 2010), pp. 230–33.

9.   Jonah Goldberg, "See You Next Tyranny Day! The experts don't know as much as they think they do," *National Review Online*, July 9, 2010, http://www.nationalreview.com/articles/243432/see-you-next-tyranny-day-jonah-goldberg (assessing Mr. Friedman's self-described "fantasy," in one of his bestselling books (*Hot, Flat, and Crowded: Why We Need a Green Revolution—and How It Can Renew America* (2009)), of the United States government becoming "China for a Day").

10.   For the best treatment of this topic, see Kurtz, *Radical-in-Chief*, *supra*.

CHAPTER SIX—THE "PROSECUTORIAL DISCRETION" CANARD

1.   DHS Secretary Janet Napolitano, Memorandum, "Exercising Prosecutorial Discretion with Respect to Individuals Who Came to the United States as Children," June 15, 2012, http://www.dhs.gov/xlibrary/assets/s1-exercising-prosecutorial-discretion-individuals-who-came-to-us-as-children.pdf; see also DHS Public Announcement, "Secretary Napolitano Announces Deferred Action Process for Young People Who Are Low Enforcement Priorities," June 15, 2012, http://www.dhs.gov/news/2012/06/15/secretary-napolitano-announces-deferred-action-process-young-people-who-are-low; Andrew Stiles, "He Can't Wait," *Washington Free Beacon*, June 15, 2012. See also Alexander Bolton, "Senate Rejects DREAM Act, closing door on immigration reform," *The Hill*, Dec. 18, 2010, http://thehill.com/homenews/senate/134351-dream-act-defeated-in-senate; Mark Krikorian, "DREAM On: The amnesty-for-illegals crowd has found some sympathetic poster chil-

dren," *National Review Online*, Dec. 1, 2010, http://www.nationalreview.com/articles/254180/dream-mark-krikorian.

2. "Obama: Young Illegals Are Americans in Every Way Except 'On Paper,'" Video, *Real Clear Politics*, June 15, 2002, http://www.realclearpolitics.com/video/2012/06/15/obama_illegal_immigrations_are_americans_in_every_way_except_on_paper.html.

3. U.S. Const., art. I, sec. 8.

4. Stiles, "He Can't Wait," *supra*.

5. Catherine E. Shoichet, "Obama: 'I need a dance partner' on immigration reform," CNN, July 25, 2011, http://www.cnn.com/2011/POLITICS/07/25/obama.la.raza/index.html?_s=PM:POLITICS.

6. Andrew Stiles, "Timeline: The Obama Administration's War on Immigration Enforcement" ("Timeline of Administrative Non-Enforcement of Federal Immigration Law" compiled by the office of Sen. Jeff Sessions), Dec. 19, 2013, http://m.nationalreview.com/corner/366776/timeline-obama-administrations-war-immigration-enforcement-andrew-stiles; Andrew Becker, "Unusual methods helped ICE break deportation record, e-mails and interviews show," *Washington Post*, Dec. 6, 2010, http://www.washingtonpost.com/wp-dyn/content/article/2010/12/05/AR2010120503230.html; "How the Obama Administration Inflates Deportation Statistics," Numbers USA, Feb. 12, 2013, https://www.numbersusa.com/content/news/february-12-2013/how-obama-administration-inflates-deportation-statistics.html.

7. Andrew C. McCarthy, "Sovereignty, Preempted," *National Review Online*, July 2, 2012, http://www.nationalreview.com/articles/304214/sovereignty-preempted-andrew-c-mccarthy.

8. John Yoo, "Executive Overreach," *National Review Online*, June 15, 2012, http://www.nationalreview.com/corner/303038/executive-overreach-john-yoo.

9. See, e.g., *Arizona* v. *United States*, 132 S.Ct. 2492 (2012) (Scalia, J., concurring in part and dissenting in part) (the Government has conceded that "even before Section 2 was enacted, state and local officers had state-law authority to inquire of DHS . . . about a suspect's unlawful status and otherwise cooperate with federal immigration officers"

(citing Brief for the United States)), http://www.supremecourt.gov/opinions/11pdf/11-182b5e1.pdf.

10. Andrew C. McCarthy, "Winning the Case, Losing the Principle: Arizona won, but the sovereignty of states suffered a setback," *National Review Online*, May 28, 2011, http://www.nationalreview.com/articles/268341/winning-case-losing-principle-andrew-c-mccarthy; Andrew C. McCarthy, "Sovereignty Preempted: Even the conservative justices don't understand states' rights," *National Review Online*, July 2, 2012, http://www.nationalreview.com/articles/304214/sovereignty-preempted-andrew-c-mccarthy; Andrew C. McCarthy, "Preemption and Prosecutorial Discretion: A response to Heather Mac Donald," *National Review Online*, Aug. 3, 2010, http://m.nationalreview.com/corner/242397/preemption-prosecutorial-discretion-response-heather-mac-donald-andrew-c-mccarthy.

11. Stephen Dinan, "Homeland Security suspends immigration agreements with Arizona police," *Washington Times*, June 25, 2012, http://www.washingtontimes.com/news/2012/jun/25/homeland-security-suspends-immigration-agreements-/.

12. "Appropriate" does not mean invidiously "selective." If the Justice Department abuses its discretion in this regard, defendants are protected: an indictment will be dismissed if the defendant can show it is vindictive or the product of impermissible discrimination. See, e.g., U.S. Attorney's Manual, "Sample Memorandum Supporting Motion Precluding Evidence of Selective Prosecution," http://www.justice.gov/usao/eousa/foia_reading_room/usam/title4/civ00138.htm.

13. Adam J. White, "Yucca Mountain: A Post-Mortem," *New Atlantis*, Fall 2012, http://www.thenewatlantis.com/publications/yucca-mountain-a-post-mortem; "Harry, Barack and Yucca Mt.: They pack the appeals court that just called out their lawlessness," Review & Outlook, *Wall Street Journal*, Nov. 22, 2013, http://online.wsj.com/news/articles/SB10001424052702304337404579214183070687104; Tennille Tracy, "NRC Chief Says Yucca Mountain Review Uncertain: Macfarlane says agency is assessing costs," *Wall Street Journal*, Sep. 10, 2013, http://online.wsj.com/news/articles/SB10001424127887324094704579067370399908200; Tennille Tracy and Keith Johnson, "Court Keeps Yucca

Mountain in Play," *Wall Street Journal*, Aug. 13, 2013, http://online.wsj.
com/news/articles/SB10001424127887323446404579011225779857
20.

14. White, "Yucca Mountain: A Post-Mortem," *supra*.

15. "Harry, Barack and Yucca Mt.," *supra*.

16. Stephen Power, "Report Slams U.S. Nuclear Regulator," *Wall Street Journal*, June 10, 2011, http://online.wsj.com/news/articles/SB1
00014241052702304259304576375961521636474.

17. Commissioner profiles, U.S. NRC website (accessed March 7, 2014), http://www.nrc.gov/about-nrc/organization/commfuncdesc.
html.

18. *In re: Aiken County, et al., Petitioners (State of Nevada, Intervenor)*, No. 111271 (D.C. Cir., Dec. 13, 2013) (granting mandamus petition in case "raising significant questions about the scope of the Executive's authority to disregard federal statutes"), http://www.cadc.
uscourts.gov/internet/opinions.nsf/BAE0CF34F762EBD985257BC6
004DEB18/$file/11-1271-1451347.pdf.

19. Ibid., citing *In re Aiken County*, No. 111271 (D.C. Cir., Aug. 3, 2012).

20. Ibid., citing and quoting James Madison, *The Federalist No. 47*, p. 269 (Clinton Rossiter ed., rev. ed., 1999); see also http://avalon.
law.yale.edu/18th_century/fed47.asp.

21. Ibid., citing and quoting 1 Montesquieu, *The Spirit of Laws*, bk. 11, ch. 6, p. 163 (Thomas Nugent trans., 1914).

22. Andrew C. McCarthy, "The Lawlessness of the 'Fix': Insurance companies would be insane to offer plans that failed to comply with the ACA," *National Review Online*, Nov. 16, 2013, http://www.
nationalreview.com/article/364117/lawlessness-fix-andrew-c-mccarthy.

ARTICLE I

1. See, e.g., McCarthy, "The Lawlessness of the 'Fix'," *supra*; Michael Barone interview by Michael Graham, "Barone Podcast: Obamacare Is Obama's Iraq War," *Weekly Standard*, Feb. 17, 2014, http://www.weeklystandard.com/blogs/barone-podcast-obamacare-obamas-iraq-war_781726.html; see also Chris Conover, "Progressive

Fascism: Obamacare's Lawless Rollout Cements Case against Single Payer Health Care," *Forbes*, March 6, 2014, http://www.forbes.com/ sites/theapothecary/2014/03/06/progressive-fascism-obamacares-lawless-rollout-cements-case-against-single-payer-health-care/.

2. Michael F. Cannon and Jonathan Adler, "Taxation without Representation: The Illegal IRS Rule to Expand Tax Credits under the PPACA," *Health Matrix: Journal of Law-Medicine*, vol. 23, no. 1 (Spring 2013), http://law.case.edu/journals/healthmatrix/Docum ents/23HealthMatrix1.5.Article.AdlerFINAL.pdf; Michael Tanner, "Obamacare: What We Know Now," Cato Institute, Policy Analysis no. 745 (Jan. 27, 2014), pp. 31–32, http://object.cato.org/sites/cato.org/ files/pubs/pdf/pa745_web_1.pdf; Michael F. Cannon, "An Update on Halbig, and Other Lawsuits That Could Make the Decrepit HealthCare. Gov Look Like a Hiccup," *Forbes*, Oct. 30, 2013, http://www.cato.org/ publications/commentary/update-halbig-other-lawsuits-could-make-decrepit-healthcaregov-look-hiccup; Scott Pruitt, "ObamaCare's Next Legal Challenge: The law says subsidies can only go through state-run exchanges," *Wall Street Journal*, Dec. 1, 2013, http://online.wsj.com/ news/articles/SB1000142405270230448204579186322449012040; Tyler Hartsfield and Grace-Marie Turner, "37 Changes to Obamacare . . . So Far," Galen Institute, March 5, 2014, http://www.galen.org/ newsletters/changes-to-obamacare-so-far/.

3. Scott Gottlieb, "Decision to Waive Obamacare Rules on Small Business Health Plans Comes with Costs," *Forbes*, March 5, 2014, http://www.forbes.com/sites/scottgottlieb/2014/03/05/white-houses-broken-rules-on-obamacare-put-law-in-jeopardy/; Tanner, "Obamacare: What We Know Now," *supra*, p. 4 & n.17 (citing Mark Mazur, "Continuing to Implement the ACA in a Careful, Thoughtful Manner," Dept. of Treasury, July 2, 2013); Congressional Research Service, Memorandum to Senator Tom Coburn, "Enacted Laws That Repeal or Amend Provisions of the Patient Protection and Affordable Care Act (ACA); Administrative Delays to ACA's Implementation," Sept. 5, 2013 (hereafter, "CRS Memo"), http://www.coburn.senate.gov/public/index. cfm?a=Files.Serve&File_id=b8e7a876-ee12-477f-8c62-a9dd9294f537; Hartsfield and Turner, "37 Changes to Obamacare . . . So Far," *supra*.

4.   Hartsfield and Turner, "37 Changes to Obamacare . . . So Far,"
supra; CRS Memo, *supra*.

5.   Patrick Brennan, "White House Delays Employer Mandate
Again," *National Review Online*, Feb. 10, 2014, http://www.nation-
alreview.com/corner/370769/white-house-delays-employer-man-
date-again-patrick-brennan; Karen R. Harned, Executive Director,
National Federation of Independent Business (Small Business Legal
Center), Letter to John Koskinen, Commissioner, Internal Revenue
Service, March 5, 2014 (pointing out that IRS issued its regulations
without allowing the public an opportunity for notice and comment,
and pointing to the absence of legal authority to define different categories of employer for purposes of mandate waiver or enforcement),
http://www.nfib.com/assets/Employer_Mandate_NFIB_SBLC_Letter-
to_IRS_030514.pdf; Hartsfield and Turner, "37 Changes to Obamacare
. . . So Far," *supra*; CRS Memo, *supra*.

6.   Andrew C. McCarthy, "Obama Adds Irrationality to Lawlessness—While Threatening Prosecution," *National Review Online*,
Feb. 12, 2014, http://www.nationalreview.com/corner/370909/
obama-adds-irrationality-lawlessness-while-threatening-prosecution-
andrew-c-mccarthy; see also Title 18, U.S. Code, Sec. 1001 (prescribing
imprisonment of up to five years for false statements to government),
Sec. 3571(b)(3), (c)(3) and (d) (prescribing the fine for a felony committed by an individual as up to $250,000, by a corporation as up to
$500,000, and further prescribing as an alternative fine an amount
not greater than twice the pecuniary gain or loss from the offense).

7.   The White House, Office of the Press Secretary, "Statement by
the President on the Affordable Care Act," Nov. 14, 2013 ("I completely
get how upsetting this can be for a lot of Americans, particularly after
assurances they heard from me that if they had a plan that they liked,
they could keep it. . . . So state insurance commissioners still have
the power to decide what plans can and can't be sold in their states.
But the bottom line is, insurers can extend current plans that would
otherwise be canceled into 2014, and Americans whose plans have
been canceled can choose to re-enroll in the same kind of plan."),
http://www.whitehouse.gov/the-press-office/2013/11/14/statement-

president-affordable-care-act; Department of Health and Human Services, Centers for Medicare and Medicaid Services, Letter of Gary Cohen, Director, Center for Consumer Information and Insurance Oversight, to State Insurance Commissioners, Nov. 14, 2013, http://www.cms.gov/CCIIO/Resources/Letters/Downloads/commissioner-letter-11-14-2013.PDF; Andrew C. McCarthy, "Obama's '5 percent' Con Job: It's a 100 percent lie, according to the White House's own figures," *National Review Online*, Nov. 18, 2013, http://m.nationalreview.com/article/364176/obamas-5-percent-con-job-andrew-c-mccarthy; McCarthy, "The Lawlessness of the 'Fix,'" *supra*; Avik Roy, "Obama to Nation: If You Like Your Plan, You Can Keep Your Plan (at Least until the Next Election)," *Forbes*, Nov. 15, 2013, http://www.forbes.com/sites/theapothecary/2013/11/15/obama-to-nation-if-you-like-your-plan-you-can-keep-your-plan-at-least-until-the-next-election/; Hartsfield and Turner, "37 Changes to Obamacare . . . So Far," *supra*; CRS Memo, *supra*; Louise Radnofsky, "Obama Gives Health Plans Added Two-Year Reprieve: Plans that don't meet ACA rules could stay in place through 2016," *Wall Street Journal*, March 5, 2014, http://online.wsj.com/news/articles/SB10001424052702303369904579421541748450598; Conover, "Progressive Fascism," *supra*; "The Endangered Senators Rule: HHS delays another ObamaCare mandate to rescue Democrats," Review & Outlook, *Wall Street Journal*, March 5, 2014, http://online.wsj.com/news/articles/SB10001424052702303369904579421624193271010?KEYWORDS=obamacare&mg=reno64-wsj.

8. Avik Roy, "Government Takeover: White House Forces Obamacare Insurers to Cover Unpaid Patients at a Loss," *Forbes*, Dec. 14, 2014, http://www.forbes.com/sites/theapothecary/2013/12/11/obamacare-exchanges-claim-258497-sign-ups-in-november-but-no-word-on-how-many-are-actually-enrolled-in-coverage/.

9. Department of Health and Human Services, Centers for Medicare and Medicaid Services, Center for Consumer Information and Insurance Oversight, "Options Available for Consumers with Cancelled Policies," public announcement, Dec. 19, 2013, http://www.cms.gov/CCIIO/Resources/Regulations-and-Guidance/Downloads/cancellation-consumer-options-12-19-2013.pdf; Avik Roy, "Utter Chaos:

White House Exempts Millions from Obamacare's Insurance Mandate, 'Unaffordable' Exchanges," *Forbes*, Dec. 20, 2013, http://www.forbes. com/sites/theapothecary/2013/12/14/government-takeover-white-house-forces-obamacare-insurers-to-cover-unpaid-patients-at-a-loss/; Tanner, "Obamacare: What We Know Now," *supra*, p. 3; Hartsfield and Turner, "37 Changes to Obamacare . . . So Far," *supra*; CRS Memo, *supra*.

10. Avik Roy, "Yet Another White House Obamacare Delay: Out-of-Pocket Caps Waived until 2015," *Forbes*, Aug. 13, 2013, http://www. forbes.com/sites/theapothecary/2013/08/13/yet-another-white-house-obamacare-delay-out-of-pocket-caps-waived-until-2015/.

11. See, e.g., Michelle Malkin, "How's That Obamacare Waiver Workin' Out for Ya?" *National Review Online*, Nov. 16, 2012, http://www. nationalreview.com/articles/333535/how-s-obamacare-waiver-workin-out-ya-michelle-malkin; "List of health reform waivers keeps growing," *The Hill*, April 2, 2011, http://thehill.com/blogs/healthwatch/health-reform-implementation/153421-list-of-health-reform-waivers-keeps-growing#ixzz2vEBcCYat; John Vinci, "The Six Types of Obamacare Waivers," The Heartland Institute, undated (accessed March 5, 2014), http://heartland.org/policy-documents/six-types-obamacare-waivers.

12. U.S. Office of Personnel Management, Benefits Administration, Letter no. 13207, "Final Rule for Federal Employees Health Benefits Program: Members of Congress and Congressional Staff," Sep. 13, 2013, http://www.opm.gov/retirement-services/publications-forms/benefits-administration-letters/2013/13-207.pdf; McCarthy, "Ron Johnson's Frivolous Obamacare Lawsuit," *supra*; Avik Roy, "Congress, Fearing 'Brain Drain,' Seeks to Opt Out of Participating in Obam-acare's Exchanges," *Forbes*, April 25, 2013, http://www.forbes.com/sites/theapothecary/2013/04/25/congress-fearing-brain-drain-seeks-to-opt-out-of-participating-in-obamacares-exchanges/; Hartsfield and Turner, "37 Changes to Obamacare . . . So Far," *supra*.

13. "ObamaCare's Union Favor: The White House may let Big Labor dodge a reinsurance tax," Review & Outlook, *Wall Street Journal*, Nov. 17, 2013, http://online.wsj.com/news/articles/SB1000142405 2702303309504579182061106839366; Hartsfield and Turner, "37 Changes to Obamacare . . . So Far," *supra*.

14. Robert Pear, "Rules for equal coverage by employers remain elusive under health law," *New York Times*, Jan. 18, 2014, http://mobile.nytimes.com/2014/01/19/us/rules-for-equal-coverage-by-employers-remain-elusive-under-health-law.html?hp&_r=0&referrer=; Hartsfield and Turner, "37 Changes to Obamacare . . . So Far," *supra.*

15. Hartsfield and Turner, "37 Changes to Obamacare . . . So Far," *supra.*

16. Ibid.; Tanner, "Obamacare: What We Know Now," *supra*, p. 40 n.8.

17. Tim Devaney, "Republicans slam administration over WARN Act waivers," *Washington Times*, Feb. 14, 2013, http://www.washingtontimes.com/news/2013/feb/14/republicans-slam-administration-warn-act-waivers/?page=all.

18. Robert Rector, "How Obama has gutted welfare reform," *Washington Post*, Sep. 6, 2012, http://www.washingtonpost.com/opinions/how-obama-has-gutted-welfore-reform/2012/09/06/885b0092-f835-11e1-8b93-c4f4ab1c8d13_story.html; Andrew M. Grossman, "Welfare Reform's Work Requirements Cannot Be Waived," Heritage Foundation, Aug. 8, 2012, http://www.heritage.org/research/reports/2012/08/welfare-reforms-work-requirements-cannot-be-waived.

19. Department of Homeland Security, Citizenship and Immigration Services, "Provisional Unlawful Presence Waivers," press release, updated May 6, 2013, http://www.uscis.gov/family/family-us-citizens/provisional-waiver/provisional-unlawful-presence-waivers; Department of Homeland Security, Citizenship and Immigration Services, "USCIS to Propose Changing the Process for Certain Waivers," press release, Jan. 6, 2012, http://www.uscis.gov/news/fact-sheets/uscis-propose-changing-process-certain-waivers; USCIS Field Guidance Memorandum, "Guidance Pertaining to Applicants for Provisional Unlawful Presence Waivers," http://www.uscis.gov/sites/default/files/files/nativedocuments/2014-0124_Reason_To_Believe_Field_Guidance_Pertaining_to_Applicants_for_Provisional_Unlawful_Presence_Waivers-final.pdf (applicant eligible for waiver if prior criminal

offenses qualify for "petty offense" or "youthful offender" exception under the INA and are not crimes involving moral turpitude).

20. U.S. Immigration and Customs Enforcement, Memorandum, "11064.1: Facilitating Parental Interests in the Course of Civil Immigration Enforcement Activities," Aug. 23, 2013, http://www.ice.gov/doclib/detention-reform/pdf/parental_interest_directive_signed.pdf; Stephen Dinan, "Obama adds to list of illegal immigrants not to deport: Parents," *Washington Times*, Aug. 23, 2013, http://www.washingtontimes.com/news/2013/aug/23/new-obama-policy-warns-agents-not-detain-illegal-i/?page=all.

21. Department of Homeland Security, Citizenship and Immigration Services, Policy Memorandum, "Parole of Spouses, Children and Parents of Active Duty Members of the U.S. Armed Forces, the Selected Reserve of the Ready Reserve, and Former Members of the U.S. Armed Forces or Selected Reserve of the Ready Reserve and the Effect of Parole on Inadmissibility under Immigration and Nationality Act § 212(a)(6)(A)(i)," Nov. 15, 2013, http://www.uscis.gov/sites/default/files/USCIS/Laws/Memoranda/2013/2013-1115_Parole_in_Place_Memo_.pdf; Lourdes Medrano, "'Parole in place': Obama's illegal-immigration order stokes amnesty worries," *Christian Science Monitor*, Dec. 9, 2013, http://www.csmonitor.com/USA/Politics/2013/1209/Parole-in-place-Obama-s-illegal-immigration-order-stokes-amnesty-worries.

22. In *Massachusetts* v. *EPA*, 549 U.S. 497 (2007), http://www.law.cornell.edu/supremecourt/text/549/497, a sharply divided Supreme Court ruled, 5–4, that it was *permissible* for the government to regulate carbon emissions under the Clean Air Act. The Court did not hold that the government was *required* to do so, nor did it resolve the implausibility of such regulation under the terms of the act. The Supreme Court is dealing with that issue this term in *Utility Air Regulatory Group* v. *EPA*, no. 121146, etc. (six consolidated cases), http://www.law.cornell.edu/supct/cert/12-1146.

23. "The 'Absurd Results' Power Grab: Can the EPA simply rewrite a law to suit its policy goals?" Review & Outlook, *Wall Street*

Journal, Feb. 23, 2014, http://online.wsj.com/news/article_email/ SB10001424052702304914204579397003756191282-lMyQjAxM-TAoMDIwNDEyNDQyWj.

24. House Committee on the Budget, "Sessions, Ryan: President Defying Law Requiring Action on Medicare," press release, March 1, 2012, http://budget.house.gov/news/documentsingle. aspx?DocumentID=282515; "Examiner Editorial: Obama ignores Medicare warnings," *Washington Examiner*, Feb. 8, 2013 (noting that, despite absence of proposal, Obama administration acting director of the White House Office of Management and Budget claimed changes to Medicare in the PPACA satisfied the requirement—even though trustees have continued to issue the warning for years after the PPACA's enactment), http://washingtonexaminer.com/examiner-editorial-obama-ignores-medicare-warnings/article/2521009; *compare* "President Barack Obama talks to Bret Baier about health care reform bill," Fox News, March 17, 2010 (Obama says the health-care bill, later to become the PPACA, "doesn't solve that big structural problem" of Medicare's being $38 trillion in debt, adding, "We're still going to have to fix Medicare over the long term" and "nobody's claiming that this piece of legislation is going to solve every problem that's been there for decades"), http:// www.foxnews.com/story/0,2933,589589,00.html?mep#ixzz1GmIytJA; Steve Eggleston, "Four years of a Medicare Funding Warning, zero years of Obama action," *Hot Air*, March 1, 2012 ("as part of the creation of the Medicare Part D prescription drug benefit, a [requirement] was put into place [that], if the Medicare trustees find in two consecutive years that general funds, be they interest on the Treasury securities held by three 'Trust Fund' accounts held by Medicare, redemptions of same, or other 'general fund' revenues, do, or will within 6 fiscal years, comprise more than 45% of total Medicare outlays (or once the Hospital Insurance Fund was depleted, the 'dedicated' funds are less than 55% of total obligations whether fulfilled or unfulfilled), the President [is] to submit to Congress legislation to deal with said excessive general funding within 15 days of submitting the following year's budget"), http://hotair.com/greenroom/archives/2012/03/01/ four-years-of-a-medicare-funding-warning-zero-years-of-obama-action/.

ARTICLE II

1.   Andrew C. McCarthy, "Our Libyan Adventure," *National Review Online*, Oct. 27, 2011, http://www.nationalreview.com/articles/281414/our-libyan-adventure-andrew-c-mccarthy; Andrew C. McCarthy, "Re: Republicans and Libya," *National Review Online*, June 30, 2011, http://www.nationalreview.com/corner/270902/re-republicans-and-libya-andrew-c-mccarthy; Andrew C. McCarthy, "Congress Has War Powers, Too: And it is time to start using them," *National Review Online*, June 1, 2011, http://www.nationalreview.com/articles/268503/congress-has-war-powers-too-andrew-c-mccarthy; Andrew C. McCarthy, "More on that Senate resolution 'authorizing' the Libya war," *National Review Online*, April 1, 2011, http://www.nationalreview.com/corner/263712/more-senate-resolution-authorizing-libya-war-andrew-c-mccarthy; Andrew C. McCarthy, "Et Tu, Yoo? Not all who opposed the Libya adventure are 'isolationist,'" *National Review Online*, Aug. 24, 2011, http://www.nationalreview.com/articles/275411/et-tu-yoo-andrew-c-mccarthy; Andrew C. McCarthy, "Decoding Libya: Sharia can tell us how this story ends," March 26, 2011, http://www.nationalreview.com/articles/263138/decoding-libya-andrew-c-mccarthy; Andrew C. McCarthy, "On the NRO Libya Editorial, I Respectfully Dissent," *National Review Online*, March 17, 2011, http://www.nationalreview.com/corner/262377/nro-libya-editorial-i-respectfully-dissent-andrew-c-mccarthy; Andrew C. McCarthy, "The 'Focused' Mission in Libya," *National Review Online*, March 18, 2011, http://www.nationalreview.com/corner/262535/focused-mission-libya-andrew-c-mccarthy; Andrew C. McCarthy, "No Intervention in Libya: In the absence of compelling national-security interests, we should stay out," *National Review Online*, March 10, 2011, http://www.nationalreview.com/articles/261793/no-intervention-libya-andrew-c-mccarthy.

2.   Robert Barnes, "Supreme Court questions Obama's recess appointment power," *Washington Post*, Jan. 13, 2014, http://www.washingtonpost.com/politics/supreme-court-skeptical-of-legality-of-presidents-recess-appointments/2014/01/13/15869f86-7c87-11e3-9556-4a4bf7bcbd84_story.html; Andrew C. McCarthy, "Reid Backs Obama on Recess Appointments," *National Review Online*, Jan. 4,

2012, http://www.nationalreview.com/corner/287218/reid-backs-obama-recess-appointments-andrew-c-mccarthy; John Berlau, "Cordray Recess Appointment Is Travesty for Government Accountability," Competitive Enterprise Institute, *OpenMarket.org*, Jan. 4, 2012, http://www.openmarket.org/2012/01/04/cordray-recess-appointment-is-travesty-for-government-accountability/; Mark Calabria, "Obama's Constitutional Gamble on Consumer Finance Nomination," Cato Institute, Jan. 4, 2012 (appointment of Richard Cordray to head Consumer Financial Protection Bureau not only unconstitutional but a violation of Dodd-Frank Act, which directs that CFPB authorities remain with the treasury secretary until director is "confirmed by the Senate"), http://www.cato.org/blog/obamas-constitutional-gamble-consumer-finance-nomination.

3. *Canning* v. *NLRB*, 705 F.3d 490 (D.C. Cir. Jan. 25, 2013), http://www.cadc.uscourts.gov/internet/opinions.nsf/D13E4C2A7B33B57A8 5257AFE00556B29/$file/12-1115-1417096.pdf.

ARTICLE III

1. See, e.g., Bill Vaughn (with Monica Morrill and Cari Blake), *Betrayed: The Shocking True Story of Extortion 17 as Told by a Navy SEAL's Father* (Molon Labe Publishing, 2013); Rowan Scarborough, "Shades of Vietnam: Spike in U.S. troop deaths tied to stricter rules of engagement," *Washington Times*, Dec. 5, 2013, http://www.washingtontimes.com/news/2013/dec/5/increase-in-battlefield-deaths-linked-to-new-rules/?page=all; "Coalition Military Fatalities by Year," icasualties.org (accessed Feb. 26, 2014), http://icasualties.org/oef/.

2. Andrew C. McCarthy, "Our Libyan Adventure," *supra*; Andrew C. McCarthy, "The Senators Sway: Before they wanted to kill Qaddafi, they were celebrating in his tent," *National Review Online*, April 2, 2011 (noting that Bush administration's restoration of diplomatic relations with Qaddafi owed in part, according to the State Department, to "the excellent cooperation Libya has provided to the United States and other members of the international community in response to common global threats faced by the civilized world since September 11, 2001"), http://www.nationalreview.com/articles/263694/senators-

sway-andrew-c-mccarthy?pg=1; McCarthy, "Re: Republicans and Libya," *supra*; Andrew C. McCarthy, "It's Not That Qaddafi Was Right, It's That We Knew He Was Right," *National Review Online*, March 28, 2011, http://www.nationalreview.com/corner/263220/its-not-qaddafi-was-right-its-we-knew-he-was-right-andrew-c-mccarthy; McCarthy, "On the NRO Libya Editorial, I Respectfully Dissent," *supra*; Andrew C. McCarthy, "Libya's Makeover: The Libyan people are no more our ally than Qaddafi," *National Review Online*, March 2, 2011, http://www.nationalreview.com/articles/261063/libyas-makeover-andrew-c-mccarthy/page/0/1; William La Jeunesse, "Did Qaddafi deserve U.S. funding? Foreign aid under scrutiny amid Mideast unrest," Fox News, March 24, 2011, http://www.foxnews.com/politics/2011/03/24/did-qaddafi-deserve-funding-foreign-aid-scrutiny-amid-mideast-unrest/; see also John Rosenthal, *The Jihadist Plot: The Untold Story of Al-Qaeda and the Libyan Rebellion* (Encounter Books, 2013); John Rosenthal, "Al-Qaeda Takes Tripoli," Gatestone Institute, Sep. 9, 2011, http://www.gatestoneinstitute.org/2409/al-qaeda-takes-tripoli; Nicole Gaouette, "U.S. Racing to Beat Terrorists in Hunt for Libya's Anti-Aircraft Missiles," *Bloomberg*, Aug. 26, 2011, http://www.bloomberg.com/news/2011-08-26/u-s-racing-to-beat-terrorists-in-hunt-for-libya-s-anti-aircraft-missiles.html; Reuters, "Al Qaeda Acquiring Weapons in Libya: Algerian Official," *World Post / Huffington Post*, April 4, 2011, http://www.huffingtonpost.com/2011/04/04/al-qaeda-weapons-libya_n_844492.html.

3.   Andrew C. McCarthy, "Denying the Libya Scandal: The vice president was dishonest during the debate," *National Review Online*, Oct. 13, 2013, http://www.nationalreview.com/articles/330318/denying-libya-scandal-andrew-c-mccarthy.

4.   Michael R. Gordon, Eric Schmitt and Michael S. Schmidt, "Libya warnings were plentiful, but unspecific," *New York Times*, Oct. 29, 2012, http://www.nytimes.com/2012/10/30/world/middleeast/no-specific-warnings-in-benghazi-attack.html?pagewanted=all&_r=0.

5.   "Al Qaeda confirms death of bin Laden confidant Libi," *Reuters*, Sep. 11, 2012, http://www.reuters.com/article/2012/09/11/us-security-qaeda-idUSBRE88A04L20120911; see also, McCarthy, "Denying

the Libya Scandal: The vice president was dishonest during the debate,"
supra.

6. Even the panel handpicked by Secretary of State Hillary Clinton
concluded that there had been "[s]ystematic failures and leadership
and management deficiencies" in the administration, specifically in
the State Department, that led to the inability to mount a defense of
the Benghazi facility and the Americans working there. See Unclas-
sified Summary of State Department Report, Dec. 18, 2012, http://
www.state.gov/documents/organization/202446.pdf; see also, e.g.,
"Benghazi attack review finds systematic State Dept failures but no
officials breached duty," Fox News, Dec. 18, 2012, http://www.foxnews.
com/us/2012/12/18/benghazi-attack-review-finds-systematic-state-dept-
failures-but-no-officials/; Jill Dougherty, "Report blames poor security,
inadequate response in Benghazi attack," CNN, Dec. 31, 2012, http://
www.cnn.com/2012/12/31/politics/benghazi-senate-investigation/.
A Senate report was scathing regarding the administration's performance—again, particularly the State Department's. Senate Committee
on Homeland Security and Governmental Affairs, "Flashing Red: A
special report on the terrorist attack at Benghazi," Fox News, Dec. 30,
2012, http://www.foxnews.com/politics/interactive/2012/12/30/latest-
senate-report-flashing-red-on-benghazi-attack/?intcmp=related; "Senate
committee report on Benghazi attack faults State Department," Fox
News, Dec. 31, 2012, http://www.foxnews.com/politics/2012/12/30/
latest-senate-committee-report-on-benghazi-terrorist-attack-faults-
state/. A subsequent interim report for the House Republican conference from the chairmen of five committees pursuing the House's
(continuing) Benghazi investigation recounted that, despite the intensifying terrorist threat, the State Department's "highest levels" had
directed security cutbacks in Benghazi. Howard P. "Buck" McKeon
(Armed Services), Ed Royce (Foreign Affairs), Bob Goodlatte (Judiciary), Darrell Issa (Oversight and Government Reform), and Mike
Rogers (Intelligence), "Interim Progress Report for the Members of
the House Republican Conference on the Events Surrounding the
September 11, 2012 Terrorist Attacks in Benghazi, Libya," April 23,

2013, http://oversight.house.gov/wp-content/uploads/2013/04/Libya-Progress-Report-Final-1.pdf; see also "House report on fatal Benghazi attack faults State Department for security," Fox News, April 23, 2013, http://www.foxnews.com/politics/2013/04/23/house-report-on-fatal-benghazi-attack-faults-state-department-for-security/. The Senate Intelligence Committee later issued a bipartisan report concluding that there had been serious security shortfalls by the Obama administration in Benghazi. Senate Select Committee on Intelligence, "Review of the Terrorist Attacks on U.S. Facilities in Benghazi, Libya, September 11–12, 2012, together with Additional Views," Jan. 15, 2014, http://www.intelligence.senate.gov/benghazi2014/benghazi.pdf; see also, e.g., Anne Gearan, "Review of Benghazi attack faults 'grossly' inadequate security, leadership failures," *Washington Post*, Dec. 19, 2013, http://www.washingtonpost.com/world/national-security/benghazi-panel-presents-findings-to-lawmakers-makes-recommendations/2012/12/18/9ada6032-495c-11e2-b6f0-e851e741d196_story.html; Jonah Goldberg, "Truth and Consequences for Benghazi: Answers won't come until 2016," *National Review Online*, Sep. 20, 2013, http://www.nationalreview.com/article/359022/truth-and-consequences-benghazi-jonah-goldberg.

7. Andrew C. McCarthy, "'Blame It on the Video' Was a Fraud for the Cairo Rioting, Too," *National Review Online*, May 13, 2013, http://www.nationalreview.com/corner/348125/blame-it-video-was-fraud-cairo-rioting-too; Andrew C. McCarthy, "The 10 p.m. Phone Call: Clinton and Obama discussed Benghazi. What did they say?" *National Review Online*, May 18, 2013, http://www.nationalreview.com/article/348677/10-pm-phone-call-andrew-c-mccarthy.

8. Andrew C. McCarthy, "On Egyptian President-Elect's Vow to Work for Blind Sheikh's Release," *National Review Online*, June 30, 2012, http://www.nationalreview.com/corner/304490/egyptian-president-elects-vow-work-blind-sheikhs-release-andrew-c-mccarthy.

9. Thomas Joscelyn, "Al Qaeda's expansion into Egypt," *Long War Journal*, Feb. 11, 2014, http://www.longwarjournal.org/archives/2014/02/al_qaedas_expansion.php; Andrew C. McCarthy,

"'Blame It on the Video' Was a Fraud for Cairo as Well as Benghazi: More Proof," *National Review Online*, Feb. 20, 2014, http://www.nationalreview.com/corner/371565/obamas-blame-it-video-was-fraud-cairo-well-benghazi-more-proof-andrew-c-mccarthy.

10. McCarthy, "'Blame It on the Video' Was a Fraud for the Cairo Rioting, Too," *supra*; Andrew C. McCarthy, "As Morsi Huddles with Hamas, Blind Sheikh's Son Threatens Siege of U.S. Embassy," *PJ Media*, July 27, 2012, http://pjmedia.com/andrewmccarthy/2012/07/27/blind-sheikhs-son-threatens-embassy/; Al-Masry Al-Youm, "Son of 'Blind Sheikh' threatens U.S. embassy employees," *Egypt Independent*, July 27, 2012, http://www.egyptindependent.com/news/son-blind-sheikh-threatens-us-embassy-employees.

11. Raymond Ibrahim, "Jihadis Threaten to Burn U.S. Embassy in Cairo," *PJ Media*, Sep. 10, 2012, http://pjmedia.com/tatler/2012/09/10/jihadis-threaten-to-burn-u-s-embassy-in-cairo/; Stephen F. Hayes, "The Benghazi Scandal Grows: The State Department, the CIA, the White House . . . ," *Weekly Standard*, May 20, 2013, http://www.weeklystandard.com/articles/benghazi-scandal-grows_722032.html; McCarthy, "'Blame It on the Video' Was a Fraud for the Cairo Rioting, Too," *supra*.

12. See, e.g., John Rosenthal, "Benghazi: A Sea of Al-Qaeda Flags," *National Review Online*, Nov. 5, 2011, http://www.nationalreview.com/corner/282353/benghazi-sea-al-qaeda-flags-john-rosenthal; John Rosenthal, "Al-Qaeda flags fly over rebel-held Syria," *Asia Times*, Aug. 14, 2012, http://www.atimes.com/atimes/Middle_East/NH14Ak01.html.

13. McCarthy, "'Blame It on the Video' Was a Fraud for the Cairo Rioting, Too," *supra*; Joscelyn, "Al Qaeda's expansion into Egypt," *supra*; "Egypt protestors torch US embassy flag, demand apology for anti-Islam film," *Ahram Online*, Sep. 12, 2012, http://english.ahram.org.eg/News/52569.aspx; see also Federation of American Scientists, "Jihad against Jews and Crusaders: World Islamic Front Statement," Feb. 23, 1998 (English translation of declaration of war by al-Qaeda and affiliated jihadist organizations), http://www.fas.org/irp/world/para/docs/980223-fatwa.htm.

14. Joscelyn, "Al Qaeda's expansion into Egypt," *supra* (observing that the other two "senior al Qaeda–linked jihadists who helped spark the

protest" in Cairo were Tawfiq al-Afani and Adel Shehato, both "longtime [Egyptian Islamic Jihad] ideologues and leaders"; and that "Shehato has since been re-arrested" by the new (non–Muslim Brotherhood) Egyptian government and "charged with leading the so-called Nasr City Cell, which had multiple ties to al Qaeda"); see also McCarthy, "'Blame It on the Video' Was a Fraud for Cairo as Well as Benghazi: More Proof," *supra*.

15. See, e.g., Jennifer Griffin and Adam Housely, "Military timeline from night of Benghazi attack begs more questions," Fox News, Nov. 11, 2012, http://www.foxnews.com/politics/2012/11/11/military-timeline-from-night-benghazi-attack-begs-more-questions/; "How the Benghazi Attack Unfolded," *Wall Street Journal*, undated, http://online.wsj.com/news/articles/SB10000872396390444620104578008922056244096.

16. Guy Benson, "Obama Campaign: Vegas Fundraiser on Day after Benghazi Massacre Was 'Appropriate,'" *Townhall.com*, Oct. 1, 2012, http://townhall.com/tipsheet/guybenson/2012/10/01/obama_campaign_vegas_fundraiser_on_day_after_benghazi_massacre_was_appropriate.

17. Fred Lucas, "Obama Has Touted Al Qaeda's Demise 32 Times since Benghazi Attack," CNS News, Nov. 1, 2012, http://cnsnews.com/news/article/obama-touts-al-qaeda-s-demise-32-times-benghazi-attack-0.

ARTICLE IV

1. Andrew C. McCarthy, "Go to Congress First: Going into Libya is bad enough; doing so without congressional approval is worse," *National Review Online*, March 19, 2011, http://www.nationalreview.com/articles/262547/go-congress-first-andrew-c-mccarthy; Sam Youngman and Jordan Fabian, "White House denies regime change is part of Libya mission," *The Hill*, March 22, 2011, http://thehill.com/homenews/campaign/151191-white-house-suggests-regime-change-is-goal-of-libya-mission; Charlie Savage and Mark Landler, "White House defends continuing U.S. role in Libya operation," *New York Times*, June 15, 2011, http://www.nytimes.com/2011/06/16/us/politics/16powers.html?pagewanted=1&_r=0&hp; Jayshree Bajoria, "Libya and the Responsibility to Protect," Council on Foreign Relations, March 24, 2011, http://

www.cfr.org/libya/libya-responsibility-protect/p24480; McCarthy, "Our Libyan Adventure," *supra*; McCarthy, "Decoding Libya," *supra*.

2. McCarthy, "Our Libyan Adventure," *supra*:

President Obama invaded without congressional authorization—just consultations with the Arab League and a Security Council resolution that called for a no-fly zone to protect civilians, not for war against Qaddafi or regime change. Even as Obama paid lip-service to this charade, promising Americans there would be no U.S. "boots on the ground," he dispatched covert intelligence operatives to guide the Islamists. Senator Graham—Qaddafi's tent guest and military-aid supporter in 2009—wondered aloud why we couldn't just "drop a bomb on" our erstwhile ally and "end this thing." No congressional approval? No U.N. mandate? No problem. "I like coalitions," Graham explained to CNN, "it's good to have the U.N. involved. But the goal is to get rid of Qaddafi. . . . I would not let the U.N. mandate stop what is the right thing to do."

Citing Gus Lubin, "Obama Deployed CIA Agent to Libya to Aid and Supply Rebels Weeks Ago," *Business Insider*, March 30, 2011, http://www.businessinsider.com/libya-wednesday-march-30-2011-3; Justin Elliott, "Maybe McCain's Libya amnesia is contagious: Now Lindsey Graham can't remember meeting with 'international terrorist' Moammar Gadhafi in 2009, either," *Salon*, March 31, 2011, http://www.salon.com/2011/03/31/graham_gadhafi_libya/; Elise Foley, "Lindsey Graham: U.S. Should Ignore U.N. Mandate in Libya," *Huffington Post*, April 24, 2011, http://www.huffingtonpost.com/2011/04/24/lindsey-graham-un-mandate-libya_n_852989.html; see also Corbett Daly, "Clinton on Qaddafi: 'We came, we saw, he died,'" CBS News, Oct. 20, 2011, http://www.cbsnews.com/news/clinton-on-qaddafi-we-came-we-saw-he-died/.

3. Kevin Baron, "For the U.S., War against Qaddafi Cost Relatively Little: $1.1 Billion," *Atlantic*, Oct. 21, 2011, http://www.theatlantic.com/international/archive/2011/10/for-the-us-war-against-qaddafi-cost-relatively-little-11-billion/247133/.

4. Karin Laub, "Libya: Estimated 30,000 Died in War; 4,000 Still Missing," *World Post / Huffington Post*, Sep. 8, 2011, http://www.huffingtonpost.com/2011/09/08/libya-war-died_n_953456.html.

5. Savage and Landler, "White House Defends Continuing U.S. Role in Libya Operation," *supra*; see also Tom Rogan, "Obama's subversion of war powers: U.S. is involved in 'hostilities' against Libya, which demands a vote in Congress. The president is in breach of the constitution," *Guardian*, June 17, 2011, http://www.theguardian.com/commentisfree/cifamerica/2011/jun/17/obama-libya-war-powers.

6. See e.g., "Prophet Film Spurs Egyptian Anger at US," *OnIslam*, Sep. 11, 2012, http://www.onislam.net/english/news/middle-east/458983-prophet-film-spurs-egyptian-anger-at-us.html; McCarthy, "'Blame It on the Video' Was a Fraud for the Cairo Rioting, Too," *supra*.

7. Andrew C. McCarthy, "It's Not Just Obama's Lies—It's the Premise of Obama's Lies," *PJ Media*, Oct. 18, 2013, http://pjmedia.com/andrewmccarthy/2012/10/18/its-not-just-obamas-lies-its-the-premise-of-obamas-lies/.

8. James Rosen, "The Benghazi Transcripts: Top Defense officials briefed Obama on 'attack,' not video or protest," Fox News, Jan. 14, 2014, http://www.foxnews.com/politics/2014/01/14/benghazi-transcripts-top-defense-officials-briefed-obama-on-attack-not-video-or/; Griffin and Housely, "Military timeline from night of Benghazi attack begs more questions," *supra*.

9. McCarthy, "The 10 p.m. Phone Call: Clinton and Obama discussed Benghazi. What did they say?" *supra*.

10. Ibid.

11. Ibid.

12. Ibid.

13. Ibid.; see also Stephen Dinan, "Obama made no phone calls on night of Benghazi attack, White House says," *Washington Times*, Feb. 14, 2013, http://www.washingtontimes.com/news/2013/feb/14/white-house-no-phone-calls-benghazi/.

14. McCarthy, "The 10 p.m. Phone Call," *supra*; see also Fred Lucas, "WH: Obama Called Hillary on Night of Benghazi Attack—More Than Six Hours after It Started," CNS News, Feb. 20, 2013, http://cnsnews.com/news/article/wh-obama-called-hillary-night-benghazi-attack-more-six-hours-after-it-started.

15. McCarthy, "The 10 p.m. Phone Call," *supra*; see also Terence P. Jeffrey, "Clinton Publicly Linked Benghazi to Video before Woods and Doherty Were Killed," CNS News, Jan. 9, 2013, http://cnsnews.com/blog/terence-p-jeffrey/clinton-publicly-linked-benghazi-video-woods-and-doherty-were-killed.

16. McCarthy, "It's Not Just Obama's Lies—It's the Premise of Obama's Lies," *supra*.

17. Stephen F. Hayes, "The Benghazi Cover-up (cont.): How the CIA's No. 2 misled Congress," *Weekly Standard*, March 3, 2014, http://www.weeklystandard.com/articles/benghazi-cover-cont_782749.html?nopager=1#.

18. Stephen F. Hayes, "The Benghazi Talking Points: And how they were changed to obscure the truth," *Weekly Standard*, May 13, 2013, http://www.weeklystandard.com/articles/benghazi-talking-points_720543.html#.

19. Ibid.

20. David E. Sanger and Jodi Cantor, "Rice's blunt style endeared her to president, but not all," *New York Times*, Dec. 13, 2012 (detailing background of Rice-Obama relationship; adding observations of Clinton administration Secretary of State Madeleine Albright, who has known Ambassador Rice since the latter was a child, that Rice and President Obama "share a common vision and a common style," and that Rice "is incredibly bright, but lots of people in Washington are bright. What separates people out here is that some are loyal."), http://www.nytimes.com/2012/12/14/us/susan-rices-bluntness-endeared-her-to-president.html?_r=0.

21. "Flashback: What Susan Rice Said about Benghazi," *Wall Street Journal*, Nov. 16, 2012, http://blogs.wsj.com/washwire/2012/11/16/flashback-what-susan-rice-said-about-benghazi/, excerpting *This Week* transcript, "U.S. Ambassador to the United Nations Susan Rice," ABC News, Sep. 16, 2012, http://abcnews.go.com/Politics/week-transcript-us-ambassador-united-nations-susan-rice/story?id=17240933#.UKQD2GfSnpg.

22. Ibid., excerpting *Face the Nation* transcripts, "Libyan Pres. Magariaf, Amb. Rice and Sen. McCain," CBS News, Sep. 16, 2012,

http://www.cbsnews.com/news/face-the-nation-transcripts-september-16-2012-libyan-pres-magariaf-amb-rice-and-sen-mccain/.

23. Ibid., excerpting *Fox News Sunday* with Chris Wallace, transcript, "Amb. Susan Rice, Rep. Mike Rogers discuss violence against Americans in the Middle East," Fox News, Sep. 16, 2012, http://www.foxnews.com/on-air/fox-news-sunday-chris-wallace/2012/09/16/amb-susan-rice-rep-mike-rogers-discuss-violence-against-americans-middle-east#p//v/1843960658001.

24. Ibid., excerpting *Fox News Sunday* transcript, *supra*, and *Meet the Press* transcripts, "September 16: Benjamin Netanyahu, Susan Rice, Keith Ellison, Peter King, Bob Woodward, Jeffrey Goldberg . . . ," NBC News, Sep. 16, 2012, http://www.nbcnews.com/id/49051097/ns/meet_the_press-transcripts/t/september-benjamin-netanyahu-susan-rice-keith-ellison-peter-king-bob-woodward-jeffrey-goldberg-andrea-mitchell/#.UyAi_txhNFw.

25. Ibid., excerpting *State of the Union with Candy Crowley* transcript, CNN, Sep. 16, 2012, http://transcripts.cnn.com/TRANSCRIPTS/1209/16/sotu.01.html.

26. Hayes, "The Benghazi Cover-up (cont.)," *supra.*

27. Ibid.

28. Ibid.

29. Glenn Kessler, "Obama's claim he called Benghazi an 'act of terrorism,'" *Washington Post*, May 14, 2013, http://www.washingtonpost.com/blogs/fact-checker/post/obamas-claim-he-called-benghazi-an-act-of-terrorism/2013/05/13/7b65b83e-bc14-11e2-97d4-a479289a31f9_blog.html. Despite his patent, conscious refusal to acknowledge a terrorist attack by what the administration knew were al-Qaeda-affiliated terrorists (not to mention that notorious terrorists had been involved in the Cairo rioting that the administration had linked to the Benghazi massacre), the president later disingenuously insisted that he had emphatically called Benghazi an "act of terrorism." Ibid. Nevertheless, the speeches from which he mined this claim, a presidential statement in the wake of the eleventh anniversary of the 9/11 terrorist attacks and campaign speeches soon

thereafter, mentioned "acts of terror" only generically, not in specific connection to Benghazi. (See, e.g., ibid., quoting the Rose Garden speech on September 12: "No acts of terror will ever shake the resolve of this great nation.")

30. "Transcript, Video: Hillary Clinton speaks at ceremony as bodies of Americans killed in Libya arrive in the US," Fox News Insider, Sep. 14, 2012, http://foxnewsinsider.com/2012/09/14/transcript-video-hillary-clinton-speaks-at-ceremony-as-bodies-of-americans-killed-in-libya-arrive-in-the-us.

31. Allahpundit, "Your tax dollars at work: State Department now running TV ads in Pakistan denouncing Mohammed movie," *Hot Air*, Sep. 20, 2012, http://hotair.com/archives/2012/09/20/your-tax-dollars-at-work-state-department-now-running-tv-ads-in-pakistan-denouncing-mohammed-movie/; "Flashback: Obama and Hillary apologize for free speech on Pakistani TV," Fox Nation, Sep. 24, 2012, http://nation.foxnews.com/president-obama/2012/09/20/obama-and-hillary-apologize-free-speech-pakistani-tv.

32. Katrina Trinko, "Obama: The Future Must Not Belong to Those Who Slander the Prophet of Islam," *National Review Online*, Sep. 25, 2012 (with link to transcript of full speech), http://www.nationalreview.com/corner/328483/obama-future-must-not-belong-those-who-slander-prophet-islam-katrina-trinko; Jim Hoft, "Obama at UN: 'The future does not belong to those who slander . . . ,'" YouTube video excerpt, Sep. 25, 2012, http://www.youtube.com/watch?v=T6uZFSj_ueM.

33. Rich Lowry, "The Benghazi patsy," *Politico*, May 9, 2013, http://www.politico.com/story/2013/05/the-benghazi-patsy-91101.html; Jeff Emanuel, "Hillary Clinton to father of American murdered in Libya: 'We'll make sure that the person who made that film is arrested and prosecuted,'" *RedState*, Oct. 26, 2012, http://www.redstate.com/2012/10/26/hillary-clinton-to-father-of-american-murdered-in-libya-well-make-sure-that-the-person-who-made-that-film-is-arrested-and-prosecuted/; "Fallen SEAL's Father: Hillary Told Me 'We're Going Arrest [*sic*] . . . the Man That Made the Video' at Funeral," *Breitbart*, Oct. 25, 2012 (with audio excerpt from the *Lars Larson Show*), http://www.breitbart.com/Breitbart-TV/2012/10/25/Fallen-Seals-Father-

Hillary-Told-M-Dont-Worry-Were-Going-To-Arrest-The-Man-That-Did-This; "Father of Navy SEAL killed at Libyan embassy reveals the shocking details of his meeting with Obama, Biden, and Clinton in interview with Glenn Beck," *Glenn Beck*, Oct. 25, 2012, http://www.glennbeck.com/2012/10/25/updating-glenn-talks-to-father-of-navy-seal-killed-during-assault-on-libyan-embassy/.

34. Evan Perez and Erica E. Phillips, "Alleged Maker of Anti-Muslim Video Jailed in Fraud Case," *Wall Street Journal*, Sep. 28, 2012, http://online.wsj.com/news/articles/SB10000872396390443328404578022953359653378; "Anti-Islam Filmmaker Nakoula Basseley Nakoula arrested on probation violation, detained without bail," ABC News, Sep. 27, 2012, http://abcnews.go.com/Blotter/anti-islam-filmmaker-nakoula-basseley-nakoula-arrested-probation/story?id=17343351.

35. Andrew C. McCarthy, "Amnesty, but Not for D'Souza," *National Review Online*, Feb. 1, 2014, http://www.nationalreview.com/article/370097/amnesty-not-dsouza-andrew-c-mccarthy/page/0/1; Lowry, "The Benghazi patsy," *supra*; Perez and Phillips, "Alleged Maker of Anti-Muslim Video Jailed in Fraud Case," *supra*.

36. "Anti-Islam Filmmaker Nakoula Basseley Nakoula arrested on probation violation, detained without bail," *supra*.

37. McCarthy, "Amnesty, but Not for D'Souza," *supra*.

38. "Anti-Islam Filmmaker Nakoula Basseley Nakoula arrested on probation violation, detained without bail," *supra*; McCarthy, "Amnesty, but Not for D'Souza," *supra*.

39. Brooks Barnes, "Man behind anti-Islam video gets prison term," *New York Times*, Nov. 7, 2012, http://www.nytimes.com/2012/11/08/us/maker-of-anti-islam-video-gets-prison-term.html.

40. McCarthy, "Amnesty, but Not for D'Souza," *supra*; Lowry, "The Benghazi patsy," *supra*.

41. Senate Select Committee on Intelligence, "Review of the Terrorist Attacks on U.S. Facilities in Benghazi, Libya, September 11–12, 2012," *supra*, Additional Views of Vice Chairman Chambliss and Senators Burr, Risch, Coats, Rubio, and Coburn.

42. McCarthy, "Obama's '5 percent' Con Job," *supra*; Roy, "Obama to Nation: If You Like Your Plan, You Can Keep Your Plan (at Least

until the Next Election)," *supra*; see also, e.g., Avik Roy, "Pants on Fire: PolitiFact Tries to Hide That It Rated 'True' in 2008 Obamacare's 'Keep Your Health Plan' Promise," *Forbes*, Dec. 27, 2013 (noting that PolitiFact later rated the president's promise as its 2013 "Lie of the Year"), http://www.forbes.com/sites/theapothecary/2013/12/27/in-2008-politifacts-2013-lie-of-the-year-that-you-could-keep-your-health-plan-under-obamacare-it-rated-true/.

43. Roy, "Obama to Nation: If You Like Your Plan, You Can Keep Your Plan (at Least until the Next Election)," *supra* (individual market accounts for 8 percent of the population, around 25 million Americans, not the 5 percent claimed by the president).

44. John Hinderaker, "Today, Obama Repeated the Five Percent Lie," *Power Line*, Nov. 14, 2013 (citing and excerpting chart, "Table 3: Estimates of the Cumulative Percentage of Employer Plans Relinquishing Their Grandfathered Status, 2011–2013," Federal Register, vol. 75, no. 116 (June 17, 2010), Rules and Regulations, p. 34553 (estimating that between 49 and 69 percent of employer plans covering Americans would "relin-quish[] their grandfathered status" by 2013—i.e., would no longer be per-missible for insurance companies to offer under the PPACA's coverage mandates), http://www.powerlineblog.com/archives/2013/11/today-obama-repeated-the-five-percent-lie.php?utm_source=feedburner&utm_medium=email&utm_campaign=Feed%3A+powerlineblog%2Flivefeed+%28Power+Line%29; see also McCarthy, "Obama's '5 percent' Con Job," *supra*; Roy, "Obama to Nation: If You Like Your Plan, You Can Keep Your Plan (at Least until the Next Election)," *supra*.

45. *Priests for Life* v. *HHS*, No. 13 cv 1261 (U.S. District Court for the District of Columbia), Brief for the respondent U.S. Dept. of Health and Human Services (Oct. 17, 2013), p. 27, http://www.americanfreedom-lawcenter.org/wp-content/uploads/caseapps/c39629e5f397e42be2f7d-0021bed01c5aadaa422.pdf; see also McCarthy, "Obama's '5 percent' Con Job," *supra*.

46. Roy, "Obama to Nation: If You Like Your Plan, You Can Keep Your Plan (at Least until the Next Election)," *supra*.

47. See, e.g., Avik Roy, "Do You Like Your Doctor? Obam-acare Drives UnitedHealth to Downsize Its Medicare Physician

Networks," *Forbes*, Nov. 18, 2013, http://www.forbes.com/sites/
theapothecary/2013/11/18/do-you-like-your-doctor-obamacare-
drives-unitedhealth-to-downsize-its-medicare-physician-networks/;
Robert Pear, "Lower health insurance premiums to come at cost of
fewer choices," *New York Times*, Sep. 22, 2013, http://www.nytimes.
com/2013/09/23/health/lower-health-insurance-premiums-to-come-at-
cost-of-fewer-choices.html?smid=tw-nytimes&_r=1&pagewanted=all&.

48. See, e.g., John Nolte, "Video: 19 Times Obama Promised to
Lower Annual Insurance Premiums by $2500," *Breitbart*, Oct. 28, 2013,
http://www.breitbart.com/InstaBlog/2013/10/28/Video-19-Times-
Obama-Promised-to-Lower-Annual-Insurance-Premiums-By-2500;
"Flashback: Obama pledged to reduce health insurance premiums
by $2,500 per family per year," *Twitchy*, June 2, 2013, http://twitchy.
com/2013/06/02/flashback-obama-pledged-to-reduce-health-insur-
ance-premiums-by-2500-per-family-per-year/.

49. Avik Roy, "49-State Analysis: Obamacare to Increase Indi-
vidual-Market Premiums by Average of 41%," *Forbes*, Nov. 4, 2013,
http://www.forbes.com/sites/theapothecary/2013/11/04/49-state-
analysis-obamacare-to-increase-individual-market-premiums-by-
avg-of-41-subsidies-flow-to-elderly/; Avik Roy, "Interactive Map: In
13 States Plus D.C., Obamacare Will Increase Heath Premiums by
24% on Average," *Forbes*, Sep. 4, 2013, http://www.forbes.com/sites/
theapothecary/2013/09/04/interactive-map-in-13-states-plus-d-c-
individual-health-premiums-will-increase-by-an-average-of-24/; Avik
Roy, "No, It's Not 'Complicated'; Obamacare Increases Premiums
for Most People," *National Review Online*, Sep. 5, 2013, http://www.
nationalreview.com/corner/357728/no-its-not-complicated-obamacare-
increases-premiums-most-people-avik-roy; Chad Terhune, "Some
health insurance gets pricier as Obamacare rolls out: Many middle-
class Californians with individual health plans are surprised they
need policies that cover more—and cost more," *Los Angeles Times*,
Oct. 26, 2013, http://www.latimes.com/business/la-fi-health-sticker-
shock-20131027,0,4888906,full.story#axzz2jttIOY71; "No cut in premiums for typical family," PolitiFact, Aug. 31, 2012 (assessing President
Obama's oft-repeated claims along the lines of his bold 2007 pledge,

"I will sign a universal health care bill into law by the end of my first term as president that will cover every American and cut the cost of a typical family's premium by up to $2,500 a year"), http://www.politifact.com/truth-o-meter/promises/obameter/promise/521/cut-cost-typical-familys-health-insurance-premium-/.

50. See, e.g., Avik Roy, "Obamacare's Website Is Crashing Because It Doesn't Want You to Know How Costly Its Plans Are," *Forbes*, Oct. 14, 2013 ("Healthcare.gov forces you to create an account and enter detailed personal information before you can start shopping. This, in turn, creates a massive traffic bottleneck, as the government verifies your information and decides whether or not you're eligible for subsidies. HHS bureaucrats knew this would make the website run more slowly. But they were more afraid that letting people see the underlying cost of Obamacare's insurance plans would scare people away"), http://www.forbes.com/sites/theapothecary/2013/10/14/obamacares-website-is-crashing-because-it-doesnt-want-you-to-know-health-plans-true-costs/.

51. Andrew C. McCarthy, "The Scheme behind the Obamacare Fraud: Lies smooth the transition to a fundamental transformation of our health-care system," Nov. 23, 2013, http://www.nationalreview.com/article/364667/scheme-behind-obamacare-fraud-andrew-c-mccarthy; Andrew C. McCarthy, "Obama's Massive Fraud: If he were a CEO in the private sector, he'd be prosecuted for such deception," *National Review Online*, Nov. 9, 2013, http://www.nationalreview.com/article/363538/obamas-massive-fraud-andrew-c-mccarthy; Lisa Myers and Hannah Rappleye, "Obama admin. knew millions could not keep their health insurance," NBC News, Oct. 28, 2013, http://www.nbcnews.com/news/investigations/obama-admin-knew-millions-could-not-keep-their-health-insurance-v21213547.

52. Andrew C. McCarthy, "Negotiate with Iran? How many more Americans do they need to kill before we get the point?" *National Review Online*, Dec. 8, 2006, http://www.nationalreview.com/articles/219452/negotiate-iran-andrew-c-mccarthy; see also Department of State, List of State Sponsors of Terrorism (Iran remains on list since designation on January 19, 1984), http://www.state.gov/j/ct/list/c14151.htm;

Department of State, Country Reports on Terrorism: "Middle East and North Africa Overview," May 30, 2013:

> In 2012, there was a clear resurgence of Iran's state sponsorship of terrorism, through the Islamic Revolutionary Guard Corps–Qods Force (IRGCQF), its Ministry of Intelligence and Security, and Tehran's ally Hizballah, who remained a significant threat to the stability of Lebanon and the broader region. Attacks in Europe, Africa, the Middle East, South Asia, and the Far East were linked to the IRGCQF or Hizballah. In fact, Hizballah's terrorist activity has reached a tempo unseen since the 1990s with attacks plotted in Southeast Asia, Europe, and Africa.

http://www.state.gov/j/ct/rls/crt/2012/209982.htm.

53. Though the president and his subordinates congratulated Iranians after Rouhani's "election," Iran is not a democracy, it is a sharia state. The Constitution of the Islamic Republic of Iran severely limits which candidates may seek office. The Guardian Council, consisting of the Islamic jurists who actually run the country, arrogates to itself the power to determine who may run and disqualifies most candidates for president. Women and religious minorities (in Iran, Sunnis and non-Muslims) are barred from candidacy. See Foundation for Defense of Democracies, "Why Iran's Elections Will Not Be Democratic," policy brief, May 16, 2013, http://defenddemocracy.org/media-hit/why-irans-elections-will-not-be-democratic/; see also Erik Wasson, "White House congratulates Iranians after Rouhani victory," *The Hill*, June 15, 2013, http://thehill.com/blogs/blog-briefing-room/news/305797-white-house-congratulates-iranians-after-rouhani-election.

54. See, e.g., Mary Bruce and Jonathan Karl, "In Israel, Obama vows to prevent nuclear Iran," ABC News, March 20, 2013, http://abcnews.go.com/Politics/obama-israel-vows-unwavering-commitment-israeli-security/story?id=18771109; Margaret Talev and Hans Nichols, "Obama at UN Vows U.S. Won't Let Iran Gain Nuclear Weapon," *Bloomberg*, Sep. 25, 2012, http://www.bloomberg.com/news/2012-09-25/obama-at-un-vows-u-s-won-t-allow-iran-to-gain-nuclear-weapons.html; Mark Landler, "Obama says Iran strike is an option, but warns Israel," *New York Times*,

March 2, 2012, http://www.nytimes.com/2012/03/03/world/middleeast/
obama-says-military-option-on-iran-not-a-bluff.html?pagewanted=all.

55. John Bolton, "Abject Surrender by the United States," *Weekly Standard*, Nov. 24, 2013, http://www.weeklystandard.com/blogs/abject-surrender-united-states_768140.html?destination=node%2F768140.

56. Eli Lake, "Why the Iranian Nuclear Deal Is Dangerous," *Daily Beast*, Nov. 24, 2013, http://www.thedailybeast.com/articles/2013/11/24/why-the-iranian-nuclear-deal-is-dangerous.html; "Iran reportedly claiming world has recognized its 'right to enrich uranium': Iranian FM Zarif says only 'one or two issues' of major significance yet to be resolved in Geneva; WH remains hopeful for deal," *Times of Israel*, Nov. 22, 2013, http://www.timesofisrael.com/iran-world-powers-agree-on-90-percent-says-zarif/.

57. Andrew C. McCarthy, "Friendly 'Moderate' Rouhani Boasts of Obama's 'Surrender to the Iranian Nation's Will,'" *National Review Online*, Jan. 14, 2014, http://www.nationalreview.com/corner/368434/friendly-moderate-rouhani-boasts-obamas-surrender-iranian-nations-will-andrew-c; Bolton, "Abject Surrender by the United States," *supra*; Michael Wilner, "Rouhani boasts of West's 'surrender' to Iran in nuclear talks," *Jerusalem Post*, Jan. 14, 2014, http://www.jpost.com/Iranian-Threat/News/Rouhani-boasts-of-Wests-surrender-to-Iran-in-nuclear-talks-338135.

58. Tom Cohen, "Iranian official on nuke deal: We did not agree to dismantle anything," CNN, Jan. 23, 2014, http://edition.cnn.com/2014/01/22/politics/iran-us-nuclear/.

59. "The Iran nuclear deal: full text," CNN, Nov. 24, 2013, http://www.cnn.com/2013/11/24/world/meast/iran-deal-text/.

60. Adam Kredo, "Congress Pressures White House to Release Iran Nuke Deal Text," *Washington Free Beacon*, Jan. 14, 2014, http://freebeacon.com/congress-pressures-white-house-to-release-iran-nuke-deal-text/; Ed Henry and Chad Pergram, "Administration accused of keeping text of Iran nuclear deal 'secret,'" Fox News, Jan. 16, 2014, http://www.foxnews.com/politics/2014/01/16/administration-accused-keeping-text-iran-nuclear-deal-secret/; Iran FM: White House Misleading Americans over Interim Deal," *The Tower*, Jan. 23, 2014,

http://www.thetower.org/iran-fm-white-house-misleading-americans-interim-deal/; Jennifer Rubin, "We should trust the secret Iran deal?" *Washington Post*, Feb. 13, 2014, http://www.washingtonpost.com/blogs/right-turn/wp/2014/02/13/we-should-trust-the-secret-iran-deal/.

61. Andrew C. McCarthy, "Kerry Sees Common Ground with Tehran's Barbaric Terror Regime," *PJ Media*, Nov. 20, 2013, http://pjmedia.com/andrewmccarthy/2013/11/20/common-ground-kerry-tehran/; Michael Ledeen, "Hey Stupid! It's Not about Nukes, It's about Life and Death," *PJ Media*, Jan. 26, 2014, http://pjmedia.com/michael-ledeen/2014/01/26/its-not-about-nukes/.

62. Spencer Hsu and N. C. Aizenman, "DHS corrects report that overstated ICE deportations under Obama," *Washington Post*, Dec. 8, 2010, http://voices.washingtonpost.com/44/2010/03/dhs-corrects-report-that-overs.html.

63. Peter Slevin, "Deportation of illegal immigrants increases under Obama administration," *Washington Post*, July 26, 2010, http://www.washingtonpost.com/wp-dyn/content/article/2010/07/25/AR2010072501790.html.

64. Shankar Vedantam, "U.S. deportations reach record high," *Washington Post*, Oct. 7, 2010, http://www.washingtonpost.com/wp-dyn/content/article/2010/10/06/AR2010100607232.html.

65. Andrew Becker, "Unusual methods help ICE break deportation record, e-mails and interviews show," *Washington Post*, Dec. 6, 2010, http://www.washingtonpost.com/wp-dyn/content/article/2010/12/05/AR2010120503230.html.

66. The White House, Office of the Press Secretary, "Remarks by the President in an 'Open for Questions' Roundtable," Sep. 28, 2011, http://www.whitehouse.gov/the-press-office/2011/09/28/remarks-president-open-questions-roundtable.

67. In fact, though detentions dropped significantly toward the end of the Bush 43 administration, to a low of 791,568 in 2008; they had sharply decreased by nearly 300,000 since then, to 516,992 in 2010. See Department of Homeland Security, Office of Immigration Statistics, *Yearbook of Immigration Statistics: 2010*, Enforcement Table 33, http://www.dhs.gov/yearbook-immigration-statistics-2010. That number has

since been revised upward, to 752,329 for 2010, and down to 641,633 for 2011. A note in the 2011 compilation explains that for years beginning in 2008, the total now "includes all administrative arrests conducted by ICE ERO"—a reference to the "Enforcement and Removal Operations" program by which ICE, among other things, removes "recent border entrants." Department of Homeland Security, Office of Immigration Statistics, *Yearbook of Immigration Statistics: 2011*, p. 91 (Table 33), http://www.dhs.gov/sites/default/files/publications/immigration-statistics/yearbook/2011/ois_yb_2011.pdf; see also Enforcement and Removal Operations, ICE website (accessed March 12, 2014), http://www.ice.gov/about/offices/enforcement-removal-operations/.

68. See Jeff Bair, "Documents from FOIA request to Immigration and Customs Enforcement," *Houston Chronicle*, June 27, 2011, including Department of Homeland Security Memorandum, John Morton, Director, Immigration and Customs Enforcement, "Civil Immigration Enforcement: Priorities for the Apprehension, Detention, and Removal of Aliens," June 30, 2010, http://blog.chron.com/newswatch/2011/06/documents-from-foia-request-to-immigrations-and-customs-enforcment/); *compare* DHS Memorandum, John Morton, ICE Director, "Civil Immigration Enforcement: Priorities for the Apprehension, Detention, and Removal of Aliens," a substantially similar memo but dated March 2, 2011, http://www.ice.gov/doclib/news/releases/2011/110302washingtondc.pdf.

69. Bair, "Documents from FOIA request to Immigration and Customs Enforcement," *supra*, Memo from Gary L. Goldman, Chief Counsel, to "All Attorneys, Houston OCC" regarding "Efficiencies in the Removal Process and Prosecutorial Discretion File Review," Aug. 12, 2010, marked "RESCINDED 8/25/10"; Susan Carroll, "Report: Feds downplayed ICE case dismissals: Documents show agency had approval to dismiss some deportation cases," *Houston Chronicle*, June 27, 2011, http://www.chron.com/news/houston-texas/article/Report-Feds-down-played-ICE-case-dismissals-2080532.php#ixzz1QUEAniIR.

70. Bair, "Documents from FOIA request to Immigration and Customs Enforcement," *supra*, emails between Gary L. Goldman and Riah Ramlogan, Aug. 6, 2010.

71. Bair, "Documents from FOIA request to Immigration and Customs Enforcement," *supra*, Memo from Gary L. Goldman to "All Attorneys, Houston OCC," Aug. 12, 2010, *supra*; see also ibid., Memo from Riah Ramlogan, Director, Field Legal Operations (ICE-HQ), to Gary Goldman, Chief Counsel (ICE-Houston), Aug. 25, 2010 (same day the Goldman memo encouraging prosecutorial discretion dismissals was rescinded) (suggesting that Goldman, though well intentioned, had perhaps misunderstood prior guidance from Ramlogan and headquarters); see also ibid., email of Raphael Choi, Acting Director, ICE-ERO, to Gary Goldman (noting Riah Ramlogan's praise of Goldman's office as being "in front of the ICE priorities"), Aug. 18, 2010; and ibid., email of Arthur E. Adams (Riah Ramlogan's Deputy Director, ICE Field Legal Ops) to Gary Goldman (noting that Goldman had "impressed Riah" with his "efficiency efforts"), Aug. 18, 2010.

72. Carroll, "Report: Feds downplayed ICE case dismissals," *supra*; Morton DHS Memo, "Civil Immigration Enforcement: Priorities for the Apprehension, Detention, and Removal of Aliens," June 30, 2010, *supra*; DHS Memorandum, John Morton, ICE Director, "Exercising Prosecutorial Discretion Consistent with the Civil Immigration Enforcement Priorities of the Agency for the Apprehension, Detention, and Removal of Aliens," June 17, 2011, http://www.ice.gov/doclib/ secure-communities/pdf/prosecutorial-discretion-memo.pdf; DHS Memorandum, John Morton, ICE Director, "Prosecutorial Discretion: Certain Victims, Witnesses, and Plaintiffs," June 17, 2011, http://www. ice.gov/doclib/secure-communities/pdf/domestic-violence.pdf; DHS Secretary Janet Napolitano, Letter to Senator Harry Reid, Aug. 18, 2011 (announcing Obama administration was implementing the June 17, 2011 "Prosecutorial Discretion" memo and would halt immigration enforcement proceedings that did not meet administration priorities), stating, among other things:

> Over the past two years, the Department of Homeland Security (DHS) has established clear and well-reasoned priorities that govern how DHS uses its immigration enforcement resources. These priorities focus our resources on enhancing border security and identifying and removing criminal aliens, those who pose a threat to

public safety and national security, repeat immigration law violators and other individuals prioritized for removal. Initially set forth in a March 2010 memorandum from U.S. Immigration and Customs Enforcement (ICE) Director John Morton, these priorities were recently reiterated and clarified in Director Morton's June 17, 2011 memorandum regarding the exercise of prosecutorial discretion by ICE personnel.

. . . .

Accordingly, the June 17, 2011 prosecutorial discretion memorandum is being implemented to ensure that resources are uniformly focused on our highest priorities. Together with the Department of Justice (DOJ), we have initiated an interagency working group to execute a case-by-case review of all individuals currently in removal proceedings to ensure that they constitute our highest priorities.

http://democrats.senate.gov/uploads/2011/08/11_8949_Reid_Dream_Act_response_08.18.11.pdf; see also Jessica Vaughn, "Catch and Release: Interior immigration enforcement in 2013," Center for Immigration Studies, March 31, 2014, http://cis.org/catch-and-release; Judson Berger, "Enforcement 'Crisis'? Documents show 68,000 'criminal aliens' released last year," Fox News, March 31, 2014, http://www.foxnews.com/politics/2014/03/31/enforcement-crisis-documents-show-68000-criminal-aliens-released-last-year/.

73. Andrew C. McCarthy, "The Solyndra Fraud: The solar-energy company was a con game," *National Review Online*, Sep. 17, 2011, http://www.nationalreview.com/articles/277512/solyndra-fraud-andrew-c-mccarthy.

74. Public Law 109-58 (Aug. 8, 2005), http://www.gpo.gov/fdsys/pkg/PLAW-109publ58/pdf/PLAW-109publ58.pdf.

75. Andrew Stiles, "Notes from the Solyndra Hearing (Part I)," *National Review Online*, Sep. 14, 2011, http://www.nationalreview.com/corner/277222/notes-solyndra-hearing-part-i-andrew-stiles.

76. Bruce Krasting, "Government Investment Disaster in the Works??" *Zero Hedge*, Aug. 30, 2011, http://www.zerohedge.com/contributed/government-investment-disaster-works.

77. Ibid.

78. McCarthy, "The Solyndra Fraud," *supra*; Stiles, "Notes from the Solyndra Hearing," *supra*.

79. Ibid.

80. Ibid.

81. John Ransom, "Solyndra Bankruptcy: Obama administration knew about debt problems," *Nevada News and Views*, Sep. 13, 2011, http://nevadanewsandviews.com/archives/12825.

82. See, e.g., Title 18, U.S. Code, Section 1031 (punishing fraud against the United States by up to ten years' imprisonment and a substantial fine).

83. Title 17 C.F.R., Sec. 240.10B-5 ("Employment of Manipulative and Deceptive Devices").

84. McCarthy, "The Solyndra Fraud," *supra*; "Obama's Full Speech to Solyndra (May 26, 2010)," YouTube, http://www.youtube.com/watch?v=7rqtPc7OuMc.

85. McCarthy, "The Solyndra Fraud," *supra*; Stiles, "Notes from the Solyndra Hearing," *supra*.

86. Ibid.

87. Ibid.

ARTICLE V

1. Department of Homeland Security, Citizenship and Immigration Services, "Administrative Alternatives to Comprehensive Immigration Reform," undated memorandum, http://abcnews.go.com/images/Politics/memo-on-alternatives-to-comprehensive-immigration-reform.pdf.

2. Department of Homeland Security, "Administrative Options," draft memorandum, Feb. 26, 2010, 5 p.m., http://media.washingtonpost.com/wp-srv/politics/documents/dhs_draft_memo_09222010.pdf.

3. Ibid.

4. Ibid.

5. *Crane* v. *Napolitano*, No. 12 cv 3247, Memorandum Opinion and Order of Reed O'Connor, U.S. District Judge (Northern District of Texas, Dallas Division) (April 23, 2013), p. 23 (quoting 8 U.S. Code, Sec. 1225 and *Heckler* v. *Chaney*, 470 U.S. 821, 833 (1985)).

6. Department of Homeland Security, Office of Inspector General, "The Effects of USCIS Adjudication Procedures and Policies on Fraud Detection by Immigration Services Officers," Jan. 5, 2012, http://www. oig.dhs.gov/assets/Mgmt/OIG_12-24_Jan12.pdf.

7. *United States* v. *Mirtha Veronica Nava-Martinez*, No. 13 Cr. 441 (Southern District of Texas, Brownsville Division) (Andrew S. Hanen, U.S. District Judge), http://www.foxnews.com/politics/interactive/2013/12/19/judge-hanen-order-on-child-smuggling/.

8. Andrew C. McCarthy, "A Brothers' Day Card for Obama: Marking visa for Blind Sheikh's terrorist organization," *National Review Online*, June 25, 2010, http://www.nationalreview.com/corner/303871/ brothers-day-card-obama-marking-visa-blind-sheikhs-terrorist-organi-zation-andrew-c-mcc.

9. See Department of Homeland Security, "FY 2013 Budget in Brief," undated, pp. 15–16 (President Obama's proposed slashing $17 million from Sec. 287(g) programs that enable immigration enforcement by state and local police, purportedly due to transition to "Secure Communities" program, which focuses on removal of "criminal and other priority aliens found in state prisons and local jails"), http:// www.dhs.gov/xlibrary/assets/mgmt/dhs-budget-in-brief-fy2013.pdf; see also Department of Homeland Security, "Delegation of Immigration Authority Section 287(g) Immigration and Nationality Act," http:// www.ice.gov/287g/.

10. Morton DHS Memos, "Civil Immigration Enforcement: Priorities for the Apprehension, Detention, and Removal of Aliens," June 30, 2010, and March 2, 2011, *supra*; Morton DHS Memo, "Exercising Prosecutorial Discretion Consistent with the Civil Immigration Enforcement Priorities of the Agency for the Apprehension, Detention, and Removal of Aliens," June 17, 2011, *supra*; Morton DHS Memo, "Prosecutorial Discretion: Certain Victims, Witnesses, and Plaintiffs," June 17, 2011, *supra*; DHS Memorandum, John Morton, ICE Director, "Civil Immigration Enforcement: Guidance on the Use of Detainers in the Federal, State, Local, and Tribal Criminal Justice Systems," Dec. 21, 2012, https://www.ice.gov/doclib/detention-reform/pdf/detainer-policy.pdf; see also DHS Secretary Janet Napolitano, Letter to Senator Harry Reid,

Aug. 18, 2011 (announcing Obama administration was implementing the June 17, 2011 "Prosecutorial Discretion" memo and would halt immigration enforcement proceedings that did not meet administration priorities), *supra*; Department of Homeland Security, Citizenship and Immigration Services, Policy Memorandum, "Revised Guidance for the Referral of Cases and Issuance of Notices to Appear (NTAs) in Cases Involving Inadmissible and Removable Aliens," Nov. 7, 2011 (directing that NTAs no longer be issued to illegal immigrants who do not meet Obama administration's deportation priorities), http://www.uscis.gov/ sites/default/files/USCIS/Laws/Memoranda/Static_Files_Memoranda/ NTA%20PM%20%28Approved%20as%20final%2011-7-11%29.pdf; Peter S. Vincent, ICE Principal Legal Advisor, Memorandum, "Case-by-Case Review of Incoming and Certain Pending Cases," Nov. 17, 2011 (urging use of "prosecutorial discretion" to achieve "administrative closure" by dismissing various cases against illegal aliens), http:// www.ice.gov/doclib/foia/prosecutorial-discretion/case-by-case-review-incoming-certain-pending-cases-memorandum.pdf; Department of Justice, Executive Office for Immigration Review, "EOIR Statement Regarding Second Stage of Case-by-Case Review Pursuant to DHS's Prosecutorial Discretion Initiative," April 3, 2012, http://www.justice. gov/eoir/press/2012/EOIRProsecutorialDiscretion04032012.htm); P. Solomon Banda (Associated Press), "Immigration courtrooms silent during ICE review," *Washington Times*, Jan. 16, 2012, http://www.wash-ingtontimes.com/news/2012/jan/16/immigration-courtrooms-silent-during-ice-review/?page=all; Madeline Buckley, "Pilot-program lessons could help in Valley," *Brownsville Herald*, Jan. 22, 2012 ("Prosecutors continue to review the approximately 300,000 deportation cases in courts throughout the country, looking for low-priority cases that can be closed under prosecutorial discretion"), http://www.brownsvilleherald. com/news/valley/article_6ea429a0-50bf-5895-b6b8-5c5e07ba97ae. html; "ICE to suspend over 16,000 deportations, immigration advocates underwhelmed," Fox News Latino, April 25, 2012, http://latino. foxnews.com/latino/news/2012/04/25/75-percent-deportations-may-get-shelved-due-to-backlogged-system/#ixzz1t4h1Ipy5; ICE statistics release, June 5, 2012 (20,648 cases involving illegal aliens to be dis-

missed due to "prosecutorial discretion"), http://www.documentcloud.
org/documents/367098-ice-review-stats.html; USCIS statistics release,
Feb. 15, 2103, "Deferred Action for Childhood Arrivals Process (February
2013)," (Obama administration has deferred enforcement action—
i.e., granted administrative amnesty—in 199,460 cases involving
illegal aliens under DACA program), available at http://www.uscis.
gov/tools/reports-studies/immigration-forms-data/data-set-deferred-
action-childhood-arrivals; Julia Preston, "Program benefiting some
immigrants extends visa wait for others," *New York Times*, Feb. 8, 2014
(due to Obama administration's giving priority to granting administrative amnesty to young illegal aliens, Americans and legal immigrants
seeking green cards for foreign spouses are experiencing processing
delays), http://www.nytimes.com/2014/02/09/us/program-benefiting-
some-immigrants-extends-visa-wait-for-others.html; Mark Krikorian,
"Legal Immigrants Go to the Back of the Line," *National Review Online*,
Feb. 10, 2014, http://www.nationalreview.com/corner/370723/legal-
immigrants-go-back-line-mark-krikorian; Alicia A. Caldwell, "AP Exclusive: DHS released over 2,000 immigrants," *AP: The Big Story*, March 1,
2013 (Obama administration used sequester as rationalization to release
over 2,000 illegal aliens facing deportation and internal budget documents indicate plans to release 3,000 more), http://bigstory.ap.org/
article/documents-us-released-more-2000-immigrants.

11. *Arizona* v. *United States*, *supra*, 132 S.Ct. 2492 (2012); Stephen
Dinan, "Homeland Security suspends immigration agreements with
Arizona police," *Washington Times*, June 25, 2012, http://www.washing-
tontimes.com/news/2012/jun/25/homeland-security-suspends-immi-
gration-agreements-/; Mike Ahlers, "Official: Obama administration
will enforce its priorities, not Arizona's," CNN, June 25, 2012.

12. *Arizona* v. *Inter Tribal Council of Arizona, Inc.*, No. 12-71 (U.S.
Supreme Court, June 17, 2013) (National Voter Registration Act does
not preclude states from "deny[ing] registration based on information
in their possession establishing the applicant's ineligibility"), http://
www.supremecourt.gov/opinions/12pdf/12-71_7l48.pdf; Department
of Justice, Office of Public Affairs, "Justice Department Files Lawsuit
against Florida Alleging Violations of the National Voter Registration

Act," press release, June 12, 2012 (Obama Justice Department claims NVRA removing ineligible voters from rolls), http://www.justice.gov/opa/pr/2012/June/12-crt-746.html; *United States* v. *Florida*, No. 12 cv 285 (Northern District of Florida, Tallahassee Division) (June 28, 2012) (state is not prohibited from removing ineligible voters from rolls).

13. Kara Rowland and Stephen Dinan, "Justice: Sanctuary Cities Safe from Law: Arizona's policy 'actually interferes,'" *Washington Times*, July 14, 2010, http://www.washingtontimes.com/news/2010/jul/14/justice-sanctuary-cities-are-no-arizona/?page=all; see also, e.g., Office of Governor Edmund G. Brown Jr., "Governor Brown Signs Immigration Legislation," CA.gov (California), Oct. 5, 2013 (prohibiting state officials from detaining illegal aliens based on ICE detainer), http://gov.ca.gov/news.php?id=18253; Los Angeles Police Department, "Chief Charlie Beck Announces Proposed Changes to the Way L.A.P.D. Handles ICE Detentions of Some Undocumented Immigrant Arrests," press release, Oct. 4, 2012, http://www.lapdonline.org/newsroom/news_view/52079; Erin Durkin and Erica Pearson, "City Council approves measure to prevent deportation of immigrants arrested for low-level offenses," *New York Daily News*, Feb. 27, 2013, http://www.nydailynews.com/new-york/council-approves-law-preventing-deportation-petty-crimes-article-1.1275445; Mihir Zaveri, "D.C. Council votes to limit reach of federal effort aimed at illegal immigration," *Washington Post*, June 5, 2012, http://www.washingtonpost.com/local/dc-council-votes-to-limit-reach-of-federal-effort-aimed-at-illegal-immigration/2012/06/05/gJQAVgm5GV_story.html; "Santa Clara County to stop honoring immigration detainers for low-level offenders," *Los Angeles Times*, Oct. 18, 2011, http://latimesblogs.latimes.com/lanow/2011/10/santa-clara-county-to-stop-honoring-immigration-detainers-for-low-level-offenders-.html; Al Dardick, "Preckwinkle ices ICE proposal: Rejects call for working group to resolve issues," *Chicago Tribune*, April 10, 2012 (Cook County persists in refusing to detain suspected illegal immigrants arrested for committing crimes so that immigration status can be checked and federal authorities can take custody of arrestees found to be in the U.S. illegally, http://articles.chicagotribune.com/2012-04-10/

news/ct-met-toni-preckwinkle-0411-20120411_1_preckwinkle-detainers-immigration-status; Cook County Legislative Reference Services, Policy for Responding to ICE Detainers, Sep. 7, 2011, http://cookcountygov. com/ll_lib_pub_cook/cook_ordinance.aspx?WindowArgs=1501; Mylan Denerstein, Counsel to New York Governor Andrew M. Cuomo, Letter to John Sandweg, Counselor to Homeland Security Secretary Janet Napolitano, June 1, 2011 (informing federal government that the State of New York was ending its cooperation with federal immigration enforcement agents in the "Secure Communities" program), http:// www.governor.ny.gov/assets/Secure%20Communities.pdf.

ARTICLE VI

1. Another federal law enforcement agent, ICE Special Agent Jaime Zapata, was ambushed and murdered in Mexico on February 11, 2011, by a notorious criminal gang. Still another ICE agent, Victor Avila, was wounded. One of the guns used in the ambush was purchased by one Otilio Osorio in Dallas, Texas. Osorio had been identified by ATF as a firearms straw purchaser months before purchasing the murder weapon, but was not arrested despite ATF's observing him transfer a cache of weapons. In addition, a second weapon used in Agent Zapata's murder was purchased six months earlier and transferred to Mexico by one Manuel Barba. Barba had been under investigation by ATF since June 2010, and was known to have recruited straw purchasers to facilitate the acquisition and exportation of numerous firearms, which he said were for the Zeta drug cartel. Barba was not arrested until February 10, 2011—in a tragic coincidence, the day before the gun he'd acquired on August 10, 2010, was used in Agent Zapata's murder. The circumstances surrounding the killing of Agent Zapata, and their potential connections to the Fast and Furious investigation, are among the matters Congress has been attempting to investigate, with limited cooperation from the president and his subordinates. See House Committee on Oversight and Government Reform, "Issa, Grassley Press for Additional Information on Death of ICE Agent Zapata, Tactics Used in Texas," press release and related documents, Oct. 26, 2011, http://oversight.house.gov/release/issa-grassley-press-

for-additional-information-on-death-of-ice-agent-zapata-tactics-used-in-texas/; Sharyl Attkisson, "Second gun used in ICE agent murder linked to ATF undercover operation," CBS News, Feb. 23, 2012, http://www.cbsnews.com/news/second-gun-used-in-ice-agent-murder-linked-to-atf-undercover-operation-23-02-2012/; Michelle Malkin, "Fast and Furious Follow-up: Issa, Grassley press Holder on ICE officer Jaime Zapata's murder," *Michelle Malkin*, Feb. 27, 2012, http://michelle-malkin.com/2012/02/27/fast-and-furious-follow-up-issa-grassley-press-holder-on-ice-officer-jaime-zapatas-murder/.

2.　*Compare* Andrew C. McCarthy, "Politicizing Justice: How would Holder fare under the Democrats' Gonzales standards?" *National Review Online*, Jan. 27, 2009:

> [N]on-Judiciary Democrats like Sen. Mark Pryor . . . pronounced months earlier: "When an attorney general lies to a United States senator, I think it is time for that attorney general to go." . . . "The attorney general is meant to be the chief law-enforcement officer of the land," [Senator Chuck] Schumer declaimed. "He must be a person of truth and candor and integrity."
>
> A tremulous Dianne Feinstein soon arrived, framing Gonzales's tragic flaw—his alleged inability to relate facts to the committee—in myth and metaphor. It was, the senator said, "almost as if the walls were actually crumbling on this huge department." . . . [Senator] Patrick Leahy[] brooded over the "discrepancy here in sworn testimony." . . . [T]he chairman declared that Gonzales must "be fair to the truth." Finally, . . . [Senators] Feinstein and Schumer[] join[ed] [Senators] Sheldon Whitehouse and Russ Feingold to demand that the Justice Department appoint an independent counsel to probe Gonzales's alleged mendacity. "It has become apparent that the attorney general has provided at a minimum half-truths and misleading statements," they wrote.

http://m.nationalreview.com/articles/226758/politicizing-justice/andrew-c-mccarthy.

3.　Katie Pavlich, *Fast and Furious: Barack Obama's Bloodiest Scandal and Its Shameless Cover-Up* (Regnery, 2012); John Dodson, *The Unarmed Truth: My Fight to Blow the Whistle and Expose Fast and Furious*

(Threshold Editions, 2013); Andrew C. McCarthy, "Fast and Furious and OCDETF: Whom is executive privilege protecting?" *National Review Online*, June 23, 2012, http://www.nationalreview.com/articles/303808/ fast-and-furious-and-ocdetf-andrew-c-mccarthy; Andrew C. McCarthy, "A 'Fast & Furious' I Told You So," *National Review Online*, June 5, 2012, http://www.nationalreview.com/corner/301910/fast-furious-i-told-you-so-andrew-c-mccarthy; Robert VerBruggen, "Fast and Furious Update," *National Review Online*, June 5, 2012, http://www.nationalreview.com/corner/301896/fast-and-furious-update-robert-verbruggen.

4. J. Christian Adams, *Injustice: Exposing the Racial Agenda of the Obama Justice Department* (Regnery, 2011); Christopher Coates, Testimony Before the U.S. Commission on Civil Rights, Sep. 24, 2010 (describing, among other things, how "The election of President Obama brought to positions of influence and power within the [Civil Rights Division] many of the very people who had demonstrated hostility to the concept of equal enforcement of the [Voting Rights Act]"; how he was forbidden by his superiors, the president's subordinates, to ask job applicants whether they "would be willing to enforce the VRA in a race-neutral manner"; and how Julie Fernandez, appointed deputy assistant attorney general for civil rights by the president, instructed subordinates that the Obama administration would only pursue "cases that would provide political equality for racial and language minorities" in its enforcement of Section 2 of the Voting Rights Act), http:// pjmedia.com/blog/full-text-of-christopher-coates-testimony-to-u-s-commission-on-civil-rights-pjm-exclusive/; Andrew C. McCarthy, "The Case against the New Black Panthers: Abigail Thernstrom is wrong to belittle this shocking episode," *National Review Online*, July 20, 2010, http://www.nationalreview.com/articles/243504/case-against-new-black-panthers-andrew-c-mccarthy.

5. In fact, congressional Democrats and the Justice Department inspector general condemned Justice Department leadership during the tenure of Attorney General Alberto Gonzales for "violat[ing] department policy and federal law and commit[ing] misconduct by considering political or ideological affiliations" in hiring decisions. Even though he was found to be unaware of the improper politicization of hiring,

Attorney General Gonzales succumbed to calls that he resign, due to both the hiring practices on his watch and his provision of inaccurate information to Congress, which several lawmakers argued caused the Congress to lose confidence in the attorney general and the administration. See Terry Frieden, "Gonzales aides politicized hirings, investigators find," CNN, July 28, 2008; McCarthy, "Politicizing Justice: How would Holder fare under the Democrats' Gonzales standards?" *supra.* Whereas Congress then complained about episodes of politicization and the frustration of Congress's oversight responsibilities, such actions have today become systematic under the leadership of the president and his subordinates.

6. J. Christian Adams, Hans von Spakovsky and Richard Pollock, "'Every Single One': *PJ Media*'s Investigation of Justice Department Hiring Practices," *PJ Media*, 2011 (collecting links to 11part series), http://pjmedia.com/every-single-one-pj-medias-investigation-of-justice-department-hiring-practices/; Adams, *Injustice: Exposing the Racial Agenda of the Obama Justice Department, supra*; Andrew C. McCarthy, *How the Obama Administration Has Politicized Justice*, Broadside Series no. 7 (Encounter Books, 2010). *Compare* Glenn A. Fine, Inspector General, Department of Justice, "Politicized Hiring at the Department of Justice," Testimony before the Senate Judiciary Committee, July 30, 2008 (finding that "staff in the Office of the Attorney General improperly considered political or ideological affiliations in screening candidates for certain career positions at the Department, in violation of federal law and Department policy"; and that "the Department must ensure that the serious problems and misconduct we found in our reports about politicized hiring for career positions in the Department do not recur in the future"), http://www.justice.gov/oig/testimony/t0807/index.htm.

7. Stephen Dinan, "Justice: Feds pick Obama supporter to lead probe into IRS tea party targeting," *Washington Times*, Jan. 8, 2014, http://www.washingtontimes.com/news/2014/jan/8/feds-pick-obama-supporter-lead-irs-tea-party-probe/; Josh Hicks, "Obama political donor leading Justice Department's IRS investigation," *Washington Post*, Jan. 9, 2014, http://www.washingtonpost.com/blogs/federal-eye/wp/2014/01/09/obama-political-donor-leading-justice-departments-

irs-investigation/; Andrew C. McCarthy, "Cruz to Holder: Appoint an Independent Prosecutor in IRS Scandal," *National Review Online*, Jan. 22, 2014, http://www.nationalreview.com/corner/369222/cruz-holder-appoint-independent-prosecutor-irs-scandal-andrew-c-mccarthy.

8.   Andrew C. McCarthy, "S&P Gets the Pitchfork Treatment: The Obama administration retaliates with a fraud suit . . . or is it a fraudulent suit?" *National Review Online*, Jan. 25, 2014, http://www.nationalreview.com/article/369430/sp-gets-pitchfork-treatment-andrew-c-mccarthy.

9.   Andrew C. McCarthy, "Amnesty, but Not for D'Souza: For Obama's Justice Department, campaign-finance law is a partisan club," *National Review Online*, Feb. 1, 2014 (also noting that D'Souza has no criminal record and the alleged contributions had no bearing on the result of the pertinent Senate election, which D'Souza's preferred candidate lost by 46 percentage points), http://www.national-review.com/article/370097/amnesty-not-dsouza-andrew-c-mccarthy; William A. Jacobson, "What if Dinesh D'Souza had waved around a 30-round magazine?" *Legal Insurrection*, Jan. 27, 2014 (recounting that the Obama campaign was merely fined, not criminally prosecuted, despite its failure to disclose millions of dollars in contributions and dragging its feet in refunding millions more in excess contributions; the campaign failed to disclose sources of 1,300 large donations totaling nearly $1.9 million), http://legalinsurrection.com/2014/01/what-if-dinesh-dsouza-had-waved-around-a-30-round-magazine/; Jennifer G. Hickey and John Gizzi, "Dershowitz, Law Enforcement Experts Slam D'Souza Targeting," *Newsmax*, Jan. 29, 2014, http://www.newsmax.com/Newsfront/DSouza-Dershowitz-targeting-selective/2014/01/29/id/549845/. It should also be noted that the investigation of D'Souza's alleged offense raises serious questions. The Justice Department has claimed that D'Souza's conduct was discovered by a routine review of campaign filings. That is difficult to conceive: D'Souza is accused of using straw donors to contribute to a Senate campaign, so it is difficult to understand how his name would have surfaced in a routine review of campaign filings. Several senators on the Senate Judiciary Committee have written to the FBI asking pointed questions about the

investigative procedures in D'Souza's case and campaign finance cases in general. Daniel Halper, "Senators Demand FBI Head Answer Questions about Indictment of Dinesh D'Souza," *Weekly Standard*, Feb. 21, 2014, https://www.weeklystandard.com/blogs/senators-demand-fbi-head-answer-questions-about-indictment-dinesh-dsouza_782781.html.

10. Andrew C. McCarthy, "For Politicized Justice Department, Zimmerman 'Civil Rights' Case in CIA Interrogators Case All Over Again," *National Review Online*, July 15, 2013, http://www.nationalreview.com/corner/353455/politicized-justice-department-zimmerman-civil-rights-case-cia-interrogators-case-all; Andrew C. McCarthy, "Holder Meets Sharpton: The attorney general heaps praise on an infamous huckster," *National Review Online*, April 14, 2012, http://www.nationalreview.com/articles/296005/holder-meets-sharpton-andrew-c-mccarthy; Andrew C. McCarthy, "Martin Case Affidavit," *National Review Online*, April 13, 2012, http://www.nationalreview.com/corner/295997/martin-case-affidavit-andrew-c-mccarthy; "Alan Dershowitz: Zimmerman Arrest Affidavit 'Irresponsible and Unethical,'" Video, *Real Clear Politics*, April 12, 2012, http://www.realclearpolitics.com/video/2012/04/12/alan_dershowitz_zimmerman_arrest_affidavit_irresponsible_and_unethical.html; "Mark Levin: Zimmerman affidavit doesn't support probable cause for 2d degree murder," *The Right Scoop*, April 13, 2012, http://therightscoop.com/mark-levin-zimmerman-affidavit-doesnt-support-probable-cause-for-2nd-degree-murder/?utm_campaign=Mark%20Levin:%20Zimmerman%20affidavit%20doesnt%20support%20probable%20cause%20for%202nd%20degree%20murder&utm_medium=twitter&utm_source=twitter; Ron Radosh, "The Evidence in the Trayvon Martin Case Is Released, and George Zimmerman Is Vindicated," *PJ Media*, May 17, 2012, http://pjmedia.com/ronradosh/2012/05/17/george-zimmerman-vindicated/; Andrew C. McCarthy, "Zimmerman Prosecution Predictably Collapsing," *PJ Media*, June 30, 2013, http://pjmedia.com/andrewmccarthy/2013/06/30/zimmerman-prosecution-predictably-collapsing/; Andrew C. McCarthy, "The Obama Administration's Race-Baiting Campaign: Democrats want 2014 to be an us-versus-them election," *National Review Online*, July 30, 2013, http://www.nationalreview.com/article/353970/

obama-administrations-race-baiting-campaign-andrew-c-mccarthy; Andrew C. McCarthy, "Politics shouldn't force a federal case vs. Zimmerman," CNN, July 17, 2013, http://www.cnn.com/2013/07/17/opinion/mccarthy-zimmerman-case/index.html; Michelle Malkin, "Eric Holder's Stand Your Ground Squirrel," *Real Clear Politics*, July 17, 2013, http://www.realclearpolitics.com/articles/2013/07/17/eric_holders_stand_your_ground_squirrel_119255.html.

11. Andrew C. McCarthy, "'The Right Man' to Protect Us from Terror? At least that's what some of Eric Holder's surprising supporters say," *National Review Online*, Jan. 13, 2009, http://www.nationalreview.com/articles/226682/right-man-protect-us-terror/andrew-c-mccarthy.

12. Scott Shane, "No charges filed on harsh tactics used by the C.I.A.," *New York Times*, Aug. 30, 2012, http://www.nytimes.com/2012/08/31/us/holder-rules-out-prosecutions-in-cia-interrogations.html?_r=0; Andrew C. McCarthy, "Drop the Investigation of CIA Interrogators: The legal and policy considerations argue against an investigation, let alone a prosecution," *National Review Online*, Aug. 11, 2009, http://www.nationalreview.com/articles/228041/drop-investigation-cia-interrogators/andrew-c-mccarthy; Andrew C. McCarthy, "Release the Terrorist, Investigate the CIA," *National Review Online*, Aug. 27, 2009, http://www.nationalreview.com/corner/186174/release-terrorist-investigate-cia-andrew-c-mccarthy; see also Andrew C. McCarthy, "Miguel Estrada on the Shoddy Partisanship of OPR: Will Holder investigate the leaks?" *National Review Online*, Feb. 20, 2010 (noting the dismissal of the professional responsibility investigation of John Yoo, deputy assistant attorney general in the Bush DOJ's Office of Legal Counsel, and the unethical leaking and "deep partisan bias" exhibited during the last year of the investigation), http://www.nationalreview.com/corner/195171/miguel-estrada-shoddy-partisanship-opr-will-holder-investigate-leaks-andrew-c-mccarthy.

13. Sari Horwitz and William Branigan, "Eric Holder says he recused himself from leak probe that obtained AP phone records," *Washington Post*, May 14, 2013:

> In a sweeping and unusual move, the Justice Department secretly obtained two months' worth of telephone records of jour-

nalists working for the Associated Press as part of a year-long investigation into the disclosure of classified information about a failed al-Qaeda plot last year. The records listed outgoing calls from more than 20 work and personal phone lines in April and May 2012, the news agency said. It said the number of employees who used those lines during that period is unknown but that more than 100 journalists work in the targeted offices.

http://www.washingtonpost.com/world/national-security/holder-recused-himself-from-leak-investigation-justice-department-says/2013/05/14/acf24cf8-bcb6-11e2-97d4-a479289a31f9_story.html?hpid=z1; see also Sari Horwitz, "Under sweeping subpoenas, Justice Department obtained AP phone records in leak investigation," *Washington Post*, May 13, 2013, http://www.washingtonpost.com/world/national-security/under-sweeping-subpoenas-justice-department-obtained-ap-phone-records-in-leak-investigation/2013/05/13/1d1bb82-bc11-11e2-89c9-3be8095fe767_story.html.

14. Ed Morrissey, "Did Eric Holder lie in congressional testimony last week?" *Hot Air*, May 24, 2013, http://hotair.com/archives/2013/05/24/did-eric-holder-lie-in-congressional-testimony-last-week/; Tom Cohen, "5 things about the controversy surrounding AG Eric Holder," CNN, May 30, 2013, http://www.cnn.com/2013/05/29/politics/five-things-holder/. To be clear, my personal view is that the relevance of the investigation of Fox News reporter James Rosen lies in the Justice Department's conflicting representations to Congress and the court. There is not anything wrong, in principle, with investigating a reporter who is legitimately suspected of violating the law. And while this is a difficult area of the law—pitting the vital interest of the nation in preserving defense secrets on which lives depend against the First Amendment's free-press principles—I am more sympathetic to Espionage Act investigations of journalists than many commentators appear to be; although I believe it is better to view the reporter as, presumptively, a witness rather than a defendant, since the more culpable offender, and the one who presents no constitutional concerns in a leak case, is the leaking government official, not the journalist. See, e.g., Andrew C. McCarthy, "Reporters and Investiga-

tions: There is no reason for delay in pursuing the CIA leak case," *National Review Online*, April 25, 2006, http://www.nationalreview. com/articles/217442/reporters-and-investigations/andrew-c-mccarthy. All that said, a prosecutor should not represent to a court, for purposes of compelling information from a reporter, that there is probable cause that the reporter has committed a crime unless the prosecutor is seriously considering indicting the reporter for the crime. The obvious thrust of the Privacy Protection Act in this regard is to permit such compulsion only in the most serious circumstances. Unless told otherwise, the judge to whom the search application is made is entitled to assume the government would not be seeking the warrant unless it was intent on prosecuting the journalist.

15. Ann E. Marimow, "A rare peek into a Justice Department leak probe," *Washington Post*, May 19, 2013, http://www.washingtonpost.com/local/a-rare-peek-into-a-justice-department-leak-probe/2013/05/19/0bc473de-be5e-11e2-97d4-a479289a31f9_story. html; Josh Gerstein, "Holder walks fine line on prosecuting journalists," *Politico*, May 20, 2013, http://www.politico.com/blogs/under-the-radar/2013/05/holder-walks-fine-line-on-prosecuting-journalists-164367.html); Erik Wemple, "Eric Holder on Fox News's James Rosen: Weaselly garbage," *Washington Post*, June 20, 2013, http://www. washingtonpost.com/blogs/erik-wemple/wp/2013/06/20/eric-holder-on-fox-newss-james-rosen-weaselly-garbage/.

16. Aaron Blake, "Holder: I didn't lie about James Rosen," *Washington Post*, June 20, 2013, http://www.washingtonpost.com/blogs/post-politics/wp/2013/06/20/holder-i-didnt-lie-about-james-rosen/.

17. Gerstein, "Holder walks fine line on prosecuting journalists," *supra*.

18. Allahpundit, "Eric Holder to State AGs: You don't have to defend your state's ban on gay marriage, you know," *Hot Air*, Feb. 25, 2014, http://hotair.com/archives/2014/02/25/eric-holder-to-state-ags-you-dont-have-to-defend-your-states-ban-on-gay-marriage-you-know/; *United States* v. *Windsor*, 133 S. Ct. 2675 (2013) (marriage is "an area that has long been regarded as a virtually exclusive province of the States"), http://www.law.cornell.edu/supremecourt/text/12-307. Inter-

estingly, in 2009, the Justice Department filed a brief defending the federal Defense of Marriage Act in which it argued for "maintaining the status quo and uniformity on the federal level, and preserving room for the development of policy in the states." Brian Montopoli, "Obama administration will no longer defend DOMA," CBS News, Feb. 24, 2011, http://www.cbsnews.com/news/obama-administration-will-no-longer-defend-doma/. Now, the attorney general is advising his state colleagues to undermine state policy if it deviates from the Obama administration's "evolving" preferences.

19. See *supra*, Notes to Chapter Four, n.14.

20. McCarthy, "How the Obama Administration Has Politicized Justice," *supra*; Associated Press, "Federal lawyers seek to drop suit against Missouri on voter rolls," *St. Louis Post-Dispatch*, March 8, 2009, http://www.stltoday.com/news/local/federal-lawyers-seek-to-drop-suit-against-missouri-on-voter/article_b1fbdb0d-48df-5904-bf30-ebecef081dbd.html; Chris Stirewalt, "Holder fires back at GOP with Florida voter suit," Fox News, June 13, 2012, http://www.foxnews.com/politics/2012/06/13/holder-fires-back-at-gop-with-florida-voter-suit/; J. Christian Adams, "Meet the Radical DOJ Lawyer Forcing Florida to Keep Foreigners on the Voter Rolls," *PJ Media*, June 1, 2012, http://pjmedia.com/jchristianadams/2012/06/01/meet-the-radical-doj-lawyer-forcing-florida-to-keep-foreigners-on-the-voter-rolls/.

ARTICLE VII

1. House Committee on Oversight and Government Reform, Staff Report, "Lois Lerner's Involvement in the IRS Targeting of Tax-Exempt Organizations," March 11, 2014, http://oversight.house.gov/wp-content/uploads/2014/03/Lerner-Report1.pdf; Internal Revenue Service, "Social Welfare Organizations" (guidance on application of Internal Revenue Code, Section 501(c)(4)), http://www.irs.gov/Charities-&-Non-Profits/Other-Non-Profits/Social-Welfare-Organizations (accessed Feb. 7, 2014); Andrew C. McCarthy, "The GOP Should Use the Power of the Purse: The way to cure the rogue behavior of Obama's agencies is not to pay for it," *National Review Online*, Feb. 8, 2014, http://www.nationalreview.com/article/370652/gop-should-use-power-purse-andrew-c-mccarthy.

2. *Citizens United* v. *Federal Election Commission*, 558 U.S. 310 (2010), http://www.law.cornell.edu/supct/html/08-205.ZS.html.

3. Laurie Kellman, "Obama Scolds Supreme Court, to the Annoyance of One Justice," CNS News, Jan. 28, 2010, http://cnsnews.com/news/article/obama-scolds-supreme-court-annoyance-one-justice.

4. See, e.g., Senator Charles E. Schumer, press release, "Senate Democrats Urge IRS to Impose Strict Cap on Political Spending by Nonprofit Groups—Vow Legislation If Agency Doesn't Act," March 12, 2012, http://www.schumer.senate.gov/record.cfm?id=336270.

5. House Committee Report, "Lois Lerner's Involvement in the IRS Targeting of Tax-Exempt Organizations," *supra*; Eliana Johnson, "Lois Lerner at the FEC: Before her IRS tenure, Lerner subjected conservative groups to heightened scrutiny," *National Review Online*, May 23, 2013, http://www.nationalreview.com/article/349181/lois-lerner-fec-eliana-johnson.

6. House Committee Report, "Lois Lerner's Involvement in the IRS Targeting of Tax-Exempt Organizations," *supra*; see also "Obama's IRS 'Confusion': New evidence undercuts White House claims about IRS motivation," Review & Outlook, *Wall Street Journal*, Feb. 7, 2014, http://online.wsj.com/news/articles/SB10001424052702304181204579365161576171176?mod=WSJ_Opinion_LEADTop.

7. Treasury Inspector General for Tax Administration, "Inappropriate Criteria Were Used to Identify Tax-Exempt Applications for Review," May 14, 2013, http://www.treasury.gov/tigta/auditreports/2013reports/201310053fr.pdf.

8. House Committee Report, "Lois Lerner's Involvement in the IRS Targeting of Tax-Exempt Organizations," *supra*.

9. "'Not even a smidgeon of corruption': Obama downplays IRS, other scandals," Fox News, Feb. 3, 2014, http://www.foxnews.com/politics/2014/02/03/not-even-smidgen-corruption-obama-downplays-irs-other-scandals/; Gregory Korte, "Lois Lerner wants immunity in exchange for IRS testimony," *USA Today*, Feb. 26, 2014, http://www.usatoday.com/story/news/politics/2014/02/26/lois-lerner-wants-immunity-in-exchange-for-irs-testimony/5834321/.

10. McCarthy, "The GOP Should Use the Power of the Purse," *supra*; see also "Obama's IRS 'Confusion,'" *supra*.

11. McCarthy, "The GOP Should Use the Power of the Purse," *supra*; see also McCarthy, "Cruz to Holder: Appoint an Independent Prosecutor in IRS Scandal," *supra*.

12. See Article of Impeachment VI, "Politicization of Investigation and Prosecution," *supra*; see also House Committee Report, "Lois Lerner's Involvement in the IRS Targeting of Tax-Exempt Organizations," *supra*; Charles S. Clark, "Justice Will Not Allow Investigator of IRS Scandal to Testify," *Government Executive*, Feb. 3, 2014, http://www.govexec.com/oversight/2014/02/justice-will-not-allow-investigator-irs-scandal-testify/78089/.

13. Cathy Burke, "Cleta Mitchell: FBI Probe of IRS Targeting Done Soviet-Style," *Newsmax*, March 13, 2014, http://www.newsmax.com/Newsfront/Cleta-Mitchell-FBI-IRS-Soviet/2014/01/13/id/546884/.

14. It should go without saying that the supremacist interpretation of Islam is not the only one. It is not our purpose to broker claims of competing interpretations, but to deal with the aggressive one—which must be dealt with because it exists, it has many adherents, and it continues to be aggressive regardless of scholars' conflicting views about its legal and theological accuracy. The government recognizes the repressive nature of Islamic blasphemy laws in various contexts. See, e.g., U.S. Commission on International Religious Freedom, Fourteenth Annual Report, March 20, 2012 (citing sixteen countries as egregious and systematic religious-freedom violators—e.g., Pakistan, due in part to its "repressive blasphemy laws and other religiously discriminatory legislation," p. 120), http://www.uscirf.gov/sites/default/files/resources/Annual%20Report%20of%20USCIRF%202012(2).pdf.

The repressive treatment of blasphemy stems, in large part, from the severe treatment of apostasy by this supremacist interpretation of sharia. Apostasy, the abandonment of Islam by a formerly believing Muslim, is deemed to be "the ugliest form of unbelief" and is punished by death. It is also construed dangerously loosely: Apostasy is said to occur not only when a Muslim renounces Islam but also, among other things, when a Muslim appears to worship an idol, when he is heard merely "to speak words that imply unbelief," when he makes statements that merely appear to deny or revile Allah or the prophet Mohammed, when he is heard merely "to deny the obligatory character of us of Muslims is part of Islam," and when he is heard merely "to be sarcastic about any ruling of the Sacred Law." See *Reliance of the Traveller: A Classic Manual of Islamic Sacred Law ('Umdat al-Salik)* (translation published by Amana Publications, 1991) (endorsed as accurate by, among other influential Islamic institutions, the Islamic Research Academy at al-Azhar University in Cairo and the International Institute of Islamic Thought), sections o8.0 & ff., p9.0 & ff; see also Silas, "The Punishment for Apostasy from Islam," *Answering Islam*, Jan. 4, 2007, http://answering-islam.org/Silas/apostasy.htm; Andrew C. McCarthy, *Spring Fever: The Illusion of Islamic Democracy* (Encounter Books, 2012).

15. The resolution accomplishes this under the rhetorical camouflage of outlawing "any advocacy of religious hatred against individuals that constitutes incitement to discrimination, hostility or violence." Incitement to violence is already illegal in the United States. Discrimination is also illegal in various contexts under federal law. Speech that could potentially incite discrimination, however, is protected by the First Amendment, and hostility itself is not illegal, much less speech that could theoretically provoke hostility. As I've argued,

> Our law permits the criminalization of incitement to violence only when an agitator willfully calls for violence. Our Constitution does not abide what the resolution is designed to achieve: the heckler's veto and, worse, the suppression of speech predicated on mob intimidation—the legitimation of barbaric lawlessness. Nor does the Constitution's guarantee of free expression tolerate the outlawing of speech that prompts discrimination, much less hostility. And contrary to administration hairsplitting, it makes no difference that the resolution would not "criminalize" expression that prompts discrimination or hostility. To quote the First Amendment, "Congress shall make no law" suppressing protected speech. It does not say "Congress shall make no *criminal* law." No law means *no law*—no civil law, rule, regulation, guideline, etc.

Andrew C. McCarthy, "Blasphemy and Islam: Our fundamental rights are under attack," *National Review Online*, Dec. 15, 2012, http://www.nationalreview.com/articles/335716/blasphemy-and-islam-andrew-c-mccarthy; see also Patrick Goodenough, "Religious Tolerance Resolution Backed by Obama Administration Aligns with Islamic Bloc's Interests," CNS News, Dec. 16, 2011, http://cnsnews.com/news/article/religious-tolerance-resolution-backed-obama-administration-aligns-islamic-bloc-s; Andrew C. McCarthy, "Coercing Conformity: A government that creates the climate for bullying is the worst of the bullies," *National Review Online*, Dec. 28, 2013, http://www.national-review.com/article/367132/coercing-conformity-andrew-c-mccarthy.

16. Robert Spencer, "Obama Administration Bans the Truth about Islam and Jihad," *Frontpage Magazine*, Oct. 24, 2011, http://frontpagemag.com/2011/robert-spencer/obama-adminstration-bans-the-truth-about-islam-and-jihad/; Department of Justice, "Deputy Attorney General James M. Cole Speaks at the Department's Conference on Post 9/11 Discrimination," press release, Oct. 9, 2011 ("I recently directed all components of the Department of Justice to re-evaluate their training efforts in a range of areas, from community outreach to national security, to make sure they reflect that sensitivity"), http://www.justice.gov/iso/opa/dag/speeches/2011/dag-speech-111019.html; AWR Hawkins, "Emerson, IPT Expose Brennan Letter: FBI Training 'Substandard and Offensive' to Muslims," *Breitbart*, Feb. 8, 2013, http://www.breitbart.com/Big-Government/2013/02/08/Nov-3-2011-Letter-From-John-Brennan-Capitulating-To-Muslim-Complaints-Against-FBI; see also Letter of Muslim organizations to John Brennan, Assistant to the President for Homeland Security and Counterterrorism, and Deputy National Security Advisor, Oct. 19, 2011, available through website of Congresswoman Michele Bachmann, http://bachmann.house.gov/sites/bachmann.house.gov/files/Letter_to_John_Brennan.pdf#overlay-context=house-members-seek-national-security-answers (note that some of the organizations listed, e.g. CAIR and ISNA, were shown to be unindicted co-conspirators in Justice Department prosecution of Holy Land Foundation terrorism financing conspiracy; see Andrew C. McCarthy, "First the Ahmadi, Then Everybody Else,"

National Review Online, Feb. 18, 2012, http://www.nationalreview.com/articles/291404/first-ahmadi-then-everybody-else-andrew-c-mccarthy); Andrew C. McCarthy, "Guess Who Decides What FBI Agents Get to Learn about Islam?" *National Review Online,* Feb. 22, 2012, http://www.nationalreview.com/corner/291737/guess-who-decides-what-fbi-agents-get-learn-about-islam-andrew-c-mccarthy.

17. See McCarthy, *Spring Fever, supra. (Allahu akbar!,* "the chillingly familiar exclamation of Muslim terrorists, is commonly translated as 'God is greatest!' But that's not exactly right. It literally means, 'Allah is *greater!'*—the greater God, the mightier, more fearsome power. It is a *comparative.")*

18. See, e.g., Jennifer Griffin, "Two U.S.-born terrorists killed in CIA-led drone strike," Fox News, Sep. 30, 2011, http://www.foxnews.com/politics/2011/09/30/us-born-terror-boss-anwar-al-awlaki-killed/; see also Andrew C. McCarthy, "The Government's Awlaki Story Does Not Pass the Laugh Test," *PJ Media,* Aug. 3, 2012, http://pjmedia.com/andrewmccarthy/2012/08/03/fed-awlaki-story-doesnt-pass-laugh-test/.

19. Thomas Joscelyn, "Missed Clues before Fort Hood Shootings," *Weekly Standard,* July 26, 2012, http://www.weeklystandard.com/blogs/missed-clues-fort-hood-shootings_649008.html; Thomas Joscelyn, "Report Highlights emails from Fort Hood shooter to al Qaeda cleric," *Long War Journal,* July 20, 2012, http://www.longwarjournal.org/archives/2012/07/report_highlights_em.php; Mary Chastain, "Emails Prove FBI Could Have Prevented Fort Hood Attack," *Breitbart,* Aug. 28, 2013, http://www.breitbart.com/Big-Government/2013/08/27/Emails-Prove-FBI-Could-Have-Prevented-Fort-Hood-Attack.

20. Sara Carter, "TheBlaze Investigation: How Obama and the Army Betrayed the Victims of Fort Hood," *TheBlaze,* Feb. 12, 2014, http://www.theblaze.com/stories/2014/02/12/theblaze-investigation-how-obama-and-the-army-betrayed-the-victims-of-fort-hood/. Hasan was born in the United States; his parents were Palestinians from the West Bank. See, e.g., "Profile: Major Nidal Malik Hasan," BBC, Nov. 12, 2009, http://news.bbc.co.uk/2/hi/8345944.stm.

21. Joscelyn, "Missed Clues before Fort Hood Shootings," *supra*; Chastain, "Emails Prove FBI Could Have Prevented Fort Hood Attack," *supra*.

22. Carter, "TheBlaze Investigation: How Obama and the Army Betrayed the Victims of Fort Hood," *supra*. The Obama administration also absurdly claimed that awarding Purple Hearts would prejudice Hasan's court martial. Andrew C. McCarthy, "The Claim That Awarding Purple Hearts to Hasan's Victims Would Prejudice His Murder Trial Is Ridiculous," *PJ Media*, April 1, 2013, http://pjmedia.com/andrewmccarthy/2013/04/01/purple-hearts-to-hassans-victims/.

23. Edward Whelan, "The HHS Mandate v. the Religious Freedom Restoration Act," *National Review Online* series, Jan. 26–Feb. 13, 2013, republished by the Ethics and Public Policy Center, http://www.eppc.org/publications/the-hhs-contraception-mandate-vs-the-religious-freedom-restoration-act/; see also Andrew C. McCarthy, "Don't Worry about Supremes' Refusal to Hear Liberty U's Challenge to Obamacare," *PJ Media*, Dec. 4, 2013, http://pjmedia.com/andrewmccarthy/2013/12/04/dont-worry-about-supremes-refusal-to-hear-liberty-us-challenge-to-obamacare/?singlepage=true.

24. Whelan, "The HHS Mandate v. the Religious Freedom Restoration Act," *supra*. ("As the head of Catholic Charities USA observed, 'the ministry of Jesus Christ himself' would not qualify for the exemption. Nor will Catholic Charities, Catholic Relief Services, Catholic hospitals, food banks, homeless shelters, most Catholic schools, and even many or most diocesan offices, much less Catholic business owners who strive to conduct their businesses in accordance with their religious beliefs.")

25. Andrew C. McCarthy, "The Contraceptive Mandate's Shaky Justification: There is no crisis in 'reproductive health,'" *National Review Online*, Feb. 11, 2012, http://www.nationalreview.com/articles/290844/contraceptive-mandate-s-shaky-justification-andrew-c-mccarthy.

26. *Hosanna-Tabor Evangelical Lutheran Church and School v. EEOC*, 132 S. Ct. 694 (2012).

27. Theodore R. Bromund, "After U.S. Signature, Dangers of U.N. Arms Trade Treaty Begin to Surface," Heritage Foundation, Jan. 14,

2014; see also "Kerry signs UN arms treaty, senators threaten to block it," Fox News, Sep. 25, 2013, http://www.foxnews.com/politics/2013/09/25/kerry-signs-un-arms-treaty-senators-threaten-to-block-it/.

    28. Bromund, "After U.S. Signature, Dangers of U.N. Arms Trade Treaty Begin to Surface," *supra*, quoting Vann Van Diepen, Department of State, "Next Steps in Realizing the Goals of the Arms Trade Treaty," Oct. 3, 2013, http://www.state.gov/t/isn/rls/rm/2013/215427.htm.

INDEX